Race and Criminal Justice

Race and Criminal Justice

Hindpal Singh Bhui

Los Angeles • London • New Delhi • Singapore • Washington DC

Editorial Arrangement © Hindpal Singh Bhui 2009

All other material © SAGE

First published 2009

Apart from any fair dealing for the purposes of research or
private study, or criticism or review, as permitted under the
Copyright, Designs and Patents Act, 1988, this publication
may be reproduced, stored or transmitted in any form, or by
any means, only with the prior permission in writing of the
publishers, or in the case of reprographic reproduction, in
accordance with the terms of licences issued by the Copyright
Licensing Agency. Enquiries concerning reproduction outside
those terms should be sent to the publishers.

SAGE Publications Ltd
1 Oliver's Yard
55 City Road
London EC1Y 1SP

SAGE Publications Inc.
2455 Teller Road
Thousand Oaks, California 91320

SAGE Publications India Pvt Ltd
B 1/I 1 Mohan Cooperative Industrial Area
Mathura Road
New Delhi 110 044

SAGE Publications Asia-Pacific Pte Ltd
33 Pekin Street #02-01
Far East Square
Singapore 048763

Library of Congress Control Number: 2008938020

British Library Cataloguing in Publication data

A catalogue record for this book is available from the British Library

ISBN 978-1-4129-4554-7
ISBN 978-1-4129-4555-4 (pbk)

Typeset by CEPHA Imaging Pvt. Ltd., Bangalore, India
Printed and bound in Great Britain by TJ International Ltd, Padstow, Cornwall
Printed on paper from sustainable resources

To my parents, whose amazing journey made so many others possible

Contents

Notes on Contributors

Abdul Haqq Baker, PhD candidate at the University of Exeter, is the chairman of Brixton Mosque and director of *Street*, a Muslim youth outreach project in London.

Hindpal Singh Bhui is an inspection team leader in Her Majesty's Inspectorate of Prisons, specializing in immigration detention, race equality, and foreign national prisoners. He has been the Inspectorate's policy lead on both race equality and foreign national prisoners. He is also a visiting senior lecturer in criminal justice at the University of Hertfordshire. He was formerly a probation officer, working both in the community and in prison. He was the editor of *Probation Journal: The Journal of Community and Criminal Justice* between 1997 and 2007, and is currently a co-editor of the *Issues in Community and Criminal Justice* monograph series, established in 2001. He has published a number of papers on probation, prisons, and race equality.

Claire Cooper joined the Commission for Racial Equality (CRE) (now the Equality and Human Rights Commission) in 2004 as Senior Policy Officer for Criminal Justice. In this role, she led the CRE's work with the criminal justice sector, including monitoring the Prison Service's response to the CRE's formal investigation into racial equality in prisons in 2003. Prior to joining the CRE, she worked on national policing policy on race and diversity and contributed to a number of Home Office publications in this area. Since January 2008, Claire has taken up a position as Senior Manager in the Race Equality Action Group at the Prison Service which leads the Service's programme of work on race equality.

Finola Farrant is a senior lecturer at Roehampton University. She has published widely on a variety of criminal-justice-related topics and has conducted extensive prison-related research. These have included studies on resettlement and desistance, young adult male offenders, substance misuse, mental health, and volunteering and citizenship.

Nathan Hall is a senior lecturer in criminology and policing at the Institute of Criminal Justice Studies at the University of Portsmouth. His main research interest lies in hate crime. He has extensively researched hate crime, particularly in relation to criminal justice responses in England and Wales and in the United States. His first book, *Hate Crime*, was published by Willan Publishing in 2005, and he is currently involved in comparative research of the policing of hate crime in London and New York. In addition to working with a number of police services across the country, Nathan has also acted in a consultative capacity to the Association of Chief Police Officers (ACPO) and Her Majesty's Inspectorate of Constabulary (HMIC).

Sam Lewis is a research fellow in the School of Law at the University of Leeds. In recent years, she has undertaken research (with colleagues from other institutions) for the Home Office, local probation areas, and youth offending services. She was a member of the research team that completed a national Home Office–funded study of minority ethnic men on probation. Her research and publications focus on minority ethnic experiences of criminal justice, youth crime and justice, probation service policy and practice, and the governance of anti-social behaviour. She has co-edited (with P. Raynor, D. Smith, and A. Wardak) *Race and Probation*, published by Willan Publishing in 2006.

Robert Lambert, research fellow at the University of Exeter, is a retired Metropolitan Police officer who was the co-founder and head of the Muslim Contact Unit (MCU) from 2002 to 2007. He is now a project consultant for *Street*, a Muslim youth outreach project in London. His PhD is about *Countering al-Qaida propaganda & recruitment in London: An insider's interpretive case study*.

Karen Mills qualified as a probation office in 1988 and worked in a range of probation settings over a period of 13 years before moving into an academic post at the University of Hertfordshire, where she is currently a senior lecturer in criminal justice. She has a particular interest in substance misuse and diversity issues – especially the extent to which policy and practice in this area are influenced by the changing political landscape. Her most recent research examined the drug treatment needs of new minority groups in Peterborough and London.

Michael Rowe is associate professor at the Institute of Criminology, Victoria University of Wellington, New Zealand. He was formerly senior lecturer in Criminology at the University of Leicester, and has written extensively on policing and minority ethnic communities, and on the broader implications of diversity for the police service. He also edited *Policing beyond Macpherson: Issues in Policing, Race and Society*, published by Willan Publishing in 2007.

David Smith is a graduate of the universities of Oxford and Exeter, where he trained as a social worker. He was a probation officer in Worcestershire from 1972 to 76, when he was appointed to a lectureship in social work at Lancaster University. He became Professor of Social Work there in 1993 and Professor of Criminology in 2002. He has researched and written on a wide range of criminological and related topics, including youth justice, probation policy and practice, inter-agency co-operation, electronic monitoring, hitch-hiking, racist violence, and minority ethnic groups' experiences of probation and criminal justice. He is the co-author, with David Lobley, of *Persistent Young Offenders: An Evaluation of Two Projects* (Ashgate, 2007), and co-author and editor, with Sam Lewis, Peter Raynor, and Ali Wardak, of *Race and Probation* (Willan Publishing, 2006).

Basia Spalek is a senior lecturer in criminology and criminal justice at the University of Birmingham. Her research interests include British Muslim communities, crime, victimization, and community safety issues; equality and diversity within the public sector; and communities, identities, and crime. Her recent publications include *Islam, Crime and Criminal Justice* (Willan Publishing, 2002), *Crime Victims: Theory, Policy and Practice* (Palgrave Macmillan, 2006), and *Communities, Identities and Crime* (Policy Press, 2008).

Séamus Taylor is the Director of Equality and Diversity at the Crown Prosecution Service and was formerly Director of Strategy at the Commission for Racial Equality, where he led on the duty to promote race equality under the Race Relations Act. Séamus has served on the Advisory Group for the Cabinet Office study on Ethnic Minorities and the Labour Market. He is a trustee of the Runnymede Trust and was on the Commission on the future of multi-ethnic Britain (The Parekh Report, 2000). Previously, Séamus worked in local government in both corporate policy and performance management and in equalities. During this time, he served as Head of Equalities and Diversity at Haringey Council when the Council initiated the mainstreaming of equalities in the early 1990s. He has worked across a range of equalities strands. Prior to this, Séamus worked in the Irish community voluntary sector. Séamus was educated at University College, Dublin, and University of London (Goldsmiths College), and graduated from both institutions with distinctions.

Acknowledgements

I am greatly indebted to all the authors for their commitment to this project and for putting up with many and varied editorial demands with such good humour. The peer review the authors offered each other was invaluable, as was the assistance of the external reviewers. Particular thanks are due to Finola Farrant, Claire Cooper, Joe Levenson, Liz Dixon, Kerry McCarthy, Keith Davies, Julia Fossi, Lol Burke, Anisha Mehta, Pauline Durrance and Julian Buchanan for going well beyond the call of duty in their readiness to assist. Thanks also to Keith McInnis, Monica Lloyd, Ashraj Gataora and Chloe Falk for their helpful comments. Finally, I am grateful to Caroline Porter and Sarah-Jayne Boyd at Sage Publications for supporting this project to its conclusion.

Introduction: Criminal Justice and Race Equality

Hindpal Singh Bhui

Why is This Book Needed?

In recent years, racism, conscious and unconscious, individual and institutional, has been uncovered in all of the major criminal justice agencies, most notably by the Stephen Lawrence Inquiry in relation to the police (Macpherson, 1999), and the Zahid Mubarek Inquiry in relation to prisons (Keith, 2006). There has also been clear evidence of discriminatory outcomes in the Crown Prosecution Service (Gus John Partnership, 2003), the Probation Service (HM Inspectorate of Probation, 2000, 2004) and, to some extent, in sentencing decisions (Hood, 1992; Shute *et al.*, 2005). However, despite the undoubted upsurge in policy-level interest in 'race'[1] and racism represented by most of these publications, criminological research has struggled to keep pace with the rapidly changing social and political context of the debate. In particular, the increased prominence of foreign nationals, asylum seekers, and Muslims in debates about race, crime, and justice – groups that are not infrequently conflated blithely with terrorism in media reports – has been little explored, and the growth of gangs divided on ethnic lines is similarly only beginning to be researched. Meanwhile, the 'old' concerns have seen little progress; these include the over-representation of black and minority ethnic people as offenders and their under-representation in staff roles (MoJ, 2007); and the ongoing lack of research into the diverse experiences of the people normally included in catch-all categories such as 'minority ethnic', 'black', and 'Asian' (Garland *et al.*, 2006).

---

[1] The use of the term 'race' as a descriptor for different peoples is much contested and now close to being intellectually redundant. Its use in the title of this volume was more to reflect contemporary usage and recognition, than endorsement of it as a useful descriptive term with an assured future. David Smith's Chapter 1 considers different terminology in detail, and the preferred terminology of different authors is followed in the remainder of this book.

The generally under-researched nature of the subject is reflected by the relatively few academic texts on race and criminal justice currently on the market. Of those that do exist, some are now dated (Genders and Player, 1989) and/or focus on one criminal justice agency (Lewis *et al.*, 2006; Rowe, 2004). The impressive *Racism, Crime and Justice* (Bowling and Phillips, 2002) is more wide-ranging, but lacks in-depth discussion of prisons and probation or a focus on criminal justice practice. Inevitably, it gives little attention to newer debates and concerns that have emerged during the last few years.

The importance of an anti-racist criminal justice system, and of underpinning research and debate, to the development of a more cohesive society is worth stressing; an anti-racist criminal justice system is arguably not simply part of the response to the social division and fragmentation created by racism, but potentially the major institution for promoting race equality. The justice system is the ultimate expression of state authority and morality, and the State imposes its will by judging right and wrong through its agencies and processes. If the criminal justice system works and is seen as a repository of justice, this promotes general social cohesion and progress. If it is seen as upholding, perpetuating, or tolerating discrimination, society itself is weakened. It is surely no coincidence that societies where intolerance and oppression are strong are also societies where the justice system is a distortion of the very concept – upholding anti-racist values means upholding the values of human rights. In short, the criminal justice system is explicitly about moral issues, and social tensions and debates are intensified within the criminal justice microcosm. It is in this context – of limited research in a changing society with a powerfully symbolic criminal justice system – that this book was conceived.

Structure and Content

The book aims to provide an up-to-date and critically stimulating introduction to race, racism, and criminal justice for academics, criminal justice and criminology students, criminal justice and race relations professionals, and others working in or alongside criminal justice agencies. The authors bring an impressive combination of academic breadth and front-line experience, and a diversity of background, experience, and approach. Each chapter is self-standing, but the book can also be read as a complementary whole without the reader having to endure excessive repetition. However, there has been no attempt to remove competing interpretations in different chapters, where they make a distinct contribution to the debate, or help to illuminate discussed issues or concepts. One of the book's key aims is to provide crisp and clear chapters that are accessible to those with little knowledge of the field, but also challenging enough to engage more experienced readers.

The book reflects the impact on criminal justice of the considerable shift in cultural and racial politics in this country over recent years, which has seen, for example, the development of deeper religious fault lines that compound and supersede traditional racialized definitions and race divides. The text summarizes and updates existing knowledge and debates about the key criminal justice agencies, all of which have experienced intense public scrutiny as well as internal soul-searching about racist attitudes and outcomes. The remaining chapters either address themes of contemporary relevance to debates on criminal justice and race equality across agencies – such as the experiences of refugees and asylum seekers as victims and offenders and the link between ethnicity and drug use; or they explore particular issues relating to single agencies in more detail – namely policing of racist hate crime and the experiences of foreign national prisoners.

The first two chapters provide the foundation for what follows. **Chapter 1** by **David Smith** discusses in broad terms many of the **concepts and debates** that recur later in the book. Smith considers the impact on existing theoretical constructs relating to race and crime of deeper religious divides, which both supersede and compound traditional race/colour divides. He outlines how 'multiculturalism' came under attack following inter-ethnic disturbances in British cities in 2001 and the suicide bombings in London in July 2005. He describes an increasingly complex conception of 'racism' whose expression varies over time, place, and social and political context – and the need for similarly multi-faceted anti-racist strategies. Smith explains some of the ambiguities involved in discussions of race and racism and, maps the changing use of terminology, particularly the way that race issues fit into the wider 'diversity' agenda currently pursued by criminal justice agencies. Smith's **Chapter 2** on **contemporary criminology, society, and race issues** explores how these concepts and debates relate to specific developments in criminal justice policy and practice. Smith briefly outlines the current evidence on various aspects of race and criminal justice, particularly the increasing attention given to discrimination within the criminal justice process itself since the publication of the Macpherson Report. He considers the criminogenic effects of social exclusion and economic marginalization and describes the widening criminological and political focus on categories other than 'African Caribbean male' in recent years.

The next four chapters focus in on each of the key criminal justice agencies and their responses to the challenges of racism and race equality. **Michael Rowe's Chapter 3** on **policing** picks up where Smith leaves off, with a more detailed look at the impact on the police service of the Macpherson report. He considers two key themes: police 'stop and search', which he argues is closely related to police interaction with the public; and recruitment of minority ethnic police officers, which relates more to the culture of the police organization. He argues that ethnic discrepancies in stop-and-search figures – which are also discussed in several other chapters – are not as clear as they appear, and that more sophisticated analysis of the figures needs to inform policing practice. He also notes that a more diverse police workforce will not necessarily lead to progress, and that more needs to be done to develop police officers' core understanding of the range of issues affecting crime, policing, and minority ethnic communities. He warns that the increasing centrality of security to contemporary policing discourse threatens to undermine a progressive agenda of anti-racism, a trend that is particularly evident in relation to the Muslim community and terrorism. This theme is picked up again later in the book, especially in relation to prisons.

There is limited research on ethnic disparities in sentencing, and key aspects of what little knowledge there is are briefly summarized in Smith's Chapter 2. However, while there are still considerable gaps in knowledge about disparities in prosecution practice, more is known about decision making in this context. As a senior official responsible for tackling racism in the **Crown Prosecution Service** (CPS), **Seamus Taylor's Chapter 4** provides a uniquely informed perspective on the CPS's faltering race equality journey. He characterizes the CPS as a 'late starter', only sparked into action by a number of negative tribunal findings brought by black and minority ethnic staff. He examines in detail the evidence relating to race bias in prosecutions, and recent progress in the handling of racist and hate crimes.

Just as the murder of Stephen Lawrence in 1993 and the subsequent mishandling of the investigation compelled change and reform within the police service, so the killing of Zahid Mubarek by his racist and mentally disordered cell mate in 2000, propelled the prison service on a similarly difficult and important journey. **Hindpal Singh Bhui's Chapter 4** on **prisons and race equality** paints a complex picture of both improvements and setbacks. He argues that while overt racism in prisons is less discernible than it was in the 1970s and 1980s, more 'subtle' and/or unwitting racism persists and is helping to fuel discontent and alienation, and undermines the legitimacy of prison amongst many black and minority ethnic prisoners. The increasing number of Muslims and foreign nationals (the latter group is considered in more detail in Chapter 10) in the minority ethnic prison population describe different dimensions to their experiences of racism and discrimination. Bhui concludes that there are three major challenges threatening to undermine the development of anti-racist prison cultures: severe prison overcrowding, which encourages a stress on security above all else; impoverished training and professional development of prison officers, who continue to do personally and professionally challenging work without adequate preparation; and the threat to positive race relations posed by unsophisticated attempts to combat radicalization of Muslim prisoners. This latter point resonates particularly strongly with Rowe's thoughts on the detrimental impact of security-focused policing, and there are some interesting similarities in these analyses.

The advent of the National Offender Management Service (NOMS) has brought the prison and probation services into closer alignment, and the problems of one are fast becoming issues for the other. **Sam Lewis's Chapter 6** on **probation and race equality** argues that anti-racist probation practice has been undermined by the lack of attention to race and other diversity issues in the development of NOMS, which now overarches both the probation and prison systems. She questions the validity of risk assessment tools and offending behaviour programmes for minority ethnic groups and highlights the way that the undermining of traditional casework skills and time for probation work have impacted negatively on anti-racist practice. Lewis considers in detail the results of the largest ever study of black and minority ethnic people subject to probation supervision.

Moving on to issues of relevance across the criminal justice system, **Finola Farrant's Chapter 7** draws together and builds upon available evidence on the **experiences of minority ethnic women**. She identifies them as a group which has been increasingly visible in the criminal justice system, while remaining virtually invisible in the literature. She examines the lessons of various theoretical perspectives such as feminism, anti-racism, and post-colonialism, and stresses the value of the concept of 'intersectionality'. This encourages recognition of different forms of oppression and how they link with each other to intensify discriminatory experience. She is critical of the fact that minority ethnic women have traditionally had their racial experiences conceived of through minority ethnic men, and their gender experiences conceived through white women. Intersectionality, she argues, can provide a valuable conceptual tool for analyzing the ways in which gender, race, class, and all other forms of identity can, in different contexts, produce situations in which people become vulnerable to discrimination.

Another group that has up to now had low visibility in serious research and literature about race and racism in criminal justice – as opposed to newspaper headlines and debate – is discussed in **Claire Cooper's Chapter 8** on **asylum seekers and refugees**. Cooper explores their experiences of relative deprivation and poverty and the impact on them of public concerns about terrorism and national security. She cites evidence of their relative social isolation and vulnerability to racial harassment and discrimination, and argues that the boundaries between the immigration and criminal justice systems are gradually being eroded as refugees and asylum seekers are subjected to a process of criminalization. Asylum, she argues, is explicitly a race relations issue, and frequent stories about the mis-treatment of asylum seekers has a deleterious effect on the perceptions and confidence of settled minority ethnic communities.

Complementing and developing some of the themes in Cooper's and Bhui's earlier chapters, **Hindpal Singh Bhui's Chapter 9** discusses the research on the experiences of **foreign national prisoners**. He draws on the largest ever study of foreign prisoners in Britain to examine commonalities and divergences in the experiences of different nationalities and ethnicities. He outlines the possible reasons for the rapid growth in the foreign prisoner population, and the implications for practice in prisons. Bhui also explores the context, origins, and long-term impact of the controversy regarding the release of over a thousand foreign national prisoners in 2006 before they were considered for deportation. He highlights concerns over the lack of effective prison service policies and procedures for the management of this group and discusses recent evidence of a marked rise in suicides amongst foreign national prisoners.

One of the main motivations for compiling this book at this time, was to explore the impact on existing constructs of race and criminal justice of **Muslims' experiences of criminal justice**. This theme recurs in various chapters, where different strands of argument are developed. For example, while Smith's Chapter 2 traces the increasing problematization of Muslim identity, Bhui's Chapter 5 discusses the specific difficulties that face a prison system attempting to identify and challenge radicalization amongst Muslim prisoners. These discussions are crystallized in **Basia Spalek, Robert Lambert, and Abdul Haqq Baker's Chapter 10** which contends that the stress on radicalization has already had considerable negative outcomes. In particular, the authors argue that legitimate religious aspirations and spiritual awareness amongst Muslims have been misrepresented in the police and prison systems, resulting in stigmatization and alienation. They argue that Muslims are faced with criminal justice agencies that problematize their faith identity, and that the common identification of minority Salafi and Islamist community groups with terrorists is unjust and counter-productive. The work of the police service's Muslim Contact Unit is discussed in detail, and the importance of 'bottom-up', partnership and community-based approaches to engagement are stressed as the most effective ways of countering terrorism and radicalization.

Spalek, Lambert, and Haqq Baker's contention that there has been a lack of attention to Muslims' vulnerability to racist attacks places some onus on the police to respond to and reduce the fear of victimization. **Nathan Hall's Chapter 11** considers the **policing of racist hate crime** in detail, examining definitions of hate crime, as well as reporting, recording, and investigative practices. Drawing on his substantial research in this area, he concludes that despite significant improvements, there is still cause for concern about the way that racist hate crimes are policed and about the police's ability to provide a service that matches the needs of victims and wider communities.

The final chapter, Karen Mills' Chapter 12 on **drug use, ethnicity, and racism** examines another arena in which service provision has historically left much to be desired, but where there has been less attention on promoting change. Mills discusses the complex reality of drug use within minority ethnic communities, where, despite high use of some drugs by some groups, overall drug use is actually less prevalent. She argues that factors such as community, family, and faith can both support and lead to the exclusion of drug users, and considers the often unmet treatment needs of minority ethnic communities. She includes emerging evidence on newer migrant communities where types and patterns of usage differ substantially from what is known about more established minority ethnic groups.

Some Conclusions?

Studying and writing about race, racism, and ethnicity is inevitably an exercise in tolerance. Researchers must commonly use imperfect and contested language to express imprecise general conclusions about non-homogenous categories. Disagreement about terminology and the research subjects is virtually inevitable, but research findings based on broad descriptive categories (e.g., 'Muslims' rather than 'Somali Muslims') will continue to make an important contribution to knowledge, even if, as Garland *et al.* (2006) rightly point out, we must guard against over-simplification.

It is also clear that no text that seeks to reflect the complexity of human experience and professional response can possibly hope to be comprehensive or unflawed. This book cannot be anything other than a partial contribution to a subject that is ever-changing, and could easily have been twice the length. However, while it does not purport to offer a 'theory of everything' to do with race equality and criminal justice, it will help to give readers a broad and up to date understanding of the influence of ethnicity, racism, and cultural difference in the development of the criminal justice system. In other words, while many convincing arguments are presented in many chapters, there are no final conclusions on offer – in their place the book offers a stronger platform for informed and critical debate and progress.

The book highlights some new directions and debates about race and criminal justice, but it is worth stressing again that the 'old' challenges – such as the marked disproportionality of African Caribbean people at all stages of the criminal justice process – have not in the meantime resolved themselves. Instead they have been overlaid by other concerns, which research and practice must continue to expose and understand, and to which the research must, wherever possible, suggest solutions.

In 2000, the Parekh Report's impressive analysis of multi-ethnic Britain considered the country to be at a turning point, where it had to decide whether it was to become narrow and inward looking, characterized by conflict between communities and regions; or develop as a 'community of citizens' and a 'community of communities', where a tolerant and pluralistic human rights culture could thrive (Parekh, 2000). The challenges of pluralism have, to say the least, posed considerable difficulties for a society that was not at ease with its diversity even before the London terrorist attacks of July 2005. The notion of multi-culturalism has come under sustained attack; inter-ethnic tensions are showing little sign of abating, and are in some respects increasing. The concept of 'racisms' (see Smith's Chapter 1) is also increasingly important in the context of destructive inner city conflicts and gang violence between different minority ethnic groups, and the marginalization of Muslim minorities in particular. A brief perusal of the British press during 2007 reveals many prominent crime-related stories, mostly speculative and unevidenced, about Irish travellers, African Caribbean family structures, foreign nationals, and, most vehemently, Muslims. The ongoing debate about anti-terror legislation and frequent attacks from politicians on the increasingly politically inconvenient Human Rights Act give more pause for thought. The research and arguments in this book are presented as a small contribution to us finding a way through these difficult times and to promoting a positive human rights ethos throughout the criminal justice system.

References

Bowling, B. and Phillips, C. (2002) *Racism, Crime and Justice*. Harlow: Longman.

Crown Prosecution Service (2001) Report of an independent inquiry into race discrimination in the Crown Prosecution Service (The 'Denman Report'). London: CPS.

Garland, J., Spalek, B. and Chakraborti, N. (2006) 'Hearing Lost Voices: Issues in Researching "Hidden" Minority Ethnic Communities', British Journal of Criminology 46: 423–37.

Genders, E. and Player, E. (1989) *Race in Prisons*. Oxford: Clarendon Press.

Gus John Partnership (2003) Race for Justice: A review of CPS decision-making for possible racial bias at each stage of the prosecution process. London: CPS.

Her Majesty's Inspectorate of Probation (HMIP) (2000) Towards Race Equality: A Thematic Report. London: HMIP.

Her Majesty's Inspectorate of Probation (HMIP) (2004) Towards Race Equality: Follow-Up Inspection Report. London: HMIP.

Hood, R. (1992) *Race and Sentencing*. Oxford: Clarendon Press.

Keith, Justice (2006) Report of the Zahid Mubarek Inquiry, Volumes 1 and 2. London: The Stationary Office.

Lewis, S., Raynor, P., Smith, D., *et al.* (eds) (2006) Race and Probation. London: Willan Publishing.

Macpherson, W. (1999) The Stephen Lawrence Inquiry. London: The Stationery Office.

Ministry of Justice (2007) Statistics on Race and the Criminal Justice System (Section 95 statistics). London: Ministry of Justice.

Parekh, B. (The Parekh Report) (2000) *The Future of Multi Ethnic Britain*. London: Profile Books.

Rowe, M. (2004) *Policing, Race and Racism*. Cullompton: Willan Publishing.

Shute, S., Hood, R. and Seemungal, F. (2005) *A Fair Hearing? Ethnic Minorities in the Criminal Courts* Devon: Willan Publishing.

ONE

Key Concepts and Theories About 'Race'

David Smith

This chapter attempts to explore the meanings of some central concepts in the field of race, ethnicity, and identity, and to show how these underpin contemporary arguments about multiculturalism, migration, and 'Britishness'. The aim is to provide initial clarification of the issues explored in more detail in subsequent chapters. In pursuit of this, the chapter moves from a discussion of fundamental theories of race, in their historical development and their current expression, to an exploration of some of the key issues in recent political and policy debates. It explores the move away from biological understandings of 'race' towards the more sociologically and culturally sensitive concept of 'ethnicity', and how racist ideology has followed a similar path, from claims based on a biological hierarchy of 'races' to claims about the threats to traditional and national identity posed by cultural diversity and difference. The chapter explores, and takes issue with, recent claims that policies of multiculturalism have promoted segregation and eroded national identity. It also shows how anti-racist arguments have also become more complex, as simple polarities of white and black, oppressor and oppressed, have been replaced by a less essentialist appreciation of the complexity and ambiguity of racial identities.

The Meanings of 'Race'

Many writers have commented on the problems of definition and usage that arise in discussions of race, racism, and associated concepts (Goldberg and Solomos, 2002; Back and Solomos, 2000). Well-founded unease about the meaning of 'race', in particular, has led to the practice of putting scare quotes around the word, to show that the writer does not suppose that it can be used unproblematically; to avoid this awkwardness, some writers have preferred the term 'ethnicity', which suggests a more socially situated, less biological concept (just as 'gender' is often preferred to 'sex' by writers wishing to convey a sense that the differences between women and men are not simply a matter of biology). This preference does not, however, remove all difficulties. Social scientists often speak of 'essentially contested concepts' when dealing with terms whose meanings are inherently unstable and liable to shift over time and in different contexts: Bowling and Phillips (2002: xvi–vii), for example, treat not only 'race', but also 'ethnicity', 'crime', and 'discrimination', as 'essentially contested'. They describe their discomfort in the face of a tension between 'empiricism' and 'social constructionism'. Empiricism, in this context, assumes that race and crime are real, that they exist in some objective, essential sense, which allows them to be observed and measured; social constructionism takes these terms to refer to 'dynamic social processes', and therefore assumes that their meanings are multiple and fluid. The dilemma for Bowling and Phillips, as for other writers in this field, is that they need to use apparently objective and factual data on racial (or ethnic) differences in offending, prosecution, sentencing, victimization, etc., for the purposes of analysis, while 'contending that race is not "real" outside the racist ideologies and discriminatory practices that bring it into being' (p. xvii). But, even though race is a social construct, it has real, material effects, and the approach of Bowling and Phillips is therefore to reject essentialist views of race while 'retaining race and ethnic categories in order to illuminate the racialised patterns of everyday human experience' (p. xvii).

This approach is broadly that which informs the following discussion. Race is the key term in the vocabulary of this field, from which many of the other terms flow, either by direct derivation from it or through a rejection of its implications. From the beginning, the idea of race was bound up with ideas of racial difference and superiority and inferiority. Considering only Europe, it is possible to find a conception of race and racial distinction in the writings of the ancient Greeks, for whom non-Greeks were generically 'barbarians' (people whose language sounded like 'Bar-bar'), and usually regarded as by definition inferior to Greeks (De Ste. Croix, 1983: 416–7) – although in the fifth century BCE Herodotus argued in the second book of his *History* that the Greeks had borrowed from the Egyptians in culture and religion, and not *vice versa* (Bernal, 1987). In mediaeval Europe, religious hatred and suspicion was mixed with ideas of racial difference in Christian hostility towards Jews, and later towards Muslims from the Middle East and North Africa. According to Wieviorka (2002), however, 'race' in something like its contemporary sense is a later European invention, associated with the beginnings of maritime empire-building in the fifteenth century. What Wieviorka (2002: 460) calls 'protoracist' conceptions of race and difference were articulated from the seventeenth century, in European accounts of the African and native American peoples whose lands they invaded. Physical differences between these peoples and the supposed European norm were noted, described, treated as signs or causes of inferiority, and explained mainly in terms of differences in the natural environment, especially climatic differences. Towards the end of the eighteenth century, the first 'scientific' conceptions of race began to appear (thus considerably preceding Darwin and the theory of evolution, which is sometimes blamed for providing the basis for a scientific classification of racial differences and the establishment of a racial hierarchy).

Scientific Racism

Gould (1996) describes the development of such a hierarchy from an originally relatively neutral description of the geographical distribution of human types (defined as races). The first account of human races with scientific claims was produced in 1758 by the Swedish Carolus Linnaeus, regarded as the founder of the modern system of biological taxonomy (genera, species, and individuals). Linnaeus proposed a four-fold classification: *homo sapiens Americanus*, *Europeus*, *Asiaticus*, and *Afer* (African). This was modified by the German naturalist J.F. Blumenbach, who by 1795 had developed Linnaeus' scheme into a five-fold classification. Humans belonged to one of five varieties: Caucasian (for light-skinned inhabitants of Europe and adjacent areas), Mongolian (for East Asian people), Ethiopian (for dark-skinned Africans), American (for the indigenous people of the Americas), and Malay (for the people of the Pacific islands and the aboriginal people of Australia). The classification was by now not merely geographical but explicitly hierarchical, ordered by Blumenbach according to the eccentric and subjective criterion of physical beauty, which supposedly had reached its apex (according to the evidence of skulls) among the Caucasus Mountains in modern Russia and Georgia. Blumenbach attributed the degeneration of the non-Caucasian races to the effects of climate, and believed that it was in principle reversible: the descendants of 'Ethiopians' transported north out of Africa might eventually become white. While such thinking is offensive to modern readers, according to Gould (1996: 405), Blumenbach 'was the least racist, most egalitarian, and most genial of all Enlightenment writers on the subject of human diversity'; he believed in the fundamental unity of humanity, and that the moral and intellectual differences among the racial groups were minor – certainly not enough to justify the exploitation of one by another. It is his classification, however, that became the most influential scientific account of human races, and elements of it remain in official use.

A simpler and more overtly racist classification of humanity was devised by the French aristocrat Gobineau, who published his views on 'the inequality of human races' between 1853 and 1855 (Darwin's *The Origin of Species* was not published until 1859). Gould (1996: 379) describes Gobineau as the 'grandfather of modern academic racism' and 'undoubtedly the most influential academic racist of the nineteenth century'. His scheme, which divided humanity hierarchically into whites, yellows, and blacks, was enthusiastically embraced by ideological racists. According to Gobineau, civilizations prospered to the degree that they maintained racial purity, and declined as a result of miscegenation; the white races would maintain their superior position only if they remained relatively pure and avoided diluting their stock by breeding with the inferior yellow and brown races. This kind of argument, of course, became familiar in the twentieth century, not only in the genocidal programme of Nazism but in advocacy of eugenics and controlled reproduction to maintain the purity and strength of national stocks. Vanstone (2004) shows that the eugenicist movement, by now reliant on a particular view of evolutionary theory for its scientific basis, was a far from negligible influence on the early development of the probation service: the only solution for offenders deemed degenerate, it was argued, was 'permanent detention and complete segregation' (Vanstone, 2004: 39). In the early years of the twentieth century, eugenic thinking often formed part of a package of 'progressive' ideas for social improvement and modernization, sometimes in the form of 'Lombrosianism'. Lombroso, as all students of criminology know, began his work with the study of differences in human skulls (on which Gobineau also based his theories), and received from this his insight that criminals were examples of evolutionary 'atavism', throwbacks to an earlier stage of human development; in this, even if 'white', they resembled the inferior races as described by Gobineau and his followers.

Eugenic plans for the maintenance and improvement of national racial stocks ceased, for most people, to be morally or intellectually defensible after the Second World War and the revelation of the Nazi programme for the extermination of Jews and other groups considered a threat to racial purity. The point of discussing the roots of racial theory here is, as it was for Gould (1996) in his additional chapters for the second edition of his book, that in spite of this discredit the basic ideas of racial theory persist in ostensibly respectable academic writing. Gould was particularly concerned to refute the arguments of Herrnstein and Murray (1994), whose book received much critical attention, especially for its supposed demonstration that intelligence was stratified not only by social class and status, but by race. Herrnstein and Murray studied IQ results, not the size and shape of skulls, but their method of argument and their results were similar to Gobineau's, and they were as confident as he had been that 'race' was a scientific biological category, not an ideological construct. Intelligence (as measured by IQ tests conducted on Americans) was treated as an irrevocable hereditary fact, and the results showed that Asians were slightly superior to Caucasians, and Caucasians substantially superior to people of African descent (Gould, 1996: 369). It is worth noting in this context that both Herrnstein and Murray have had considerable, though controversial, influence in the fields of criminology, criminal justice, and social policy, in Britain as well as the USA (e.g., Wilson and Herrnstein, 1985; Murray et al., 1996). Herrnstein and Murray themselves claimed after its publication that their arguments about racial differences were only a minor topic of their book; but its publication and reception showed the continued vitality of ideologies of racial difference, when given a new veneer of science and statistical rigour.

Identity and Difference

Essentialism and Hybridity

Rejecting the claim that race is a natural category that denotes a biological reality, we must, like Bowling and Phillips (2002), recognize that in using the term we are referring to an 'imagined community' (Anderson, 1983) – but it is an imagined community with real, material effects. Race and ethnicity need to be understood as social constructions, a means by which differences can be recognized and accorded meaning (Goldberg and Solomos, 2002). As socially constructed categories, they are liable to change their boundaries across time and context, depending on who deploys the terms and for what social or political purposes. For example, 'black' has quite different meanings when employed by Gobineau and his intellectual descendants and when used as a signifier of political affiliation and solidarity by groups formed to resist racism and its effects, as it was in USA from the 1960s. In this instance, a term whose origins lie in ideologies of racial difference and hierarchy was subverted and used as an element in a political struggle against racism; 'black' came to refer not primarily to race or even colour, but to the experience of social subordination and oppression. But this subversion also illustrates the difficulty of using a term that implies a fixed, biological essence in a non-essentialist way. Whatever its value and success as a political statement, this use of 'black' arguably obscures important differences among minority ethnic groups. Modood (1994), for example, suggests that in resisting the categories of racial difference, the term risks implying another false essentialism, that the experience of all minority ethnic groups in Britain is the same. Modood argues that the political conception of blackness that was dominant in the 1980s denied the particularities of the experience of racism among Asian communities, by equating racial discrimination with discrimination on the basis of colour, not culture, and that the majority of Asians rejected the attempt to impose on them an overly politicized 'black' identity. In the contemporary probation context, this tension is reflected in the different positions of the Association of Black Probation Officers and the National Association of Asian Probation Staff, the first promoting a political 'black' identity and the second insisting on the specificity of Asian experiences of discrimination, for example, over religion and dress (e.g., Heer, 2007).

Modood's (1994: 859) support for the 'new emphasis on multi-textured identities' is reflected in much recent work that has sought to break with the over-simple formulations of the past and to develop concepts that reflect the complexity and differentiation within categories like 'Asian' or 'African-Caribbean', or the catch-all category of 'Black and Minority Ethnic' (BME) groups which is now generally used by the Home Office and other government departments (e.g., Jansson, 2006). Hall (1992) for example, wrote of 'new ethnicities' that call into question what it means to be black and, in a local context, 'the dominant coding of what it means to be British' (Back, 1996: 4). Others (e.g., Gilroy, 2000) have explored the nature of 'hybrid' identities (such as African American or British Asian) in increasingly cosmopolitan and globalized societies in which the traditional distinctions of nation and race have (it is argued) become less important. In a more critical spirit, May (2002) distinguishes hybridity theory from multiculturalism (which is discussed below), arguing that the idea of hybridity, conceived as a positive resource for social change, entails a rejection of ethnic and cultural rootedness as a basis for identity; such traditional sources of identity are, according to those who celebrate hybridity, inherently conservative, introverted, and backward-looking. May argues that hybridity theory exaggerates the extent to which 'postmodern' identities are in fact hybrid rather than singular, and that it removes a political resource for resistance to racism and discrimination by suggesting that 'all group-based identities are essentialist' (May, 2002: 133) – and therefore liable to practices of exclusion, racism, and violence. As part of a defence of multiculturalism, May distinguishes between race and ethnicity, and argues that while categorizations based on race have historically always been essentialist, and associated with hierarchy and exploitation, categorizations by ethnicity or nationhood need not be essentialized, nor do they necessarily entail exclusion and conflict (Jenkins, 1997).

Ethnicity

As used in these contexts, 'ethnicity' has been stripped of virtually all the biological connotations of 'race', and the use of the plural 'ethnicities' is intended to signal a clean break with essentialism and a recognition of diversity and difference; similarly, the use of 'racisms' recognizes that 'there is no one monolithic racism but numerous historically situated racisms' (Back, 1996: 9). But ethnicity too *can* be used in an essentialist way, even when referring to social and cultural, rather than biological and hereditary, difference: culture rather than biology is conceived as an essential characteristic of a particular group. Some of the literature on the Irish in Britain provides an example. The most influential position on this, at least until recently, was that the Irish were the largest minority ethnic group in Britain ('ethnic' here surely makes sense only as a cultural category), and that their long-term experience of deprivation and disadvantage was under-recognized because of their 'invisibility' (Hickman and Walter, 1997). The claim about the size of the Irish minority is based on the assumption that everyone with at least one Irish-born parent should be counted (and will self-categorize) as Irish, and this was accepted without argument by the 'Parekh Report' (Commission on the Future of Multi-Racial Britain, 2000: 31, 374), which declared that, with an estimated population of 1,969,000 in England and Wales, the Irish were 'by far the largest migrant community' (the figure was arrived at by multiplying the number of Irish-born people recorded by the 1991 census by 2.5). In the event, 641,804 people in England and Wales described themselves as ethnically Irish in the 2001 census (Office of National Statistics, 2003). Howard (2006) describes the campaign by 'ethnic activists' for a question about Irish ethnicity to be included in the 2001 census, and what he sees as their special pleading after the results appeared, and showed that nothing like the predicted number of people saw themselves as Irish, or at least defined themselves as such for census purposes. Howard argues that the campaign to include the category 'Irish' in the ethnicity options in the census was a predictable consequence of policies of multiculturalism, which depend on the official recognition and institutionalization of a range of ethnic groups; if a group is excluded from an existing system of ethnic classification, it can be expected to mobilize for its inclusion. Official 'ethnic' categories are thus the product of political pressures and decisions within the context of multiculturalism.

Multiculturalism and its Critics

Policies of multiculturalism have long been attacked by the political right, since they first emerged as an alternative to assimilation, initially in the Greater London Council and London local authorities in the early 1980s. The basis of this attack is essentially that multiculturalism undermines national unity and identity and is thus unpatriotic (May, 2002). More recently, as immigration has acquired a renewed political salience with the enlargement of the European Union in May 2004, such policies have been criticized from elsewhere on the political spectrum, and on rather less familiar grounds. One strand of criticism can be associated with the French republican tradition, and insists that no ethnic or cultural group should have any special legal standing; what matters is shared citizenship, and (in principle) equality in education, housing, and employment. This is why the idea of using a census to count the size of minority ethnic groups is anathema to many politicians and social commentators in France. A more influential kind of criticism has been articulated since 2005 by the Commission for Racial Equality and latterly by its successor the Equality and Human Rights Commission, both chaired by Trevor Phillips. As expressed on the CRE's website (see the page on 'Integration, multiculturalism and the CRE', archived since the reorganization at http://83.137.212.42/sitearchive/cre/diversity/integration/index.html, accessed 24.2.2008), the argument is that multiculturalism has led to more polarized communities and promoted social and residential segregation. Multiculturalism is said to be characterized by particularism rather than universalism, and a stress on group differences rather than common identity and membership of some wider society (such as might be represented by 'Britishness'). It is criticized for claiming that 'all cultures are of equal value and must be publicly recognized as such', and accommodated by the 'wider society' without any expectation of reciprocation or compromise. It is said to entail a view of ethnic and cultural groups as closed and conservative in their beliefs and practices, and as regarding membership of these groups as the key defining feature of the identity of their members. The results, it is said, are that public policy is shaped on the basis of dubious assumptions that cultural organizations represent the interests of minority ethnic groups more authentically than any other organizations can, and thus participation in institutions and political activities based on cultural identity is privileged over engagement with common democratic processes and involvement in the civic and political institutions of the wider society.

'Sleepwalking to Segregation'?

Multiculturalism's recognition of difference is then blamed for a supposed increase in social and residential segregation. Phillips made a speech in September 2005 on 'Sleepwalking to segregation' after '7/7' (the attacks by Islamist suicide bombers on the London transport network on 7 July 2005). He revived the long-expressed fear that parts of British cities would soon experience the 'hyper-segregation' and ghettoization of many urban areas in the USA. This anxiety had to some extent been laid to rest, or at least shown to be exaggerated, by the findings of the 1991 census (Ratcliffe, 1996), but Phillips apparently accepted the claim, to be found in much of the media and some political rhetoric, that it had increased more recently (the latest Census findings, which suggest the opposite, are discussed below). In the CRE/Phillips argument, segregation is bad by definition, because it prevents integration, the preferred policy goal, and integration is distinguished from assimilation, defined on the website cited above as (in the form it took in the 1950s and 1960s):

the absorption of minority migrant communities into the majority community with no noticeable effect on the culture and way of life of the majority, while expecting that the culture and way of life minorities brought with them would disappear.

Minority cultures are not to be suppressed in order to establish a shared identity of Britishness, but they are to co-exist with this 'national identity' in 'a common sense of belonging'. Phillips describes integration as 'a two-way street', meaning that 'settled communities accept that new people will bring change with them', and the newcomers reciprocate by accepting that they too will need to change.

There are problems with some of these formulations; for example, how long does it take to become a settled community, and how long does one remain a newcomer? While Phillips was writing in the aftermath of the 7 July bombings, he may also have had in mind the recent arrival in Britain of migrants from central and eastern Europe, to whom the term 'newcomers' could be applied more accurately than to the British-born suicide bombers. The implications of this new pattern of migration for concepts of multiculturalism, integration, and Britishness are discussed below. A more obvious problem with Phillips' account is that the weight of evidence suggests that residential segregation on ethnic lines has declined rather than increased since 1991. The interpretation of the census data is complex and has been disputed by geographers and demographers (Simpson, 2004; 2005; Johnston *et al.*, 2005), but the data certainly do not provide clear support for Phillips' thesis about increasing segregation – which is not to deny that some members of some groups, in some parts of the country, do live in highly segregated conditions.

Segregation and Integration

Simpson (2007) gives a clear and accessible account of the main issues, in terms both of demography and of the implications of his analysis for public policy. He argues that the census figures do not support either 'white flight' or 'Muslim self-segregation' arguments, and that some degree of concentration of ethnic groups is inevitable, for purely demographic reasons. The argument, in summary, is this: initial immigration follows demand for labour in urban areas, and brings people to particular localities where cheap rented housing is available. Friends and family members follow the pioneer immigrants into the same places. If the minority ethnic population in a locality increases and the white population decreases, we should not assume that this is because of movement and retreat; births and deaths change populations naturally, and since most immigrants are in their twenties, they have many years ahead of them in which they are 'much more likely to have children than to die' (Simpson, 2007: 5). Housing shortages in the areas of original settlement create pressure for movement elsewhere, and those who move, and who move furthest away, tend to be those who are relatively advantaged, for example, in terms of income and marketable skills. This process of dispersal can lead to new clusters of minority ethnic populations outside the original areas of settlement, and Simpson concludes that concentrations of minority populations can thus grow without any segregation, and in fact with more mixing.

Between 1991 and 2001, all minority ethnic populations in Britain, except for Chinese and African groups, grew more through natural change than through immigration, as is to be expected a generation or so after the period of initial settlement. But this happened with no increase in segregation; instead, for all minority groups there was a decrease in the 'index of dissimilarity'. For example, in 1991, the index of dissimilarity (which measures evenness of distribution) for Pakistanis was 75.1, and in 2001 it was 71.7; it would be 100 if all Pakistanis lived in areas where no members of any other group lived. It shows that the Pakistani population became more dispersed, with its members more likely to live in ethnically mixed areas. The other index used by Simpson, the index of isolation, measures lack of exposure to other ethnic groups; it would also be 100 if all members of a particular group lived in areas where no one else lived. In 2001, on average, whites lived in areas that were 93.5 per cent white (95.3% in 1991); for all other groups, the figure was under 20 per cent – that is, minority ethnic people tend to live in ethnically mixed areas, not areas in which their own group predominates. The index of isolation increased for African, Pakistani, Bangladeshi, and Chinese groups, but this is purely because these were the groups whose size grew most between 1991 and 2001. The third measure used by Simpson is the number of 'polarized enclaves' – wards in which one minority group is dominant. The number of these remained tiny over the decade, at eight in both 1991 and 2001. In fact, there was movement away from the areas of the greatest concentration of their population by all minority ethnic groups, and movement into areas of lower concentration, in a process of dispersal and mixing, not self-segregation and retreat. Looking at the local authorities in which at least one ward had a minority white population in 2001, Simpson finds only two cases where there was movement out on the part of whites and a movement in on the part of BME groups. The pattern one would find if increasing ghettoization was happening, as a result of white flight and minority self-segregation, thus barely exists; the two cases identified by Simpson, Harrow and Waltham Forest, are ethnically diverse areas in which there is no ward in which the white population is less than a quarter of the total. Thus, figures that have been used to show increasing segregation, such as the forecast Simpson (2007) makes for Birmingham, that white people will be in a minority by 2027, in fact reflect only the natural growth of populations in which there are more births than deaths; and in 2007, Birmingham was still ethnically diverse, with a white population about twice the size of the population of Pakistani origin.

Figures and projections derived from censuses of course have their limitations: a full census is conducted only every ten years, and even then not everyone is counted; homeless people and people in institutional care or custody are not counted, and nor, on the whole, are Gypsy and Traveller communities (treated as a distinct ethnic group by the Commission on the Future of Multi-Racial Britain [2000]). Furthermore, as was noted above in the case of the Irish, the ethnic groups covered by the census and other surveys are social constructions and subject to change over time; Simpson (2007) gives the example of 'British Bangladeshi' as an ethnic category that many people might find acceptable in 2007, but was barely available ten years before. Population surveys in Britain have still hardly begun to take account of the East European migrants who began to appear as a major element in media panics about migration after the enlargement of the European Union in May 2004, forming a relatively new target for racist and xenophobic fears and media panics. With all due qualifications, though, the Phillips/CRE analysis – that segregation has increased, and that this is at least partly because of the excesses of policies of multiculturalism – does not survive scrutiny in the light of the work of geographers and demographers.

The Politics of Identity

That analysis, however, reflected a widespread set of concerns. Simpson (2007) concludes his paper by asking why such persistent political attention is paid to segregation, and why political discourse tends to exaggerate the differences among ethnic groups. A possible answer is in the rise of 'the new identity politics' (Muir, 2007), a result of the forces of globalization and in particular the greatly increased scale of movement of peoples, whether in pursuit of economic opportunities or in flight from social dislocation, conflict, and war. An important outcome has been a dramatic increase in the number of ethnic and cultural groups with substantial populations in Britain. Treating language as an indicator of identity, the CRE (2007) reports that when the census team in 2001 consulted with local authorities about what languages should be used for the dissemination of census forms and information, they obtained a list of 24. The census itself showed that around three million people in Britain were born in countries where English is not the first language, but many of them will have been competent in English; the problem for those concerned with segregation and separation – social if not geographical – is people who are not competent in English. The Commission on Integration and Cohesion, established by the government in August 2006, made a particular point in its report, published in June 2007, of questioning whether local authorities should continue automatically to translate their materials into locally used languages, and suggested a more selective approach, based on assessment of need and the vulnerability of particular groups (Commission on Integration and Cohesion, 2007: 159). Translations into a wide variety of languages are clearly a product of a commitment to policies of multiculturalism, so the Commission's scepticism about their effects is an aspect of its scepticism about these policies more generally.

Muir (2007: 4) suggests that the mobilities of globalization have 'led some to fear that older forms of solidarity and identity are being weakened while all too familiar tensions and hostilities have gained a new lease of life'. These are the tensions of racism and xenophobia, which of course arose in part from 'older forms of identity'. As Simpson (2007) argues, we should not assume, as politicians, often do assume, that the erosion of old identities is always a negative and regrettable process; indeed, the hardening and strengthening of some such identities into what Giddens (1994) calls 'fundamentalisms' could be a major source of racist and nationalist, as well as religious and cultural, hostility. It is this kind of consideration that has traditionally led the political left to be wary of identities based on national tradition and appeals to patriotism, but Muir (2007: 5) argues that a sense of national identity is necessary for the realization of some of the 'key collective goals' of the left in Britain, such as support for public goods like the health service and greater participation in civic and political activities. Hence, the revival of interest in 'Britishness' and what this means, which according to Gordon Brown (2006) includes 'a sense of fair play, a belief in individual liberty and a sense of civic responsibility'. Whether there is anything particularly 'British' about this list is open to question, and it is vague enough to command general assent (which was perhaps the intention); it is quite compatible with the established appeal to Britishness, and sometimes Englishness, as a justification for xenophobia and nationalism, often expressed politically as opposition to the European Union. But the fact that the liberal, social democratic left has begun to explore the meanings of Britishness as part of its concern with questions of citizenship and social cohesion (ETHNOS, 2005) reflects a growing sense that the question of identity has both become problematic (it can no longer be taken for granted) and is crucial for the achievement of peaceful, reasonably harmonious social relations and a safe, mutually supportive fabric of social life. National identity, it is argued, needs to interact with local senses of identity and belonging in the interests of 'community cohesion' – authoritatively defined as the means of reducing inter-ethnic conflict (Cantle, 2001; 2005).

Racism, Anti-racism, and Diversity

The catalyst for the community cohesion agenda, and the origin of widespread anxieties about segregation and identity, was the rioting in Bradford, Burnley, and Oldham in the early summer of 2001. While the vocabulary of 'community cohesion' tends to avoid specific engagement with issues of racism, there is no doubt that racist hostilities and exclusions lay behind much of the anger and resentment that were eventually expressed in collective violence (for Oldham in particular, see Ray and Smith, 2004; Ray et al., 2004). Like 'race', racism is difficult to define. Back (1996: 9) discusses the development of the term as he moves towards his own definition (I have removed several references from the quotation):

Early writers concentrated on criticizing the legitimacy of the 'idea of race' or they accepted the existence of 'races' and focused on the way in which they were constructed in congenitally superior/inferior relationships. I will refer to racism as an ideology that defines social collectivities in terms of 'natural' and immutable biological differences. These are invested with negative connotations of cultural difference and inferiority, whereby the presence of other 'races' can be correlated with the economic and social health of either a specific region or the nation as a whole. Racism is defined within particular historical and social contexts where past racial ideology can be used alongside new elements; thus there is no one monolithic racism but numerous historically situated racisms.

This is a useful explanation in that it acknowledges much of the complexity of racism and the ways in which it is expressed, and Back's work itself fully illustrates this complexity in showing how racist sentiments and attitudes are often only one element in subtle and nuanced relationships among young people from different ethnic and cultural backgrounds. Arguably, though, Back's definition does not cover the full range of ways in which racism is manifested in contemporary Britain (and elsewhere). Back (1996: 67) himself writes of the 'new racism' that defines outsiders (in this case, Vietnamese people) in terms of cultural rather than 'racial' difference, and this shift from biology to culture is also identified by Wieviorka (2002) as an important development in European racism since 1945. Racist rhetoric came to place less emphasis on a biologically based hierarchy of superiority and inferiority, and instead argued that cultural differences could be such as to produce an inherent incompatibility between national or European values and practices and those of some minority groups (Wieviorka, 2002).

This process, of defining and justifying racist hatred in cultural rather than biological terms, can be seen, for example, in the propaganda of the British National Party, which has increasingly been directed at 'Asians', especially Muslims, on the grounds of cultural incompatibility, while disavowing overt racism. Most of the white perpetrators of racist violence interviewed by Ray *et al.* (2004) also denied holding racist views, even when there was plentiful evidence that their offending had involved terms of racist abuse. Since they were quite ready to talk about their use of violence, it is unlikely that they were simply giving the interviewer what they judged would be socially acceptable (or politically correct) answers. While this may have motivated some (just as it may partly explain why broader surveys consistently show low levels of support for overtly racist opinions (e.g., Ipsos MORI, 2007), another interpretation is that at a rational, cognitive level, they did not regard themselves as racist, at least in relation to a biological conception of race. What they felt is another matter, and Ray *et al.* argue that strong, barely acknowledged emotions of shame and resentment lay behind their outbursts of violence against South Asian people whom they perceived as undeservedly more successful, socially and economically, than themselves. Very few articulated racism as an ideology, and they generally saw themselves as disadvantaged relative to their South Asian victims, not in a position of racial, or even cultural, superiority. It is clear that some forms of racism, or some racisms, cannot be understood in terms of an ideology of superiority derived from scientific rationalizations of imperialism, but in terms that are cultural, situationally specific, and rooted in emotions rather than beliefs.

Further shifts in the meanings of racism have emerged from the new patterns of migration in the twenty-first century. In Britain and other Western European countries, refugees and asylum seekers from countries devastated by war, ethnic conflict, or civil breakdown, in parts of Africa and the Middle East, have featured prominently in political and media discourse, often with an implication that their claims to be fleeing from persecution and possible death are false, and that they are actually motivated by the hope of economic improvement (see Chapter 8 by Claire Cooper in this book). This is certainly the motive attributed to those who are supposedly the latest threat, migrants from Central and Eastern Europe, and particularly from Poland, since May 2004, when ten countries were admitted to membership of the European Union. An Ipsos MORI survey (2007) found that anxieties about immigration had grown over the past five years, and that generally positive attitudes towards ethnic diversity co-existed with a widely held view – among people from minority ethnic groups as well as the white population – that there were too many immigrants in Britain. The survey cites (p. 4) the European Social Survey of 2002–03, which found that only a quarter of British respondents would like to live in an area where almost nobody was of a different ethnic group than themselves, a lower proportion than in other European countries apart from Germany and Sweden. On the other hand, according to Ipsos MORI (2007), more people identified immigration and race relations as the most important political issue than any other, ahead of education, health, and international terrorism. In relation to migrants from within Europe, many of whom intend their stay in Britain to be temporary, racist sentiments are most often justified not on biological or even cultural, but on economic grounds – though no doubt economic arguments often mask less socially acceptable hostilities. Enthusiasts for a globalized economy must logically support the free movement of labour across national boundaries (Legrain, 2007), and it is widely accepted that migrants have contributed to the British economy by bringing scarce skills, particularly to the building industry, and being prepared to do low-paid, often seasonal work that no one else will do, particularly in agriculture (Travis, 2007). The dominant political rhetoric, however, emphasizes the economic threats posed by migrants, in undercutting wages, taking jobs that would otherwise be done by British citizens, and placing an extra burden on local housing, health, and social services – and the criminal justice system.

As the expressions of racism have become more complex and their targets more diverse, anti-racist policies have had to discard the relatively simple formulations used when they were first articulated in local government, welfare, and criminal justice organizations in the 1980s. Then, racism tended to be seen as monolithic, all-pervasive, and institutionalized (cf. Macpherson, 1999); the political conception of 'blackness' criticized by Modood (1994) was generally accepted without much critical scrutiny; and multiculturalism was rejected as a patronizing, if well-intentioned, concept that was a legacy of colonialism and served only to reinforce the 'power of the white community' (Gardiner, 1985). Walker (2002) discusses the origins of anti-racist discourse in the field of social work, the successful efforts by groups of black practitioners to incorporate it into social work training in the late 1980s, and the eventual reaction in the name of common sense and resistance to 'political correctness' on the part of Conservative ministers and media commentators. Practical competences came to replace anti-racist and anti-oppressive values at the core of the curriculum, and the discourse of diversity joined, if it did not quite replace, that of anti-racism. 'Diversity' is clearly a broader, more diffuse term than 'anti-racism', and it perhaps lacks the same sense of political purpose and commitment to action. It covers, in a sample text from 1995 cited by Walker (2002: 111):

> people from ethnic minority groups, people with disabilities, people with HIV/AIDS, people with different religions and cultures, people with different class backgrounds, people whose first language is not English, gay and lesbian people.

As Walker notes, in the discourse of diversity, the emphasis is on numerical minorities and lack of representation, not on the experience of exclusion and disadvantage. It is about valuing and respecting difference, not taking political action against discrimination. In view of the shifts in meaning of 'race' and 'racism' outlined here, however, and the demographic changes that have accompanied them, it has become impossible to use the terms with the former sense of certainty and confidence. A simple black/white binary division, in which the whites have all the power and only they can be racist (since racism involves not only the expression of prejudice but the exercise of power), is inadequate for understanding the complexities of inter-cultural relations, tensions, and conflicts in globalized twenty-first century societies.

Conclusion

This chapter has tried to explain some of the complexities and ambiguities of the key concepts and debates involved in discussing race and racism. It has argued that the term from which the others flow, 'race', is a social and historical construction whose meanings and uses have changed over time. It denotes an 'imagined community' (Anderson, 1983), but an imagined community that has real, material effects, through processes of exclusion, discrimination, and violence. This sense of 'race' is far removed from that given to it by biologists and psychologists who, with or without the aid of Darwin's account of evolution, claimed that it had an objective, scientific status which allowed for the hierarchical ordering of hereditary human types. While much of their work now seems (or ought to seem) little more than historical curiosity, it is important to remember that scientific racism is far from dead, and continues, lightly disguised, to inform supposedly objective studies of the distribution of intelligence across social groups. Contrary to the assumptions of some commentators in the period immediately after the Second World War, the biological conception of race survived the holocaust.

Rejecting biologically essentialist conceptions of race, social scientists and, for different reasons, political activists, began in the 1960s to use the term to describe social divisions and patterns of exploitation and discrimination, particularly in the USA and Europe. 'Black' became a politically charged term, denoting the experience of racism perpetrated by dominant white groups; later, it became the banner under which a wide variety of disadvantaged groups united in an anti-racist struggle. But this was itself criticized from the early 1990s for substituting a cultural and political essentialism for a biological one: ethnicity, the term preferred to 'race' because it carried less biological baggage and recognized that the categories in question were socially constructed, could itself be used in narrow and exclusionary ways. The case of the supposedly distinctive ethnic character of the Irish in Britain provides an example. It was argued (Modood, 1994) that different minority ethnic groups had distinctive experiences of racism and discrimination which needed to be acknowledged. Furthermore, ethnic identities were not simple and singular but complex and multiple: in a world of global flows and mobility, identities were increasingly hybrid. Patterns of migration also became more diffuse and varied, bringing to Western Europe and North America people with whom there had previously been little direct interaction, for example, from parts of the former Soviet Union and Yugoslavia.

Policies of multiculturalism, entailing the institutional recognition of a range of ethnic groups, developed to take account of this increasing diversity. After the riots in northern English towns in 2001, however, and still more after the suicide bombings in London by British-born Islamists in July 2005, these policies came under attack, not only from their traditional enemies on the political right but from Trevor Phillips, the Chair of the Commission for Racial Equality. He argued that multiculturalism encouraged a sense of the essentialism of difference and, by accepting uncritically the equal validity of the beliefs and attitudes of all minority cultural groups, promoted mutual ignorance and suspicion instead of participation by all groups in common social and political institutions. In particular, he blamed multiculturalism for fostering increased residential segregation, which had been identified as an important contributor to the divisions and hostilities that lay behind the 2001 riots (Cantle, 2001). Work by demographers and geographers suggests that in fact there is very little sign of the processes of 'white flight' or Muslim withdrawal into mono-cultural enclaves identified as the motors of ghettoization and ethnic separation, but the critique of multiculturalism has led to a new stress in government policy on national identity – what it means to be British, and how a shared sense of Britishness can be encouraged.

Understandings of racism also became more complex in response to the growing complexity of patterns of discrimination and inter-group conflict.

The old political conception of racism as 'prejudice plus power' came to seem inadequate to reflect new patterns of hostility and conflict, in which whites constructed themselves as victims, and tensions between minority groups became increasingly apparent (as in the violence between young black and Asian people in Lozells, Birmingham, in October 2005). While there was some evidence of a decline in overtly racist attitudes among the white population by 2005 compared with five years before (and certainly compared with three decades earlier), there was also evidence of a heightened concern about immigration, not only among whites but among minority ethnic groups. In response to these contradictions and the increase in the number of minority ethnic groups with substantial populations in Britain, as a result of new patterns of movement and migration, commentators began to think of racism as complex and polymorphous, its expression varying over time, place, and social and political context. It followed that anti-racist strategies needed to evolve beyond the simple didactic certainties of their original formulation, and from this process emerged the concept of 'diversity', encompassing not only ethnic difference but differences of faith, (dis)ability, and sexual preference. Public bodies were encouraged to develop policies that recognized and valued diversity; they were to foster diversity among their own staff, and ensure that they provided services appropriate to the different needs of different groups. Anti-racism's focus on relations of oppression and subordination was replaced by a blander, but perhaps more politically manageable, commitment to achieving a diversity of services that mirrored the diversity of service users. This is the diversity agenda to which all the agencies of the criminal justice system are ostensibly committed.

Summary

This chapter explains some of the complexities and ambiguities of the key concepts and debates involved in discussions of race and racism, and provides a grounding for the chapters that follow. It argues that while the term 'race' is a social and historical construction whose meanings and uses have changed over time, to some degree 'scientific' racism persists. Rejecting biologically essentialist conceptions of race, social scientists and, for different reasons, political activists, began in the 1960s to use the term 'race' to describe social divisions and patterns of exploitation and discrimination. 'Black' became a politically charged term, denoting the experience of racism perpetrated by dominant white groups; later it became the banner under which a wide variety of disadvantaged groups united in an anti-racist struggle. But this was itself criticized from the early 1990s for substituting a cultural and political essentialism for a biological one: ethnicity, the term preferred to 'race' because it carried less biological baggage and

(Continued)

(Continued)

recognized that the categories in question were socially constructed, and could itself be used in narrow and exclusionary ways. Furthermore, ethnic identities were not simple and singular but complex and multiple: in a world of global flows and mobility, identities were increasingly hybrid.

Policies of multiculturalism, entailing the institutional recognition of a range of ethnic groups, developed to take account of this increasing diversity. After the riots in northern English towns in 2001, however, and still more after the suicide bombings in London by British-born Islamists in July 2005, multiculturalism came under attack, and was blamed by the Commission for Racial Equality for fostering residential segregation and contributing to the divisions and hostilities that lay behind the 2001 riots. Although work by demographers and geographers suggests that in fact there is very little sign of the processes of 'white flight' or Muslim withdrawal into mono-cultural enclaves, the critique of multiculturalism has led to a new stress in government policy on national identity and on encouraging a shared sense of Britishness.

Understandings of racism also became more complex in response to the growing complexity of patterns of discrimination and inter-group conflict. The old political conception of racism as 'prejudice plus power' came to seem inadequate to reflect new patterns of hostility and conflict, in which white people constructed themselves as victims and tensions between minority groups became increasingly apparent (as in the violence between young black and Asian people in Birmingham in October 2005). While there was some evidence of a decline in overtly racist attitudes among the white population, there was also evidence of a heightened concern about immigration amongst all ethnic groups. In response to such developments, racism has increasingly come to be seen as complex and polymorphous, its expression varying over time, place, and social and political context.

Key Texts

Goldberg, D.T. and Solomos, J. (2002) (eds) *A Companion to Racial and Ethnic Studies*. Oxford: Blackwell.
Back, L. and Solomos, J. (eds) (2000) *Theories of Race and Racism: A Reader*. London: Routledge.

References

Anderson, B. (1983) *Imagined Communities: Reflections on the Origins and Spread of Nationalism*. London: Verso.
Back, L. (1996) *New Ethnicities and Urban Cultures: Racisms and Multiculture in Young Lives*. London: UCL Press.

Back, L. and Solomos, J. (eds) (2002) Theories of Race and Racism: A Reader. London: Routledge.

Bernal, M. (1987) *Black Athena: The Afroasiatic Roots of Classical Civilization*. London: Free Association Books.

Bowling, B. and Phillips, C. (2002) *Racism, Crime and Justice*. Harlow: Longman.

Brown, G. (2006) 'The Future of Britishness', speech to the Fabian Society, 14 January (at www.fabian-society.org.uk/press_office/news_latest_all.asp?pressid=520).

Cantle, T. (2001) *Community Cohesion: A Report of the Independent Review Team*. London: Home Office.

Cantle, T. (2005) *Community Cohesion: A New Framework for Race and Diversity*. Basingstoke: Palgrave.

Commission on the Future of Multi-Racial Britain (The Parekh Report) (2000) *The Future of Multi-Ethnic Britain*. London: Profile Books.

Commission on Integration and Cohesion (2007) *Our Shared Future*. London: Department of Communities and Local Government (at http://www.integrationandcohesion.org.uk/upload/assets/www.integrationandcohesion.org.uk/our_shared_future.pdf).

Commission for Racial Equality (2007) *Ethnic Minorities in Britain* (Factfile2). London: CRE (at http://www.cre.gov.uk/downloads/factfile02_ethnic_minorities.pdf).

De Ste. Croix, G.E.M. (1983) *The Class Struggle in the Ancient Greek World*. London: Duckworth.

ETHNOS (2005) *Citizenship and Belonging: What is Britishness?* London: CRE.

Gardiner, D. (1985) *Ethnic Minorities and Social Work Training* (Paper 21.1). London: Central Council for Education and Training in Social Work.

Giddens, A. (1994) *Beyond Left and Right: The Future of Radical Politics*. Cambridge: Polity Press.

Gilroy, P. (2000) *Between Camps: Nations, Cultures and the Allure of Race*. London: Allen Lane/The Penguin Press.

Goldberg, D.T. and Solomos, J. (2002) 'General introduction', in D.T. Goldberg and J. Solomos (eds) *A Companion to Racial and Ethnic Studies*. Oxford: Blackwell.

Gould, S.J. (1996) *The Mismeasure of Man* (revised and expanded edition). New York: Norton.

Hall, S. (1992) 'New ethnicities', in J. Donald and A. Rattansi (eds) *'Race', Culture and Difference*. London: Sage.

Heer, G. (2007) 'Asian employees in the probation service', *Probation Journal*, 54 (3), 281–5.

Herrnstein, R.J. and Murray, C. (1994) *The Bell Curve: Intelligence and Class Structure in American Life*. New York: Free Press.

Hickman, M.J. and Walter, B. (1997) *Discrimination and the Irish Community*. London: CRE.

Howard, K. (2006) 'Constructing the Irish of Britain: ethnic recognition and the 2001 censuses', *Ethnic and Racial Studies* 29 (1), 104–23.

Ipsos MORI (2007) *Race Relations 2006: A Research Study*. London: CRE.

Jansson, K. (2006) *Black and Minority Ethnic Groups' Experiences and Perceptions of Crime, Racially Motivated Crime and the Police: Findings from the 2004/05 British Crime Survey (Home Office Online Report 25/06)*. London: Home Office.

Jenkins, R. (1997) *Rethinking Ethnicity*. London: Sage.

Johnston, R., Poulsen, M. and Forrest, J. (2005) 'On the measurement and meaning of residential segregation: a response to Simpson', *Urban Studies*, 42 (7), 1221–7.

Legrain, P. (2007) *Immigrants: Your Country Needs Them*. London: Little, Brown.

Macpherson, W. (1999) *The Stephen Lawrence Inquiry. Report of an Inquiry by Sir William Macpherson of Cluny (Cm 4262)*. London: HMSO.

May, S. (2002) 'Multiculturalism', in D.T. Goldberg and J. Solomos (eds) *A Companion to Racial and Ethnic Studies*. Oxford: Blackwell.

Modood, T. (1994) 'Political blackness and British Asians', *Sociology*, 28 (4), 859–76.

Muir, R. (2007) *The New Identity Politics*. London: IPPR.

Murray, C., with Lister, R., Field, F., Brown, J.C., Walker, A., Deakin, N., Alcock, P., David, M., Phillips, M., Slipman, S. and Buckingham, A. (1996) *Charles Murray and the Underclass: The Developing Debate*. London: IEA Health and Welfare Unit in association with the *Sunday Times*.

Office of National Statistics (2003) *Census 2001: National Report for England and Wales*. London: The Stationery Office.

Ratcliffe, P. (ed) (1996) *Ethnicity in the 1991 Census, Volume 3: Social Geography and Ethnicity in Britain: Geographical Spread, Spatial Concentration and Internal Migration*. London: Office of National Statistics.

Ray, L. and Smith, D. (2004) 'Racist offending, policing and community conflict', *Sociology*, 38 (4), 681–99.

Ray, L., Smith, D. and Wastell, L. (2004) 'Shame, rage and racist violence', *British Journal of Criminology*, 44 (3), 350–68.

Simpson, L. (2004) 'Statistics of racial segregation: measures, evidence and policy', *Urban Studies*, 41 (3), 661–81.

Simpson, L. (2005) 'On the measurement and meaning of residential segregation: a reply to Johnston, Poulsen and Forrest', *Urban Studies*, 42 (7), 1229–30.

Simpson, L. (2007) 'Demographic contributions to the debate on segregation, integration and diversity', paper to Conference on 'Segregation or integration: what's going on?', University of Manchester, 17 May (at http://www.ccsr.ac.uk/events/segint/conference/documents/Simpson17Mayscript withslides.doc)

Travis, A. (2007) 'Shortage of pickers may hit strawberry crop', *The Guardian*, 28 May.

Vanstone, M. (2004) *Supervising Offenders in the Community: A History of Probation Theory and Practice*. Aldershot: Ashgate.

Walker, H. (2002) *A Genealogy of Equality: The Curriculum for Social Work Education and Training.* London: Woburn Press.

Wieviorka, M. (2002) 'The development of racism in Europe', in D.T. Goldberg and J. Solomos (eds) *A Companion to Racial and Ethnic Studies.* Oxford: Blackwell.

Wilson, J.Q. and Herrnstein, R.J. (1985) *Crime and Human Nature.* New York: Simon and Schuster.

TWO

Criminology, Contemporary Society, and Race Issues

David Smith

The first chapter explored how some of the key concepts in debates about race and racism have become increasingly complex. This chapter explores how criminological researchers have responded to that complexity as they examine the relationships between crime, minority ethnic groups, and discrimination in the criminal justice process. The critique of multiculturalism discussed in the previous chapter is particularly relevant in making sense of developments in policy and criminal justice practice. While there is little evidence that multiculturalism has in fact fostered a sense of identity that emphasizes minority group membership rather than citizenship (Hussain and Bagguley, 2005), the supposed lack of integration of young Muslims in Britain, mostly of Pakistani origin, was already a concern of government even before the riots in towns in the north of England in the spring of 2001. Since then, and especially since the suicide bombings on the London transport system of July 2005, this concern has grown; in particular, official (and public) anxiety has grown about the extent of support for violent *jihad* among Muslims in Britain, whatever their national or ethnic origins. Even before the July 2005 bombings, the then Home Office minister Hazel Blears told the House of Commons that Muslims must expect to be particular targets of stops and searches by the police (Dodd and Travis, 2005).

Blears was in effect referring to what Matza (1969) called the 'method of suspicion' – the police practice of targeting those who seem to them to be the sort of people most likely to commit a particular type of crime. Matza meant the term critically: for him, the police's authoritative imposition of a negative label was part of the process of 'becoming deviant'. But, to put the matter rather simplistically, it is not clear what other method the police can use when, for example, they have to decide whom to stop and search. No one would argue that they should stop or arrest people at random; they therefore need some criteria to inform their selection of suspects. What we can reasonably expect is that these criteria will be based on good intelligence and substantial grounds for suspicion, and not on racist attitudes and beliefs or hostility towards particular groups. When the first anti-terrorism legislation of modern times was passed in 1974, it was principally intended to combat Irish republican violence, and it has been plausibly argued that one of its effects was to bring entire communities under suspicion (Hillyard, 1993). More recent legislation in 2000, 2001, 2005, and 2006, each Act broadening the scope of the preceding ones, has been principally aimed at combating 'Islamist' political violence, and the focus has shifted from Irish to South Asian people, because they make up the majority of the Muslim population. It is not surprising that this legislation, and its interpretation in police practice, has been criticized in similar terms to the 1974 Act; for example, Spalek and Lambert (2007) cite the view of the Muslim Council of Britain that there is a risk that a generation of young Muslim men will be criminalized (see also Chapter 10 by Spalek, Lambert, and Baker in this volume).

Black People and the Criminal Justice System: The Emergence of an Issue

About 30 years previously, the same concern about criminalization of a generation of young men began to be expressed, but then the focus was on black (African-Caribbean) youth. As a number of commentators have noted (e.g., Phillips and Bowling, 2007: 429), official anxiety about the criminality of the black population in Britain only began to be strongly expressed in the last quarter of the twentieth century. Until then, the 'expert' view tended to be that rates of offending were lower among minority ethnic groups than among the white population; certainly, Asians were seen as a low-crime group, and, with more qualifications, this was also the dominant view of African-Caribbeans (House of Commons Home Affairs Committee, 1972). Only four years later, the police at least took a very different view – that crime rates were high in the black population, and that the task of policing them was being made more difficult by anti-police campaigning by black activist groups (Smith, 1997: 1053). Gilroy (1987) suggests that the explanation for this change lies in a number of collective confrontations between the police and young black people, of which the best publicized were those at the Notting Hill Carnival in 1976–78. Hall *et al.* (1978), in their classic analysis of the construction of 'mugging' as a major crime problem, argue that the media presented this as a characteristic crime of young black men, and that the moral panic that developed out of this racialization of crime helped in the development of a new authoritarian consensus on criminal justice policy. Black communities were criminalized, and 'their culture [was] portrayed as essentially deviant, fragmented and incapable of instilling the correct values into its young people' (Blagg and Smith, 1989: 23). This image of some forms of criminality as a peculiarly black phenomenon appeared not only in the public pronouncements of senior police officers but in the work of commentators who regarded themselves as being on the political left, as in the 'left realist' criminology of Lea and Young (1982). The left realist argument was, in summary, that experiences of racism – for example, in schools and in the labour market – led to social and economic exclusion and a consequently increased risk of criminal involvement.

Concern about high crime rates in black communities, and especially among young black men, has persisted over the years; a recent manifestation is the report by the House of Commons Home Affairs Committee (2007) on young black people and the criminal justice system. The authors of the report are sensitive to the possibility that discrimination within the criminal justice system may contribute to the over-representation within it of young black people (see Feilzer and Hood, 2004), but – like Lea and Young – they regard the key reason as being social exclusion, noting (p. 5) that 80 per cent 'of Black African and Black Caribbean communities live in Neighbourhood Renewal Fund areas' (i.e., areas identified as particularly deprived and as requiring special intervention). They also argue that in at least some of these deprived areas negative social and cultural influences, including disrupted families, lack of legitimate opportunities, and lack of trust in the police and other official agencies, may encourage the development of a subculture of machismo and violence (reflected in a small number of high-profile cases that suggest that the use of weapons, mainly knives but occasionally guns, has become routinized). There is no doubt that a sense of the need to defend and assert oneself through violence could become, and perhaps has become, widespread among young men in some deprived urban areas (the account given by Robins [1992] suggests that this is not a new problem). But it is also important to retain a sense of perspective. Not all of the evidence points to a higher-than-average rate of criminal involvement among the black population as a whole. Sharp and Budd (2005) analysed self-reported involvement in crime from the 2003 Offending, Crime and Justice Study, and found that white respondents and those of mixed heritage were more likely than black and Asian respondents to say that they had offended, both in the last year and ever, and they were also more likely to report serious and frequent offending. This held good even after age was controlled for. Nor, contrary to what might be assumed from the Home Affairs Committee report, are the risks of victimization markedly higher among minority ethnic groups than in the white population, the apparently greater risk being largely a result of the younger age profile of the non-white population; younger people in all ethnic groups are more likely than their elders to be victims of crime. People in minority ethnic groups were, however, generally more worried about crime than the white population (Allen, 2006; Home Office, 2006).

Discrimination and Criminal Justice: Policing

In the early 1980s, research began to focus on the possibility that the apparent over-representation of black people – but not of Asians – in the crime statistics might be at least in part a product of discriminatory decision-making in the criminal justice system. The riots in Brixton that led to the Scarman Report (1981) were the most extreme indication of hostility between black communities and the police, but, as noted above, black activists had been claiming since the mid-1970s that racist assumptions and behaviour were endemic in the police, an argument that developed into the claim that black people were over-policed as potential offenders, and under-policed as potential or actual victims. Scarman presented (or was interpreted as presenting) what is often called the 'bad apple' thesis, which suggested that antagonism between the police and young black people arose from insensitive behaviour by a minority of police officers with racist attitudes. Other studies from the period, however, suggested that racist attitudes and language were common among the lower ranks of the police and were an accepted element of the 'canteen culture' (Smith and Gray, 1983; Holdaway, 1983). Smith and Gray argued that such attitudes are not necessarily translated into action in the course of everyday policing practice; their observations suggested that interactions between the police and black and minority ethnic people were friendlier and more relaxed than might have been expected. But these were, of course, interactions that were being observed; and Bowling and Phillips (2002: 162) are not alone in their scepticism about whether attitudes and behaviour can be separated as sharply and consistently as Smith and Gray suggest.

One of the key issues raised by the Scarman Report was the disproportionate use against young black people of the power to stop and search on the grounds of suspicion that they intended to commit an offence. The Police and Criminal Evidence Act of 1984, partly in response to concerns about the wide use of this power and the vagueness of the grounds on which it could be exercised, tightened up the definition of what constituted a reasonable basis for stopping and searching someone: the police officer must have a 'reasonable suspicion' that the person is carrying stolen or prohibited articles. The official guidance for the police on the use of this power specifically warns of the dangers of stereotyping on the basis of appearance, age, or cultural style (Bowling and Phillips, 2002: 140), but, as Bowling and Phillips note, one of the most consistent findings of subsequent research on race and criminal justice is that black people are more likely to be stopped and searched than white people or Asians. The most recent Home Office monitoring report confirms the well-established pattern: relative to the general population, black people were six times as likely to be stopped and searched as white people, and Asians were twice as likely (Home Office, 2006; see also Michael Rowe's chapter in this volume). Black people were three times as likely as white people to be arrested, relative to the general population. As a proportion of all searches, 14 per cent were of black people and 7 per cent of Asians. Since, according to the 2001 census (Commission for Racial Equality, 2007), the percentage figures for these groups in the total population were 2.3 and 4.6 per cent, respectively, it is tempting to conclude (as some have concluded) that these figures show an unreasonable use of the method of suspicion and amount to evidence of police racism (see, e.g., commentary on the use of stop-and-search powers on the Institute of Race Relations web pages; www.irr.org.uk).

The figures by themselves, though, cannot justify such a conclusion; indeed, Bowling and Phillips (2002) doubt that statistical data like these will ever allow for a confident inference of racist motives on the part of the police or anyone else. Firstly, it is important to remember the continuing socio-economic disadvantage of all minority ethnic groups compared with white people (Phillips, 2005). People in disadvantaged groups are more likely than the better off to come to police attention. Black and minority ethnic people are more likely to live in high-crime urban areas, and a higher proportion of the ethnic minority population is young – under 25 – and is therefore, in terms of age, part of the most crime-prone section of the population. Even if the proportion of searches that are of ethnic minority people is compared not – misleadingly – with the national population but – much more sensibly – with the local population, there remain problems of interpretation (FitzGerald and Sibbitt, 1997). Not all the people stopped and searched in a particular area will be residents of that area, and not all residents are equally available to be stopped and searched – that is, out and about in public (and being out and about in the early hours of the morning is, other things equal, more likely to attract suspicion than being in the same place in the middle of the day). These factors make it impossible simply to read off racism from figures that show an apparent over-representation of any minority group at any stage of the criminal justice process.

The next stage in the process by which someone enters the criminal justice system involves a decision about whether they should be charged or cautioned, warned, or dealt with informally, and similar problems of interpretation arise here. On the whole, research has confirmed the findings of early work on this question: black people are more likely to be charged after arrest than white people (Home Office, 2006). Early research in London by Landau (1981) and Landau and Nathan (1983) suggested that for some offences black juveniles were more likely than whites to be charged immediately rather than referred to a juvenile liaison bureau (involving the police and representatives of social services and education) for a decision on whether to caution or charge them, and that, when their cases were referred to the bureau, black juveniles were much more likely than whites to be charged rather than cautioned. This was true even when the nature of the offence and previous record were taken into account. Black juveniles were more likely than whites to come from deprived and disrupted family backgrounds (reflecting the general disadvantage of minority ethnic groups), and this (arguably a form of indirect discrimination) may explain the difference in decision-making. Landau and Nathan did not, however, take into account whether the juvenile admitted the offence; since an admission was a prerequisite for a caution, a lower rate of admission among black people would reduce the proportion of them who were eligible to be cautioned. Subsequent research suggests that black suspects are less likely to admit offences (Phillips and Brown, 1998); this is what one would expect if they are more likely to be arrested when they are innocent, or if they have less faith than white people in the fairness of the police and the criminal justice system as a whole – but it entails that a lower proportion of them will be cautioned. (See Rowe, Chapter 3, for a more detailed consideration of policing.)

Moving Through the System

Phillips and Brown's (1998) study is perhaps the most comprehensive attempt to track progress through the criminal justice system from arrest to sentence (for cases which get that far). It was based on a sample of people arrested and brought to ten police stations in 1992–93. They found that the evidence in cases involving ethnic minority suspects was less likely than in cases involving white people to be sufficient for them to be charged at the time of arrest, and that this was not explicable by differences in the type of offence that led to the arrest. White suspects were more likely to confess and less likely than black and Asian suspects to seek legal advice or to remain silent. Arrests of black and Asian suspects were more likely than those of white people to lead to no further action. Ethnic minority suspects were more likely to be refused bail than white people charged with similar offences and with similar records. (Asian suspects were substantially less likely, and black suspects slightly less likely, than white people to have a criminal record.) Among cases that went on to the Crown Prosecution Service, the proportions that were terminated were 27 per cent for Asians, 20 per cent for black people, and 12 per cent for white people. All of this suggests that black people and Asians were more likely than white people to be arrested and charged when there was not sufficient evidence to proceed with a prosecution against them.

At the final stage of the process, of trial and (if the defendant is convicted) sentence, there is evidence, quite consistent over time, that black and Asian defendants are more likely to plead not guilty, and more likely to be acquitted. Bowling and Phillips (2002) observe that they might more often be 'over-charged' – charged with the more rather than less serious offence in cases where the police or the Crown Prosecution Service have a choice – and thus be more likely to want to contest the case. They may also, of course, be more likely to be innocent. Pleading not guilty and choosing to be tried in the Crown Court rather than a magistrates' court are both high-risk strategies, since someone who has pleaded not guilty and is subsequently convicted will not benefit from any guilty plea discount of the sentence, and Crown Courts, while more likely to acquit than magistrates' courts, also have greater sentencing powers. Both these factors tend to increase the length of sentences imposed on black and Asian defendants, and thus contribute to their over-representation in the prison population. The acquittal rate for minority ethnic groups may also be higher in magistrates' courts. The Home Office (2006) reported that, in 2004, in a sample of courts, white people were more likely to be convicted (59%) than black people (51%) or Asians (45%). The same pattern was found from a sample of Crown Courts, though with less difference between the black and Asian rates.

Sentencing

Much of the research on differences across ethnic groups in criminal justice decision-making stemmed from the recognition in the late 1980s that black people, though at that time not Asians, were massively over-represented in the prison population. This was a major consideration in the provision in the 1991 Criminal Justice Act (Section 95) that the Home Office should publish annual information on race and the criminal justice system that sentencers and criminal justice staff could use to inform their decisions. (A similar provision was made in relation to women in the system, in response to concern about differential treatment.) Interest in explaining the make-up of the prison population also lay behind the influential research of Hood (1992), which examined sentencing patterns in Crown Courts in the West Midlands in 1989. At that time, black people formed a quarter of the male prison population, a proportion that remained fairly constant over the next fifteen years (Home Office, 2006). Although Hood found differences among the courts, overall 57 per cent of African-Caribbeans received a custodial sentence, compared with 48 per cent of white people and 40 per cent of Asians. Hood's analysis suggested that the number of custodial sentences on African-Caribbeans was 5 per cent higher than could have been expected. He also estimated, on the basis of his sample, that 70 per cent of the over-representation of black males in prison arose from the number who appeared in court, and that a further 10 per cent could be explained by offence seriousness and other legally relevant factors. Of the remainder, 13 per cent of the excess was explained by the longer average sentence length imposed on black defendants, which was partly a result of their pleading not guilty, and therefore not benefiting from any guilty plea discount. Seven per cent of the over-representation of black men in prison therefore arose from a higher use of custody than would have been predicted from a consideration only of legally relevant factors. As Bowling and Phillips (2002) argue, the cumulative effect on the prison population of an annual 7 per cent surplus in custodial sentences would be substantial.

Considering community penalties, Hood (1992) found that minority ethnic defendants were less likely than white people to be given probation orders, no doubt partly because probation officers were less likely to recommend them. More recently, the national survey reported by Calverley *et al.* (2004) found that black, Asian, and mixed-heritage men who received probation orders (or community rehabilitation orders, as they became in the course of the study) tended to have lower levels of criminogenic need than their white counterparts; despite this, the orders they received tended to be longer. Calverley *et al.* argue that differential sentencing could at least partly explain this finding: minority ethnic offenders may have been more likely than white people to be given community penalties rather than lower-tariff sentences; and those who have criminogenic needs comparable with those of white offenders given community penalties may be more likely to receive a higher-tariff sentence. Again, the evidence of differences in sentencing does not amount to evidence of racist discrimination, but, as Bhui (2004: 264) noted, it 'does suggest a need to maintain a critical focus on possible biases in both sentencing and the content of pre-sentence reports'.

Problems of Interpretation

In raising questions rather than providing definite answers to questions about discrimination in the criminal justice system, the work of Calverley *et al.* (2004) resembles several earlier studies. Typically, they find differences in decision-making at all stages of the process, from apprehension to sentencing, but with rare exceptions (Hood's 1992 study being one), they have not found clear-cut evidence of discrimination on the basis of race. Black people, especially young black men, are certainly more likely than white people to be arrested, but it is difficult to establish how far this is because they are more likely to live in areas with high arrest rates, rather than because they are black. Black people seem to be less likely to be cautioned or warned than white people, but this is likely to be partly or mainly because they are less likely to admit offences, and therefore are not eligible to be cautioned. Black people are at greater risk of being sentenced to custody than white people, and for longer, but this can be partly explained by the fact that they are more likely to plead not guilty, and to be sentenced in Crown Courts. The respondents in Calverley *et al.'s* study reported negative experiences of the criminal justice system which they believed would be less likely to happen to white offenders, such as racist abuse and frequent stops and searches; but many people who are sentenced in court feel some sense of grievance, and it is difficult to be sure that white offenders feel more fairly treated. Recent findings from the British Crime Survey (covering England and Wales) suggest that minority ethnic groups (with the exception of those of mixed heritage) are more likely than white people to say that their local police were doing an excellent job, though, as with white people, they are less likely to say this if they have been in recent contact (in any capacity) with the police (Jansson, 2006). So, the evidence of direct racism on the part of the police and other criminal justice workers is inconclusive, and therefore, as Cole and Wardak (2006: 92) put it: 'Most studies have settled for various definitions of "indirect" racism ... In recent years, the debates have moved swiftly towards the position that these discriminatory practices may indeed be institutionalised'.

Institutional Racism?

The idea of institutionalized or institutional racism was central to the argument of the Macpherson Report (1999), which examined the killing in 1993 of the black teenager Stephen Lawrence and the failure of the police investigation to find enough evidence for a successful prosecution. Macpherson examined the conduct of several police officers involved in the case and concluded that, while they did not express conscious racist attitudes, their decisions often reflected unwitting or unconscious racism, a set of assumptions about young black men and criminal involvement that prevented them from pursuing their inquiries effectively. Right at the start of the investigation, when they arrived at the scene of the crime, they ignored the evidence of Stephen's friend Duwayne Brooks and acted on the assumption that Stephen was the victim of an attack by other black youths, and not of a racist attack by a group of young white men. While the Scarman Report had not rejected the idea of institutional racism as a broad social characteristic as firmly as was subsequently claimed, it did not make it central to its analysis as the Macpherson Report did. Macpherson's use of the term, however, has itself been criticized for being ambiguous and shifting. Foster *et al.* (2005: 4), for example, argue that Macpherson used 'institutional racism' to mean unwitting discrimination on the part of individuals, conscious racism, and 'collective or systemic discrimination', thus tending to conflate three distinct processes. It might have been better to confine the term to the last of these – the embedded, taken-for-granted policies and practices of an organization that express racist and exclusionary assumptions (e.g., about what kinds of people count as trustworthy witnesses). Even if this had been done, the dominant reaction to the Report might have been the same – that institutional racism meant widespread racism among individual officers. It was this interpretation that, according to Foster *et al.*, aroused resentment and a sense of being unfairly criticized within the police, especially the Metropolitan Police – though black and minority ethnic officers were much more likely than their white colleagues to regard the Report as fair (Foster *et al.*, 2005: 23–4); outside London, the reaction tended to be that the Report reflected the incompetence – rather than the racism – of the police in London, and was not equally relevant elsewhere.

Foster *et al.* (2005) conclude that, despite this sense of unfairness, police practice improved in several respects following the Macpherson Report. Among these were the recording and monitoring of racist incidents, which had developed in line with Macpherson's definition, that an incident is racist if it is perceived to be so by the victim or anyone else involved. (Another relevant influence on police practice was the enactment of the first 'hate crime' legislation in Britain in the 1998 Crime and Disorder Act's provisions on racial aggravation of offences.) The organization and management of murder investigations and liaison with the families of murder victims – both criticized in the Macpherson Report – had improved. Racist – although not sexist – language had virtually disappeared. Efforts had been made, with uneven results, to improve relations with minority ethnic groups. This was done most effectively where specialist posts had been set up, but these could be marginalised; good practice had not entered the mainstream of police routines (a point also made by Docking and Tuffin, 2005). The establishment in the Metropolitan Police of Community Safety Units to specialize in responding to reports of hate crime, including racially motivated offences, was a positive move and a signal that the police had begun to take racist offending seriously. Officers felt they were under greater scrutiny than before, particularly in relation to stop-and-search decisions, over which some felt inhibited by the possibility that they would be accused of discriminatory practice. Foster *et al.* noted, however, that these improvements were unevenly spread geographically: there had been most progress in London, while in some other forces the impact of the Macpherson Report seemed barely to have been felt. Even where it was felt, it has arguably been overtaken by recent events, and particularly by a revived enthusiasm for the vigorous use of stop-and-search powers under the 2000 Terrorism Act. Dodd (2007) reported a 34 per cent increase in 2005–06 over the previous year in the number of stops and searches under this Act, a figure which included an increase of 84 per cent in the number of Asians stopped and searched. Over half these searches were conducted by the Metropolitan Police, and 15 per cent by the City of London Police, suggesting that at least in London Hazel Blears' prediction on the use of these powers against suspected 'terrorists' was beginning to prove accurate. It is worth noting, though, that only 4.8 per cent of all stops and searches were recorded as having been conducted under the provisions of the Terrorism Act rather than the 1984 Police and Criminal Evidence Act; the great majority were carried out on the grounds that the police reasonably suspected that they might uncover an arrestable offence, not that they suspected that the person stopped was involved in terrorism.

Just as the Woolf Report of 1991 specified the changes that were needed to restore legitimacy to the prison system (Sparks and Bottoms, 1995), so the Macpherson Report can be seen as an effort to map a route back to legitimacy for the police in their relations with black and minority ethnic groups. 'Legitimacy' here refers to the sense people have that the authority represented through the criminal justice system is entitled to respect and compliance. People are more likely to obey laws if they see them as just, reasonable, and fairly administered (Tyler, 1990), and their perceptions of the criminal justice system can be shaped by their experiences not only as suspects and defendants, but also as victims and witnesses. There is still no clear answer to the question: in general, are minority ethnic groups less likely than white groups to see the system as legitimate? There is plentiful evidence that some black and Asian people, in some places, perceive it as unjust, particularly because of the actions of the police, who are the first point of contact with the system for most people; but there is much less evidence that this is true of any minority population taken as a whole. Successive reports from the British Crime Survey of minority groups' experiences of crime and policing (Clancy et al., 2001; Salisbury and Upson, 2004; Jansson, 2006) have suggested that, if anything, minority ethnic respondents view the police more positively than the white population does, even though, in the most recent analysis (of the 2004–05 survey), households with an Asian or mixed-heritage respondent were slightly more likely than others to report having been victimized. It remains an open question whether Asians' generally positive perceptions of the police will survive increased surveillance and intervention under anti-terrorism legislation; the avowed target of this is 'Muslims', which of course is not an ethnic category, and it is not clear how the police are meant to identify Muslims by sight. Resentment on the part of those who feel that they have been unjustifiably stopped and searched – or arrested – might lead to a loss of police legitimacy among Asian groups; on the other hand, almost everyone shares an interest in safety and social peace, and intensified police activity could therefore be seen as justified and legitimate, provided it was also seen as proportionate and constrained by legal safeguards.

Racially Motivated Offending

The 2004–05 survey produced an estimate of 179,000 racially motivated crimes, a slightly lower figure than in the previous two surveys (Jansson, 2006). Two per cent of minority ethnic respondents said that they had been the victim of a racially motivated crime, double the proportion reported by white respondents; and people from minority groups who had been victims were much more likely than white people to believe that the offending to which they were subject was racially motivated. (Eleven per cent of crimes with minority group victims were thought to be racially motivated, as compared with 1 per cent of crimes with white victims.) There are inherent problems of definition in deciding if a crime is racially motivated, since motives cannot always be inferred from behaviour; the most common reason given by victims for believing that racism played some part in the offence was the use of racist language. People may, however, use racist language but continue to deny that they are racists; as noted in Chapter 1, research on racist offending in Greater Manchester found that offenders were relatively willing to talk openly about their use of violence, but much less likely to agree that it was motivated by racism – even when the language used strongly suggested that it was (Ray and Smith, 2004; Ray et al., 2004). In the Greater Manchester sample, racist attitudes and beliefs were rarely the sole motivating factor in offending; the victims were in most cases known to the offenders, and there was often a history of antagonism between them. There were very few instances of offending that conformed to the classic image of a hate crime, in which the parties to the offence are strangers, and the victim is selected because of his or her perceived membership of a hated social group. The relative rarity of 'pure' racially motivated offending helps to explain why the number of convictions for racially aggravated offences is much lower than the number of such offences estimated by the British Crime Survey, or the number recorded by the police; it is easier to prove that (say) an assault took place than to show that it was motivated by racist hatred, so where a charge of racially aggravated assault might fail, a charge of assault might succeed, and decisions by prosecutors reflect this (Burney and Rose, 2002).

Racially aggravated offending is necessarily a social construction, the product of a complex set of interpretations and decisions that are influenced by emotions, attitudes, beliefs, the immediate situational context, and wider forces, including the policy changes set in train by the Macpherson Report. The difficulty of defining and measuring it illustrates the ambiguities and interpretive problems that are inherent in trying to understand the relevance of race issues in the criminal justice process. (We have seen that it is equally problematic to infer motives from the apparent differences in the decisions made on white and black suspects and defendants.) While the British Crime Survey is the best source we have, it is worth remembering its limitations: it covers only households and people aged sixteen and over, and its findings may be valid for a total population (based on as representative a sample as possible) but not for all sections of that population (e.g., the young, the homeless, people in various kinds of institution, and people who are not willing to be interviewed). All surveys have such limitations and present problems of interpretation; and this as true (or more true) of surveys of attitudes and beliefs among Muslims in Britain as of any other survey.

Muslims as a Suspect Community

For example, one of the best-known polling organizations, Ipsos Mori, conducted a survey (for *The Sun* newspaper) of Muslims in Britain immediately after the suicide bombings in London on 7 July 2005 (see http://www.ipsos-mori.com/polls/2005/s050722.shtml). The results were presented as giving grounds for optimism – 86 per cent of those interviewed felt very or fairly strongly that they belonged to Britain; a slightly smaller proportion agreed that they felt part of British society; they were more than twice as likely to say that they felt accepted by white British people as that they had been subject to negative discrimination. There is no reason to doubt that the findings were in general a reasonable reflection of mainstream opinion among Muslims in Britain on these issues. But if you were outside the mainstream, felt loyalty to the international community of Islam, the Ummah, rather than to Britain, believed that sharia law should be implemented in its full rigour, that democracy was incompatible with Islam, and so on, you might well prefer not to disclose this to an interviewer, two weeks after bombers apparently motivated by such beliefs had killed 52 people in London. (In the survey, 14 per cent of respondents agreed or tended to agree with the idea that Islam is incompatible with the values of British democracy, a surprisingly high figure in the circumstances.)

Spalek and Lambert (2007) cite the fear of the Muslim Council of Britain that the institutional racism identified by Macpherson is turning into institutional prejudice against young Muslims. They also suggest that sections of the Muslim population have become 'suspect communities', as, according to Hillyard (1993), sections of the Irish population in Britain had been in the 1970s and 1980s. But the threat from Islamist political violence is qualitatively different, and greater, than that presented by extremist Irish republicans; it can recruit active adherents from many countries, and it has manifested itself in ways that have produced slaughter on a scale never achieved, or perhaps intended, by the Irish groups, in the form of suicide bombings and hijackings of aircraft. It is this sense of a new, widespread, and technologically sophisticated threat that has been used to justify the extension of anti-terrorism legislation, and underpins the continuing debates on how far the power to detain suspects without charge should be extended. Spalek and Lambert argue that while, as was the case with Irish people, the police and security services do discriminate among Muslim groups, they do so in a way that does not sufficiently recognize their diversity, and, for example, stigmatizes all Salafi Muslims – those who take a literal approach to the interpretation of the Koran – as fundamentalists and therefore suspect. The consequent exclusion of the Salafi minority from government efforts to establish co-operative relations with Muslim communities entails the risk of further alienation, and is likely to be counter-productive from the government's point of view, since information about extremist activity among Salafi groups will become harder to obtain if they are not regarded as potentially helpful partners in reducing the influence of extremists. Meanwhile, some media commentators and politicians are prepared to present all Muslims as by definition hostile to 'western' values of democracy and mutual tolerance (Dalrymple, 2004), ignoring the centuries of peaceful cohabitation between Muslim and Christian communities in Southeastern Europe (to look no further afield).

A paradox of this criminalization of (particularly) South Asian Muslims is, as Hudson (2007: 162) notes, that the characteristics of their communities that were long – and, according to Wardak (2000), rightly – regarded as protective against criminality (in a sharp contrast with the dominant representations of black neighbourhoods) – strong family bonds, a sense of tradition, powerful religious faith – are now presented as causes or at least facilitators of criminality (a point also made by Dalrymple, 2004). The negative imagery is not confined to extremist violence, but includes such supposedly normal features of Islam as forced marriages and so-called 'honour' killings; and, according to Hudson, stereotypical ideas that were more or less confined to the tabloid press in the 1990s have entered the mainstream discourses of politics and criminal justice. Like Spalek and Lambert, she compares the criminalization of Muslims in the 1990s and 2000s with that of African-Caribbeans in the 1970s and 1980s, and argues that the 'Muslim Asian is now well established as an "enemy within"; in the light of recent events, perhaps as *the* enemy within' (Hudson, 2007: 163). How long this special stigmatized status will endure is not, of course, a question whose resolution is within the power of the agencies of the criminal justice system; global political developments, among them the trend of British and American foreign policy, and the response to them of the leaders of extreme Islamism, will remain the major factors shaping events. But, if the criminal justice system's legitimacy among Muslim communities were to be eroded, for example by the extension of internment without trial, this could only serve to increase, for a small minority of violent fundamentalists, a continued sense of beleaguered righteousness that could be used to justify further acts of mass murder.

Conclusion

Since the early 1970s, the focus of criminological attention to issues of ethnic and cultural difference and conflict has shifted in response to a dynamically changing context. Concerns about the criminogenic effects of social exclusion and economic marginalization have remained, but they have been accompanied by growing attention to the ways in which the workings of the criminal justice system itself may exacerbate these effects through discriminatory decisions at all stages of the process. Research has continued to show that African-Caribbean people – and especially men – are particularly liable to attract the attention of the police as suspects, as they have been since the 1970s; more recently, the relative cultural isolation of sections of South Asian communities – and especially of Muslims – has ceased to be seen as a guarantee of the effectiveness of informal social controls and has been reconstituted as a criminogenic factor. Conflicts across the world have been increasingly reflected in inter-group conflicts in Britain, and changed patterns of migration, following the collapse of the communist states of Eastern and Central Europe and the enlargement of the European Union, have increased the cultural diversity and complexity of many urban areas, while also making an important contribution to the rural economy. The revival of fundamentalist Islam as a global political force has brought some Muslim communities under a new kind of suspicion, and led to an extension of the powers of the police and the courts that many commentators have seen as a threat to basic legal rights; and there are demands that these powers be further extended. The racialization of crime that was identified as a problem for criminology in the 1970s has continued to construct some African-Caribbean communities as the site of particular problems, but these have now been joined not only by some South Asian Muslim communities but by a fluid variety of other groups – asylum seekers, refugees, and migrant workers.

There have, no doubt, been improvements over the period, in that awareness of race issues and the importance of avoiding discriminatory practices have become formally recognized by all agencies in the criminal justice system. The need for ethnic monitoring is now widely accepted, even if it is still patchy in practice (e.g., in the probation service, according to Calverley *et al.*, 2004, even though this is an agency with a long-standing official commitment to the values of diversity). The Macpherson Report signalled an important shift of attention away from the supposedly problematic characteristics of African-Caribbean communities and onto the problematic behaviour and organizational assumptions of the police. Overtly racist attitudes are now more widely perceived as socially unacceptable and perhaps as morally indefensible, not only within state agencies but more widely, if the evidence of surveys can be trusted; even offenders convicted of offences with an apparently racist element are reluctant to admit to racism (Ray *et al.*, 2004). These are grounds for tentative optimism about the future development of inter-ethnic and inter-cultural relations in Britain, but there are grounds for pessimism too. Most minority ethnic groups remain massively disadvantaged compared with the overall white population, and one element of this disadvantage is their exposure to the criminal justice system. Bowling and Phillips (2002: 260) conclude pessimistically with a prediction that 'present trends in criminal justice practices will increasingly marginalise, criminalise and socially exclude ethnic minority communities in England, especially those of African/Caribbean origin'. Developments since they wrote are unlikely to have made them more optimistic, but they are among the community of criminologists and criminal justice analysts who have highlighted problems of inequality and discrimination, and in doing so sensitized practitioners and policy-makers in a way that suggests that research and scholarship can make a worthwhile difference, even in times as difficult as these.

Summary

This chapter explores the relationships between crime, minority ethnic groups, and discrimination in the criminal justice process. It considered how the concepts and debates described in chapter one – particularly the critique of multiculturalism – relate to developments in contemporary criminal justice policy and practice. Concerns about the criminogenic effects of social exclusion and economic marginalization have been accompanied by greater attention to

(Continued)

the ways in which the criminal justice system itself may exacerbate these effects through discriminatory decisions.

The 'racialization' of crime that was identified as a problem for criminology in the 1970s continues to construct some African-Caribbean communities as problematic. They have lately been joined by a fluid variety of groups, including asylum seekers, refugees, migrant workers and, in particular, some South Asian Muslim communities. African-Caribbean people, especially men, continue to be overrepresented at all stages of the criminal justice system, and South Asian Muslim communities have increasingly been seen as suspect groups, leading to controversial extensions of police and sentencing powers.

The research to date has rarely found straightforward evidence of racism in the criminal justice process, and the debate has shifted towards a greater focus on institutional or unwitting racism. There have been some advances, including greater awareness of race issues and the recognition that all criminal justice agencies have a duty to avoid discrimination. The Macpherson Report signalled an important shift of attention away from the supposedly problematic characteristics of African-Caribbean communities and onto the problematic behaviour and organizational assumptions of the police. However, despite this progress, most minority ethnic groups remain disadvantaged within the criminal justice system.

Key Texts

Bowling, B. and Phillips, C. (2002) *Racism, Crime and Justice*. Harlow: Longman.
Phillips, C. and Bowling, B. (2007) 'Ethnicities, racism, crime and criminal justice', in M. Maguire, R. Morgan and R. Reiner (eds) *The Oxford Handbook of Criminology* (4th edition). Oxford: Oxford University Press.

References

Allen, J. (2006) *Worry about Crime in England and Wales: Findings from the 2003/04 and 2004/05 British Crime Survey (Home Office Online Report 15/06)*. London: Home Office.

Bhui, H.S. (2004) 'Black and Asian perspectives on probation', *Probation Journal*, 51(3), 264–5.

Blagg, H. and Smith, D. (1989) *Crime, Penal Policy and Social Work*. Harlow: Longman.

Bowling, B. and Phillips, C. (2002) *Racism, Crime and Justice*. Harlow: Longman.

Burney, E. and Rose, G. (2002) *Racist Offences: How is the Law Working? The Implementation of the Legislation on Racially Aggravated Offences in Crime and Disorder Act 1998 (Home Office Research Study 244)*. London: Home Office.

Calverley, A., Cole, B., Kaur, G., Lewis, S., Raynor, P., Sadeghi, S., Smith, D. and Vanstone, M. (2004) *Black and Asian Offenders on Probation (Home Office Research Study 277)*. London: Home Office.

Clancy, A., Hough, M., Aust, R. and Kershaw, C. (2001) *Crime, Policing and Justice: the Experience of Ethnic Minorities – Findings from the 2000 British Crime Survey (Home Office Research Study 223)*. London: Home Office.

Cole, B. and Wardak, A. (2006) 'Black and Asian men on probation: social exclusion, discrimination and experiences of criminal justice', in S. Lewis, P. Raynor, D. Smith, and A. Wardak, (eds) *Race and Probation*. Cullompton: Willan.

Commission for Racial Equality (2007) *Ethnic Minorities in Britain (Factfile2)*. London: CRE (at http://www.cre.gov.uk/downloads/factfile02_ethnic_minorities.pdf).

Dalrymple, W. (2004) 'Islamophobia', *New Statesman*, 19 January.

Dodd, V. and Travis, A. (2005) 'Muslims face increased stop and search', *The Guardian*, 2 March.

Docking, M. and Tuffin, R. (2005) *Racist Incidents: Progress since the Lawrence Inquiry (Home Office Online Paper 42/05)*. London: Home Office.

Dodd, V. (2007) 'Only 1 in 400 anti-terror stop and searches leads to arrest', *The Guardian*, 31 October.

Feilzer, M. and Hood, R. (2004) *Differences or Discrimination? Minority Ethnic Young People in the Youth Justice System*. London: Youth Justice Board.

FitzGerald, M. and Sibbitt, R. (1997) *Ethnic Monitoring in Police Forceds: A Beginning (Home Office Research Study 173)*. London: Home Office.

Foster, J., Newburn, T. and Souhami, A. (2005) *Assessing the Impact of the Stephen Lawrence Inquiry (Home Office Research Study 294)*. London: Home Office.

Gilroy, P. (1987) *There Ain't No Black in the Union Jack*. London: Hutchinson.

Hall, S., Clarke, J., Critcher, C., Jefferson, T. and Roberts, B. (1978) *Policing the Crisis*. London: Macmillan.

Hillyard, P. (1993) *Suspect Community: People's Experiences of the Prevention of Terrorism Act in Britain*. London: Pluto Press.

Holdaway, S. (1983) *Inside the British Police*. Oxford: Blackwell.

Home Office (2006) *Statistics on Race and the Criminal Justice System – 2005*. London: Home Office.

House of Commons Home Affairs Committee (1972) *Police/Immigration Relations*. London: HMSO.

House of Commons Home Affairs Committee (2007) *Young Black People and the Criminal Justice System. Second Report of Session 2006–07*. London: The Stationery Office.

Hood, R. (1992) *Race and Sentencing*. Oxford: Clarendon Press.

Hudson, B. (2007) 'Diversity, crime and criminal justice', in M. Maguire, R. Morgan and R. Reiner (eds) *The Oxford Handbook of Criminology* (4th edition). Oxford: Oxford University Press.

Hussain, Y. and Bagguley, P. (2005) 'Citizenship, ethnicity and identity: British Pakistanis after the 2001 "riots"', *Sociology*, 39(3), 417–25.

Jansson, K. (2006) *Black and Minority Ethnic Groups' Experiences of Crime, Racially Motivated Crime and the Police: Findings from the 2004/05 British Crime Survey (Home Office Online Report 25/06)*. London: Home Office.

Landau, S.F. (1981) 'Juveniles and the police', *British Journal of Criminology*, 21(1), 27–46.

Landau, S.F. and Nathan, G. (1983) 'Selecting juveniles for cautioning in the London metropolitan area', *British Journal of Criminology*, 23(2), 128–49.

Lea, J. and Young, J. (1982) 'The riots in Britain: urban violence and political marginalisation', in D. Cowell (ed.) *Policing the Riots*. London: Junction Books.

Macpherson, W. (1999) *The Stephen Lawrence Inquiry. Report of an Inquiry by Sir William Macpherson of Cluny (Cm 4262)*. London: HMSO.

Matza, D. (1969) *Becoming Deviant*. Englewood Cliffs, NJ: Prentice Hall.

Phillips, C. (2005) 'Ethnic inequalities under New Labour: progress or entrenchment?', in J. Hills and K. Stewart (eds) *A More Equal Society? New Labour, Poverty, Inequality and Exclusion*. Bristol: Policy Press.

Phillips, C. and Bowling, B. (2007) 'Ethnicities, racism, crime and criminal justice', in M. Maguire, R. Morgan and R. Reiner (eds) *The Oxford Handbook of Criminology* (4th edition). Oxford: Oxford University Press.

Phillips, C. and Brown, D. (1998) *Entry into the Criminal Justice System: a Survey of Police Arrests and their Outcomes (Home Office Research Study 185)*. London: Home Office.

Ray, L. and Smith, D. (2004) 'Racist offending, policing and community conflict', *Sociology*, 38(4), 681–99.

Ray, L., Smith, D. and Wastell, L. (2004) 'Shame, rage and racist violence', *British Journal of Criminology*, 44(3), 350–68.

Robins, D. (1992) *Tarnished Vision: Crime and Conflict in the Inner City*. Oxford: Oxford University Press.

Salisbury, H. and Upson, A. (2004) *Ethnicity, Victimisation and Worry about Crime: Findings from the 2001/02 and 2002/03 British Crime Surveys (Home Office Research Findings 237)*. London: Home Office.

Scarman, Lord (1981) The Brixton Disorders 10–12 April 1981 (Cmnd. 8427). London: HMSO.

Sharp, C. and Budd, T. (2005) Minority Ethnic Groups and Crime: Findings from the Offending, Crime and Justice Survey 2003 (2nd edition) (Home Office Online Report 33/05). London: Home Office.

Smith, D.J. (1997) 'Ethnic origins, crime, and criminal justice', in M. Maguire, R. Morgan and R. Reiner (eds), *The Oxford Handbook of Criminology* (2nd edition). Oxford: Clarendon Press.

Smith, D.J. and Gray, J. (1983) *Police and People in London*. London: Policy Studies Institute.

Spalek, B. and Lambert, R. (2007) 'Muslim communities under surveillance', *Criminal Justice Matters*, 66, 12–3.

Sparks, J.R. and Bottoms, A.E. (1995) 'Legitimacy and order in prisons', *British Journal of Sociology*, 46(1), 45–62.

Tyler, T.R. (1990) *Why People Obey the Law*. New Haven: Yale University Press.

Wardak, A. (2000) *Social Control and Deviance: A South Asian Community in Scotland*. Aldershot: Ashgate.

THREE

Policing and Race Equality: Thinking Outside the (Tick) Box

Michael Rowe

Introduction

Questions relating to race and racism have recurred in debates about policing in Britain for three decades or more. Public discourse about policing has revolved around media-driven exposes of police deviance and malpractice, which lead to a cycle of reaction, response, and reform. During recent years, many of these have related to allegations of police racism. In the last decade or so, the police response to the murder of Damilola Taylor, the failure to convict the killers of Stephen Lawrence, the shooting dead of Jean Charles de Menezes at Stockwell tube station in the aftermath of the July 2005 London bombings, the TV documentary *The Secret Policeman* which exposed the racist attitudes of police recruits at a training centre in Manchester, and numerous other controversies have formed an authoritative narrative account of policing in Britain (Rowe, 2007). This interpretative framework poses important questions and strategic dilemmas for anti-racists and those committed to developing a more inclusive police service for the complex society of twenty-first-century Britain.

This chapter will review some of the key themes that have emerged relating to recent debates about policing, race, and racism. The report of the public inquiry into the police response to the racist murder of Stephen Lawrence and the Commission for Racial Equality investigation into employment issues within the Metropolitan Police Service have provided a framework for transforming the position of minority ethnic communities within the public sector more generally (Macpherson, 1999; Commission for Racial Equality, 2005; Morris *et al.*, 2004). Rather than providing a brief discussion of a wide-range of sub-topics within the broader picture, a more detailed analysis of a few central issues provides a more nuanced consideration of underlying themes. To this end, the discussion focuses on recent developments in terms of police use of stop and search and the recruitment and retention of minority ethnic police officers. Debates about security, terrorism, and the policing of the Muslim community in Britain are examined in conclusion, where it is argued that reform must be considered against the broader context of crime, policing, and racialization. Inevitably, space constraints mean that this chapter is unable to consider related topics such as police diversity training, the response to hate crimes (see Nathan Hall's chapter in this volume), or the system for investigating complaints against the police, all of which have also shaped broader debates about policing and minority ethnic communities. While some of these discussions have continued for many decades, there has, more recently, been growing recognition that the police service must be fundamentally reconfigured if it is to meet the needs of an increasingly diverse society. Other communities of interest, including rural communities, lesbian, gay, bisexual, and transgender people, victims of domestic violence, the elderly, the disabled, and others, pose particular challenges for police services that have been concerned, when such matters have been considered, to ensure equal opportunity by providing a standard level of service for all, rather than one that meets the specific needs of particular groups. The extent to which on-going developments in Neighbourhood Policing, which promise to reconnect police with local communities and to provide opportunities for the co-identification of priorities and solutions, will develop an environment in which diverse needs can be met will be a key item on research agendas for the next decade or more (Hughes and Rowe, 2007).

Stop and Search: Policing, Race, and Space

Claims that the British police disproportionately stop and search people of a minority ethnic background are long-standing, reflect similar allegations made in many other countries, and have become axiomatic in debates about the current state of policing in a multicultural society. In the 1970s, official statistics began to be released that suggested that black British people were more likely to be stopped and searched by the police than other sections of the community. During that period, the legal basis of stop and searches lacked clarity such that officers could carry out a stop and search on the most slender of pretences. Anecdotal and other evidence formed a picture whereby groups of officers in certain districts would routinely and deliberately use these powers to target and harass young black people. The official inquiry report into the 1981 Brixton riots noted that the stopping and searching of young black people had been a major cause of increasing public anger with the police service in the build-up to unrest (Scarman, 1981). During this period, there was a lack of authoritative statistical information about stop-and-search practices and claims and counter-claims were not easily scrutinized. Often, allegations that stop and search was targeted in a racist manner were rebuffed in terms which suggested that it was the disproportionate involvement of young black males in forms of street crime, drug dealing, and so on that explained police attention. Stop-and-search practice, it was argued, 'followed the crime' (Fitzgerald, 2000), although only 11 per cent of 'PACE stops' resulted in an arrest in 2004–05 (Home Office, 2006).

Over subsequent decades, relatively reliable and rigorous data has emerged and 'objective' quantifiable evidence is easily located in Home Office and other reports. A number of developments have broadened the evidential base against which debates about stop and search can be evaluated. Section 95 of the 1991 Criminal Justice Act required that police services collate and publish a range of information relating to ethnicity, including the ethnic profile of those who are stopped and searched under the provision of the 1984 Police and Criminal Evidence Act (PACE). These data showed that, in England and Wales in 2004–05, 15 white people per 1,000 of the resident population were stopped and searched by the police; the comparative figure for the black community was 90 in 1,000, and for Asian people it was 27 per 1,000 in the resident population. On that basis, it seems that black people were six times more likely to be stopped and searched than whites, and that Asians were also over-represented in the data, although to a lesser degree.

The data also provides for a more detailed breakdown of stop-and-search practices, which show that ethnic disparities also appear in terms of the reasons why stop and searches are conducted. Table 3.1 indicates that around half of stop and searches carried out on black or Asian people are drug-related, whereas this accounts for only 38 per cent of those conducted on white people. On the other hand, 14 per cent of stops and searches carried out on whites related to suspicions of 'going equipped' (to commit burglary or theft), which accounted for only 8 and 7 per cent of those relating to black or Asian people, respectively.

Such trends have appeared consistently in the Home Office data in recent years. Although the amount of stop and searches in overall terms fell in the

Table 3.1 Percentage of stop and searches under s1 of the PACE 1984 and other legislation, by reason for stop and ethnic appearance, England and Wales, 2004–05

Reason for search	Ethnic appearance of person searched					
	White	Black	Asian	Other	Not known	Total
Stolen property	30	24	18	31	28	28
Drugs	38	51	55	40	36	41
Firearms	1	2	2	1	1	1
Offensive weapons	8	12	13	11	7	9
Going equipped	14	8	7	11	10	13
Other	8	3	4	6	16	7
Total	627,579	118,165	59,954	12,733	21,546	839,977

Source: Home Office, 2006: 28.

years after publication of the Lawrence Report, there has subsequently been an increase: the 839,977 cases recorded in 2004–05 represented a 14 per cent rise on the previous year. Moreover, the use of other legislation, such as the 2000 Terrorism Act or the 1994 Criminal Justice and Public Order Act, which do not require 'reasonable suspicion' of the person stopped, has risen dramatically in recent years. The apparent ethnic disparities identified in respect of 2004–05, however, have been a consistent feature since the data began to be collected in the mid-1990s. Official sources – such as the annual Home Office section 95 reports – have added authority to this important element of accounts of police racism.

However, explaining patterns of police stop-and-search practice on the basis of these recorded statistics requires caution. First, the ethnic classification itself is problematic, since 'white' is an omnibus category that does not directly correspond to ethnicity, and 'Asian' conflates sub-groups that have sharply contrasting socio-economic profiles. Moreover, the statistics are based upon the appearance as perceived by the police officer conducting the stop and search. Clearly, this introduces a problematic subjectivity to the recording process. Furthermore, the recent rise in the number of stop and searches recorded seems likely, in part at least, to be an artefact of continuing debates about the implementation of stop and search and efforts to promote good practice. As with officially recorded crime figures, the increasing number of stop and searches might be a result of changes in recording practice rather than a reflection of true prevalence. Problems with recording practices have also been identified that might explain the disparities reflected in Table 3.1 in ways that do not relate simply to police racism. Fitzgerald and Sibbit (1997) found that officers were more likely to record stop and searches conducted on minority ethnic people than on whites, in part because they were more concerned about demonstrating that they had followed procedures when dealing with the former than they were with the latter. Clearly, this means it is more likely that encounters with minority ethnic people make their way into official records than are similar interactions with white people. The tendency for minorities to be treated more formally has also been noted in the context of the response of senior officers to internal matters of complaints and discipline. One reason why concerns about the performance of minority ethnic officers are more likely to activate disciplinary processes and result in formal investigation is that middle-ranking officers, most of whom are white, lack the confidence needed to resolve issues informally as they would with white officers (Morris *et al.*, 2004).

In addition to concerns about categories and recording practices, recent research findings show that the use of alternative population benchmarks suggests a wholly different perspective in which minority ethnic communities are not over-represented. The data published annually by the Home Office is presented in terms of stop and searches per 1,000 of the resident population. However, this benchmark is not the most appropriate since it is known that stop and searches tend to be conducted in particular times and particular places. The resident population comprises all those in the police area, many of whom are unlikely to be present when and where stop and searches are likely to be performed. In response to this limitation, efforts have been made to establish a more appropriate benchmark based on those available to be stopped and searched in the times and places were this is most likely to be done. MVA and Miller (2000) compiled a measure of the available population in five sites and used that to determine the ethnic proportionality of stop and search. Their report suggested that this measure led to a conclusion radically at odds with the predominant narrative based upon Home Office data outlined earlier (MVA and Miller, 2000: 84):

> the findings of this research did not suggest any general pattern of bias against those from minority ethnic backgrounds. This was true for minority ethnic groups as whole, as well as any particular minority ethnic group. Asian people tended to be under-represented in those stopped or searched, compared to their numbers in the available population, with some notable exceptions. The general picture for black people was mixed. For example, in Greenwich, and Chapeltown, they were mostly under-represented among those stopped or searched, yet in Hounslow and Ipswich, they were far more likely to be stopped or searched in vehicles than their available numbers would suggest. Perhaps surprisingly, the most consistent finding across sites was that white people tended to be stopped and searched at a higher rate than their numbers in the available population would predict.

Waddington *et al.* (2004) reproduced MVA and Miller's methodology in Reading and in Slough. They too found that this measure of police stop and search led to an important change in prevailing explanatory frameworks. They argued that (Waddington *et al.*, 2004: 900):

> ...it seems that a very different conclusion is reached from comparing stop and search figures with the composition of the 'available population' than with residential figures ... it is difficult to see how these figures could be interpreted as an outcome of officers' stereotyping: if anything, it is white people who are disproportionately stopped and searched.

As these studies tend to note, and as I have argued elsewhere (Rowe, 2004), these findings do not end concern about racism and police stop and search. If officers are not discriminating against minority ethnic communities available in areas where stop and search is carried out, then it seems that explanations in terms of frontline officers exercising discretion on the basis of racist stereotypes need to be rethought. However, questions about racism and discrimination remain since stop-and-search practices are concentrated on deprived areas where some minority ethnic groups are more likely to reside. Furthermore, 'availability' to be stopped and searched ought to be determined by intelligence, rather than whoever happens to be out on the streets for officers to encounter. Moreover, socio-economic factors, coupled in some contexts with racism, shape the availability of populations to be stopped and searched. Poverty and exclusion determine availability; in some areas, this impacts on visible minority ethnic communities, and they might be over-represented in police stop-and-search data, as they seem to be dispro-portionately treated at almost every step of the criminal justice process. In other districts, though, white communities, whether minority ethnic, such as the Irish, or otherwise, might be most affected and so have disproportionate contact with the police, an unequal impact that also mirrors broader trends within the criminal justice system (Stenson and Waddington, 2007). Race and racism are crucial to understanding patterns of stop and search, but other issues, such as class and place, need to be incorporated into a convincing explanation.

Black in Blue: The Recruitment and Retention of Minority Ethnic Police Officers

The Lawrence Report reiterated long-held concerns about the failure of the police service to recruit minority ethnic officers in proportion to their numbers in the overall population. Recommendation 65 of the report was that the Home Office and police service more generally ought to develop initiatives to increase the number of minority ethnic recruits. The Home Secretary established a steering group to oversee implementation of most of the recommendations of the report and provided a detailed series of targets outlining the number of officers that each service in England and Wales needed to recruit in order to reflect the ethnic composition of the local population. The 'action plan' specified, for example, that Nottinghamshire police ought to employ an additional 20 minority ethnic officers by 2009 in order to reflect that 3.5 per cent of the local population was minority ethnic. At the other end of the spectrum, the Metropolitan Police Service was set a target of recruiting an additional 5,661 minority ethnic officers in order to reflect that one quarter of the population of London is classified as minority ethnic (Rowe, 2004: 35).

The considerable efforts that police services have put into recruiting and retaining minority ethnic staff have clearly had a positive impact, although the dividend on this substantial investment has been minimal. In 2002–03, 2.9 per cent of officers were black or Asian; by 2004–05, that figure had increased to 3.5 per cent (Home Office, 2006). While this represents a degree of progress, it is clear that the post–Lawrence Report targets are unlikely to be met. Clearly, these developments follow a longer-term trend. Although the police service was broadly unwilling to employ minority ethnic officers for much of the immediate post-war period (Whitfield, 2004), there has been a succession of recruitment campaigns seeking to attract minorities into the service since the early 1970s. The 1981 Scarman Report provided further impetus, arguing that the development of a 'multi-racial' police service ought to be a priority for reasons of morality and police effectiveness. Subsequently, there was a plethora of outreach work and recruitment campaigns designed to attract minorities to the police service. Typically, elite voices from the Home Office, senior police organizations, the media, and policy communities promote the principle of developing a more diverse police workforce without stipulating what benefits this might bring to either the service or to society more generally. Nonetheless, although they are rarely articulated, it is possible to identify in broad terms several implied advantages of establishing a more ethnically diverse police service. First, there are legal and regulatory 'drivers' of the move to recruit more minority ethnic police officers. In an era of New Public Management and central auditing, police services have an instrumental interest in promoting minority ethnic recruitment. The cultural politics of police governance in recent years has encouraged senior officers to demonstrate their commitment to the diversity agenda. The embedding of staff associations, most notably the Black Police Association, into management and governance processes of many police services has been a key feature of the post–Macpherson Report era and demonstrates the central position that issues such as minority ethnic recruitment and retention have come to occupy in contemporary debates about policing (Holdaway and O'Neill, 2006, 2007). In this context, police managers have little option but to implement programmes to increase the recruitment of minority ethnic officers.

More positively, improving the recruitment and retention of minority ethnic officers is promoted in terms of the 'business case' – the advantages that it confers in terms of meeting the core law and order mandate of the police. Most recently, in the British context, this argument has been advanced in respect of the policing of Muslim communities. The deployment of Muslim officers, versed in the cultural values of Muslim communities and with appropriate language skills, are better placed, it is argued, to penetrate problematic sections of the Muslim population and so to develop intelligence central to contemporary policing methods. Senior police officers have argued that their inability to attract black and Asian officers, and the likelihood that they would fail to meet the Home Office recruitment targets by 2009, has a detrimental impact on operational effectiveness (Dodd, 2006). Tactical benefits of a diverse workforce have long been claimed, however, and were apparent in many colonial policing systems that recruited 'native' officers in order to enhance the control and reach of police forces (Brogden, 1987; Hill, 1989; Palmer, 1988).

While it is clear that operational advantages can be wrought from employing more minority ethnic officers, it is also apparent that potential problems might also develop, and that matching of this kind relies on an essentialist analysis that places too great an emphasis on ethnic identity. The implications that the recruitment of minority officers in order to reap benefits in terms of policing ethnic communities has for the officers concerned is one problematic feature of recent debates about the development of a more diverse workforce.

Newspaper reports in February 2007 suggested that Islamist terrorist groups working in Britain had planned to kidnap a Muslim soldier, and that Muslim police officers had expressed concern that they might also be targeted (Dodd *et al.*, 2007). Clearly, public pronouncements about the role of Muslim officers in thwarting terrorist activity raises the cultural and symbolic capital surrounding them and might make them more attractive targets for extremists. Additionally, although less violently, concerns arise about pigeon-holing minority ethnic officers into such roles and imposing responsibilities upon them that are not extended to other staff. Minority ethnic officers have frequently been used by police services in recruitment drives, and establishing them as ambassadors has raised similar concerns about bestowing particular tasks upon certain ethnic groups. More fundamentally, efforts to ethnically match police officers and communities reflect an essentialist position that reifies ethnicity in relation to other dimensions of identity. Like many other public institutions, the police service has a poor record in terms of recognizing the subtleties of ethnic identity or the implications that this might have when it comes to operational policing. Suggestions that an officer who ethnically 'matches' a significant proportion of the population of any given area will more easily develop a positive working relationship with that community are clearly naïve, and fail to recognize the significance of other elements of identity such as class, gender, age, education, and so forth. Research findings have suggested that the attitudes of minority ethnic officers toward minority ethnic communities are often not dissimilar to the stereotyped negative views held by many white officers (Holdaway, 1996; Sherman, 1983).

In addition to meeting legal requirements and securing operational benefits, the other main reason underlying efforts to recruit and retain minority ethnic officers is the symbolic capital that this represents. Developing and sustaining a diverse workforce is regarded as a litmus test that reveals a wider truth about organizational change and efforts to transform police culture in the post-Lawrence era. Since one reason why minority ethnic people have not joined the service is that they perceive it to be a racist environment, it follows that attracting under-represented groups will indicate that such subjective preconceptions are not borne out. The centrality of recruitment to arguments about the state of racialized relations within the police service was evident following the collapse of the Metropolitan Police charges of corruption against Ali Dizaei in 2003.[1] The Met's Black Police Association advised black and

---

[1] Chief Superintendent Ali Dizaei has been a high profile senior officer in the Metropolitan Police; at the time of writing (March 2007) he was borough commander of Hounslow. In 1999 a series of internal investigations began into allegations relating to drug-taking, prostitutions, financial irregularities relating to expenses claims, threatening behaviour, and that he was an agent for the Iranian security services. After several years and court proceedings, Dizaei was cleared of the most serious of these charges. Various disciplinary charges were also dropped and Dizaei was awarded a financial settlement and returned to work. Controversially, he published his account of these events in a 2007 book *Not One of Us: The Trial That Changed Policing in Britain Forever* (London, Serpent's Tail).

Asian people not to join the police service, since Dizaei's experience indicated a lack of commitment to tackling racism within the service.

Confusingly, the recruitment of a diverse workforce is seen as both a necessary precondition of effecting cultural change within the service and as evidence that such a transformation has already taken place. As with other groups under-represented in the police service, it has often been argued that negative attributes of police occupational subculture can be transformed by recruitment drives that dilute predominant white male machismo. However, repeated studies of the experiences of minority ethnic recruits and women police officers have emphasized that officers often embrace pre-dominant regressive sub-cultures as a way of avoiding prejudice and marginalization. Westmarland (2001) showed that female officers sometimes seek to demonstrate their compliance with predominant normative values in the police service by subscribing to macho and sexist elements of 'canteen culture'. Efforts to transform police subculture by recruiting a more diverse workforce employ a model of police behaviour that focuses on the prevailing characteristics of those who join the service. The conservative and insular nature of police occupational culture has often been attributed to the profile of new recruits as it is held that the prejudices and preconceptions, such as those relating to minority ethnic communities, to women, and to sexual minorities, reflect the prevailing cultural norms and values of those sections of society from which police officers are recruited. Claims that the norms and values associated with police culture reflect the prevailing disposition of officers as they enter the service draw upon the notion of the 'authoritarian personality', developed by Adorno et al. (1950) after the Second World War. Colman and Gorman (1982) measured the attitudes of new recruits to the police service on a range of controversial issues, such as the death penalty and migration, and compared the results to those obtained from a control group. They concluded that newly recruited police officers were significantly more illiberal and intolerant than the control group. Although criticized on methodological and other grounds (Butler, 1982), the notion that police officers enter the service with regressive and insular values has remained a primary explanation of police culture. This is reflected in those efforts to change problematic dimensions of police culture by re-engineering the profile of police service personnel so as to include more minority ethnic and female officers (Cashmore, 2000; Paoline et al., 2000). More detailed analysis of the nature and origins of police culture have tended to emphasise not only that it is less ubiquitous than is often assumed, but also that it is an emergent property of police work. Elements of police culture, such as stereotyping and suspicion, often understood as having negative implications for minority ethnic staff and public, arise from the broader context of police work, and so are unlikely to simply be transformed by recruiting a more diverse body of recruits. Problems of alleged police racism cannot be attributed solely to culturally unsophisticated racist junior officers. The killing by police of Sean Bell in New York City in 2006 led to considerable debates about racial profiling and aggressive police tactics in black neighbourhoods. New York Police Commissioner Kelly noted that concerns had continued despite the substantial increase in the recruitment of non-white officers in recent years. Allegations of racism arose, even though three of the five officers involved in Bell's shooting were black (Cardwell, 2007).

While efforts to recruit more minority ethnic staff as police officers have had only marginal success, the profile of non-police staff has become increasingly ethnically diverse in recent years. Home Office (2006) data shows that while 3.5 per cent of sworn police officers were of a minority ethnic background in 2004–05, other categories of police staff show a greater representation of minority ethnic people. Although voluntary Special Constables are a small proportion of police human resources, totalling less than 12,000 in 2004–05, 21.8 per cent were of a minority ethnic background in that year. Tangentially, women are also more strongly represented among 'specials' than sworn officers, amounting to 32.3 per cent of the special constabulary in 2004–05. The newer, and numerically to become more significant, auxiliary post is that of Police Community Support Officer (PCSO), a role created by the 2002 Police Reform Act to provide for public reassurance by enhancing patrols. Of the 6,214 PCSOs employed in 2004–05, 14.3 per cent were of a minority ethnic background. Similarly, minority ethnic people were relatively well-represented among police civilian staff, including traffic wardens, at 5.9 per cent in 2004–05. This data suggests ethnic diversity is emerging amidst some sectors of an increasingly pluralized police service, but that this has not extended into the core of the organization in relation to the sworn constabulary. An optimistic view of these trends is that the ethnic diversity evident in the peripheral police roles will eventually extend to the organization as a whole. Johnston (2006) noted that Home Office and Metropolitan Police policy documents have explicitly promoted the development of the role of PCSOs as one method of making the service more representative in ethnic, and other, terms. Since public perceptions of police subculture and racism are based on exaggerated or dated media coverage, it is implied that minorities have positive experiences in civilian roles, and that these will counter-balance inaccurate stereotypes of contemporary policing. Certainly, Johnston (2006) found that some PCSOs fitted the model of 'wannabe cops', who had joined in order to develop the experience necessary to become a sworn police officer. Moreover, minority ethnic staff saw their role as a PCSO as an opportunity to 'test' the police service reputation for racism prior to committing to the extensive application and training process required to become a police officer. To some extent, it is too early to say whether the stronger representation of minority ethnic communities, and females, among PCSOs will subsequently have a positive impact on recruitment into the police service, more generally. If police 'canteen culture' really has been transformed in recent years, then it might be that the results of the 'litmus recruitment test' are positive. However, there are grounds for some caution. In narrow terms, evaluation of the role of PCSOs suggest that efforts to bolster minority ethnic recruitment might be counter-productive since some of those admitted have had poor credentials and do not prove suitable (Johnston, 2006). Also, in relation to the role of the PCSO are wider problems of poor management and supervision and a lack of opportunities for career development, which although not directly or solely related to race or ethnicity, might still discourage minority staff from pursuing a career as police officers. If the future prospects in terms of recruitment appear to be mixed, the broader context of policing, race, and racism also constrain some of the positive policy developments that have been devised in recent years. It is to these that the final section of this chapter now turns.

Conclusion

While debates about trends in police practice, both in terms of interactions with the public (such as stop and search) and internal recruitment and personnel issues, continue to be contested, it is apparent that 'race' has become a salient category in terms of organizing and governing the contemporary police service. In a decade and a half, ethnic monitoring in the police service has moved from the margins to the centre, establishing a plethora of research reports around which debates are framed and re-framed. This has been both the cause and effect of continued political emphasis on racism and policing. In many respects, this has led to the promotion and reinforcement of ethnic identity in ways that has had negative, as well as positive, consequences. Internal procedures to manage staff may sometimes become problematic as a result of these trends. The Morris Inquiry (2004), for example, reported that concerns about the performance of minority ethnic officers in the Met became formalized more quickly than those relating to white officers, because line managers lacked the confidence to make decisions about minority staff and resorted more quickly to official procedures. The Morris Report (2004: 5) explained this in terms of concerns:

> ... that there is no common understanding of diversity within the organisation and that it is not embedded in the culture of the MPS. We fear that it remains, at worse, a source of fear and anxiety and, at best, a process of ticking boxes.

As has been noted, the reification of race as an organizing category within the contemporary police service raises concerns about the marginalization of other aspects of identity and other forms of discrimination. The development of the Black Police Association as an authoritative voice in debates about contemporary policing reflects the increasing centrality of race and racism in discourse about police work. However, this has reinforced racialized identity in ways that raises concerns about the status of other groups, such as female or gay police staff. Representatives of these groups have often had to resist senior management conceptualization of a 'hierarchy of oppression' with racism the pre-eminent concern at the top of the pyramid, with other problems relegated to a subordinate position (McLaughlin, 2007: 24). As McLaughlin (2007) argues, the proliferation of identity groups within the cultural landscape of twenty-first-century police work raises the prospect of 'balkanization', whereby groups of officers coalesce around essentialist and exclusive identities and compete for position. Given the complexity of contemporary society and the breadth of diversity that surrounds police work, unidimensional expressions of identity focusing on ethnicity, religion, gender, or sexuality bear little relation to the lived reality that confronts officers in their routine work. Essentialist forms of identity that inform the Black Police Association, or those groups representing officers who are Italian, Jewish, Turkish, Greek, Sikh, Hindu, Muslim, Christian, or Irish, might be politically pragmatic, but they do not reflect the complex ways in which identities are constructed and sustained (Holdaway and O'Neill, 2007: 96–7). A more meaningful conceptualization of diversity is required, reflecting the ambiguities and complexities of identity. Officers need to be given the confidence to ask questions and seek information about the cultures and communities in which they work and to become professional reflective practitioners. An embedded understanding of diversity that extends beyond 'race' and is robust enough to recognize complexities and tensions needs to be developed. Recruiting more minority ethnic officers, and more women, might help to do this, but this is not a panacea in terms of developing an antiracist police service. That requires effort to address the normative whiteness of the police service, it cannot be assumed that minority ethnic officers will affect predominant police culture by some form of cultural osmosis.

Even the earlier brief discussion of developments relating to just two topics demonstrates that the intense heat that has surrounded issues of policing, ethnicity, and racism in recent years has not always produced very much light. In statistical terms, more is known about the representation of minority ethnic people in police stop-and-search data. Claims of over-representation are undermined when the picture is considered in the light of the population available to be stopped and searched at those times and in those places where this police tactic is most used. This seems to suggest that the problem of racism is not, in this respect, just to do with the inappropriate exercise of discretion by officers who are unduly influenced by racist stereotypes. However, broader questions remain about the policy of stop and search, and concerns persist about the use of stop and search as a general tactic and its impact on public confidence. Some of these questions relate to issues to do with racism and discrimination, and so these continue to be important debates. Additionally, if routine police work impacts proportionately in terms of the ethnic profile of those available to be stopped and searched, questions remain about why certain ethnic groups are more likely to be present on the streets during those periods. This discussion will inevitably raise questions relating to racism and marginalization, which indicates that analysis of policing, race, and ethnic relations needs to be cognisant of broader social processes. The continuing racialization of crime forms an authoritative narrative of contemporary urban life against which routine police work is carried out. The most obvious example of this in recent years has been the problematization of Muslim communities and the pervasiveness of the security agenda. The bombings in London in July 2005 led to a recalibration of debates about community policing, racial profiling, and stop and search. As the security agenda has come to dominate governance more generally, so too previous insistence on ensuring equity and transparency in terms of stop and search were subsumed beneath demands that the police target Muslim communities in order to prevent further terrorist activity. Notably, the Home Office minister Hazel Blears stated that the Muslim community should expect to be stopped by the police more often, and the Chief Constable of the British Transport Police argued that his officers would properly target Asians in stop-and-search operations. Both claimed that this was not an instance of 'racial profiling', but rather an example of 'intelligence-led' policing and a valid response to an internal security threat. Subsequent data suggested that Asian people were disproportionately subjected to stop and searches under the 2000 Terrorism Act. In the month after the 7/7 bombings, British Transport Police stopped and searched 6,747 people, mostly in London (Dodd, 2005). Their data showed that 35 per cent of these involved Asian people, who comprised only 12 per cent of the London population. None of these had led to terrorism-related charges, which suggest that the intelligence on which these were based was either absent or flawed. Implicitly, the securitization of contemporary governance and policing suggests that the promotion of good community relations and the avoidance of disproportionality become only secondary concerns. This does not mean that the antiracist agenda established in the period following the Lawrence Report has been wholly jettisoned, but there is a danger that it is subsumed beneath a crime control security–oriented model of policing. If the promotion of good community and race relations helps the police to develop good sources of intelligence and so contribute to combating crime and terrorism, then it ought to be continued. Such a utilitarian reconfiguration of debates about policing, race and racism poses important concerns relating to social justice and equity.

Summary

Issues relating to police racism have formed an authoritative narrative account of policing in Britain in recent times. Efforts to reform the police service have followed an agenda established by the 1999 Lawrence Report, which has also

(Continued)

(Continued)

influenced the public sector more generally. This chapter provides a detailed exploration of debates relating to police stop and search, which in turn relates to police interaction with the public. It also considers in detail the recruitment of minority ethnic staff to the police service, which relates to internal personnel issues and to the culture of the organization. In terms of stop and search, the ethnic monitoring of police activity has led to the development of a body of statistical evidence which clearly indicates that minority ethnic people are over-represented when compared to their presence in the population as a whole. The data from 2004–05 suggests that black people are six times more likely to be stopped than whites, and Asians are twice as likely. However, these data are usually compiled using a benchmark drawn from residential populations. Since stop and search tends to be practiced in a highly focused way, in spatial and temporal terms, concern has been expressed that residential population is not the most meaningful measure to use when it comes to assessing disproportionality. An alternative measure, based on the population 'available' to be stopped and searched, has been developed by a number of studies, which have tended to find that ethnic discrepancies are not apparent. It is argued that these findings require more attention be focused on matters relating to space and social class when it comes to explaining the disproportionate impact of stop and search. This does not mean that issues relating to race and ethnicity are not relevant, but rather that they should not be the sole criteria considered.

Efforts to recruit a more ethnically diverse police service have been made for several decades, but have had added impetus in recent years. Detailed targets for each police service were introduced in the wake of the Lawrence Report. Nonetheless, progress has been slow and minority ethnic representation remains significantly lower when compared to overall demographic trends. Various implied advantages of better representation can be discerned. Often, it is suggested that the issue of recruitment acts as a litmus test in terms of the extent of racism within police subculture(s), and it is claimed that the development of a diverse workforce will help overcome problems of institutional racism. It is argued that this is not necessarily the case, and that other factors, relating to management, for example, also need to be addressed. Research also shows that the centrality of concerns about race and racism might have a detrimental impact on forms of discrimination and that a tendency to ethnic essentialism, while politically understandable, tends to marginalize the complexities and contradictions of identity politics. It is argued that more needs to be done to develop an embedded sense of diversity that will allow officers to understand and recognize the significance of a wider range of issues affecting crime and policing issues. The wider context of the nexus of policing, security, and racialization in contemporary British and global society is considered in the final part of the chapter. It is argued that internal police service reforms cannot be considered apart from this broader picture and that the increasing centrality of security to contemporary policing discourse threatens to undermine a progressive agenda of

(*Continued*)

antiracism in policing. This has been particularly evident in the continuing racialization of some forms of crime, and particularly in relation to the Muslim community and terrorism. Advances made in recognizing the importance of police community relations are jeopardized when they come to be regarded as of secondary importance relative to primary goals about security.

Key Texts

Rowe, M. (2004) *Policing, Race and Racism*, Cullompton: Willan Publishing.
Rowe, M. (ed.) (2007) *Policing Beyond Macpherson: Issues in Policing, Race and Society*, Cullompton: Willan Publishing.
Phillips, C. and Bowling, B. (2007) 'Ethnicities, Racism, Crime, and Criminal Justice', in Maguire, M., Morgan, R. and Reiner, R. (eds) *The Oxford Handbook of Criminology*, Oxford: Oxford University Press.

References

Adorno, T. (1950) *The Authoritarian Personality*, New York: Harper Row.

Brogden, M. (1987) 'The emergence of the police - the colonial dimension', *British Journal of Criminology*, 27(1), 4–14.

Butler, A.J.P. (1982) *An Examination of the Influence of Training and Work Experience on the Attitudes and Perceptions of Police Officers*, Bramshill: Police Staff College.

Cardwell, D. (2007) 'After Bell, Critics Want Mayor to Broaden Focus on Police', *New York Times*, March 21.

Cashmore, E. (2000) 'Behind the window dressing: ethnic minority police perspectives on cultural diversity', *Journal of Ethnic and Migration Studies*, 28(2), 327–41.

Colman, A. and Gorman, P. (1982) 'Conservatism, dogmatism and authoritarianism in British police officers', *Sociology*, 16(1), 1–26.

Commission for Racial Equality (2005) The Police Service in England and Wales: Final Report of a Formal Investigation by the Commission for Racial Equality, London: Commission for Racial Equality.

Dodd, V. (2005) 'Asian Men Targeted in Stop and Search', *Guardian*, 17 August.

Dodd, V. (2006) 'Diversity Target is Unrealistic say Police Chiefs', *Guardian*, 31 March.

Dodd, V., Morris, S. and Lewis, P. (2007) 'Tighter Security for Muslim Police Officers in Fear of Kidnap by Islamic Extremists', *Guardian*, 2 February.

Fitzgerald, M. (2000) Final Report into Stop and Search, London: Metropolitan Police.

Fitzgerald, M. and Sibbit, R. (1997) Ethnic Monitoring in Police Forces: a Beginning, Home Office Research Study 173, London: Home Office.

Hill, R.S. (1989) *The Colonial Frontier Tamed – New Zealand Policing in Transition*, 1867–86, Wellington: GP Books.

Holdaway, S. (1996) *The Racialisation of British Policing*, Basingstoke: Macmillan.

Holdaway, S. and O'Neill, M. (2006) 'Institutional racism after Macpherson – an analysis of police views, *Policing and Society*, 16(4), 349–69.

Holdaway, S. and O'Neill, M. (2007) 'Black Police Associations and the Lawrence Report', in Rowe, M. (ed.) *Policing Beyond Macpherson – Issues in Policing, Race, and Society*, Cullompton: Willan Publishing, pp. 88–106.

Home Office (2006) *Statistics on Race and the Criminal Justice System 2005*, London: Home Office.

Hughes, G. and Rowe, M. (2007) 'Neighbourhood policing and community safety: researching the instabilities of the local governance of crime, disorder and security in contemporary UK', *Criminology and Criminal Justice*, 7(4).

Johnston, L. (2006) 'Diversifying police recruitment? The deployment of police community support officers in London', *The Howard Journal*, 45(4), 388–402.

Macpherson, Sir W. (1999) The Stephen Lawrence Inquiry – Report of an Inquiry by Sir William Macpherson of Cluny, CM 4262–1, London: HMSO.

McLaughlin, E. (2007) 'Diversity or anarchy? The post-Macpherson blues', in Rowe, M. (ed.) *Policing Beyond Macpherson – Issues in Policing, Race, and Society*, Cullompton: Willan Publishing, pp. 18–42.

Morris, Sir W., Burden, Sir A. and Weekes, A. (2004) The Case for Change: People in the Metropolitan Police Service, the Report of the Morris Inquiry, London: Metropolitan Police Authority.

MVA and Miller, J. (2000) Profiling Populations Available for Stop and Search, Police Research Series Paper 131, London: Home Office.

Palmer, S.H. (1988) *Police and Protest in England and Ireland 1780–1950*, Cambridge: Cambridge University Press.

Paoline, E.A., Myers, S.M. and Worden, R.E. (2000) 'Police culture, individualism and community policing: evidence from two police departments', *Justice Quarterly*, 17(3), 575–605.

Rowe, M. (2004) *Policing, Race and Racism*, Cullompton: Willan Publishing.

Rowe, M. (ed.) (2007) *Policing Beyond Macpherson – Issues in Policing, Race, and Society*, Cullompton: Willan Publishing.

Scarman, Lord (1981) The Scarman Report – The Brixton Disorders, 10–12 April 1981, Cmnd 8427, London: HMSO.

Sherman, L. (1983) 'After the riots: police and minorities in the US 1970–1980', in: N. Glazer and K. Young (eds) *Ethnic Pluralism and Public Policy*, London: Heinemann.

Stenson, K. and Waddington, P.A.J. (2007) 'Macpherson, police stops and institutional racism', in Rowe, M. (ed.) *Policing Beyond Macpherson – Issues in Policing, Race, and Society*, Cullompton: Willan Publishing, pp. 128–47.

Waddington, P.A.J., Stenson, K. and Don, D. (2004) 'In proportion: race and police stop and search, *British Journal of Criminology*, 44(6), 889–914.

Westmarland, L. (2001) *Gender and Policing – Sex, Power and Police Culture*, Cullompton: Willan Publishing.

Whitfield, J. (2004) *Unhappy Dialogue – the Metropolitan Police and Black Londoners in Post-War Britain*, Cullompton: Willan Publishing.

FOUR

The Crown Prosecution Service and Race Equality

Séamus Taylor[1]

Introduction: Terminology and Limitations

As is made clear elsewhere in this book, race is a term with a high level of usage in public policy and a relatively low level of shared meaning. To that extent, it is a term that remains contested and contentious. This chapter draws on the concepts of race as reflected in public policy in England and Wales, notwithstanding their shortcomings. They are largely based on a colour-based paradigm, which has its origins in the USA and has great explanatory power, particularly in helping to explain colour-based experiences involving discrimination and disadvantage. However, this paradigm does not explain the multiple racisms that public service providers encounter today; for example, it does not adequately explain anti-Semitism or the experience of groups such as Gypsies and Travellers.

I subscribe to the social constructionist view that there is ultimately one race, the human race; but I recognize that various peoples have been racialized on the basis of assumed racial characteristics, resulting in experiences of exclusion, discrimination, and disadvantage, manifested at structural, institutional, and individual levels. This chapter focuses largely on the institutional context, and covers the following main areas: a short history on race equality and the CPS, employment, prosecutions, engagement with diverse communities, the policy-making process, and current approaches and challenges.

---

[1]Writing on race, race equality, and the CPS from within the Service has potential benefits and disbenefits. It brings the benefit of practice and detailed knowledge at a senior level. It has the potential disbenefits of being the perspective of a senior-level actor in the process that deals with race and race equality on a daily basis within the Service, and lacks to some extent the outsider's eye.

A Little History – from Agenda Setting to Outcomes

As a large public sector employer and independent public prosecutor, the CPS responded slowly to the equal opportunities agenda (CPS, 2001). In fact, in its first 10–15 years of existence, the CPS tended to operate a 'raceblind' or 'race neutral' approach, which remained in place until it was fundamentally challenged by employees within the Service and by the findings of the Lawrence Inquiry (Macpherson, 1999). It was only in the mid–late 1990s that management attention appears to have focused on race equality, prompted by a small number of findings against the CPS from employment tribunals brought by black and minority ethnic staff. At the same time, some communities also expressed concerns about the way the CPS prosecuted crime and about potential racial bias in decision-making. Both issues brought the CPS to the attention of the Commission for Racial Equality (CRE).

The CRE and the Denman Inquiry

In December 1999, the CRE wrote to the CPS indicating that it was minded to announce a comprehensive formal investigation into racial discrimination in the Service. However, following urgent discussions, in January 2000, the CRE suspended this decision, having agreed with the CPS to set up an independent inquiry and to bring forward an action plan on race equality. The Inquiry became known as the Denman Inquiry after its chair, Sylvia Denman, and produced a preliminary report in April 2000, which referred to evidence of possible segregated working at the Croydon CPS branch in South London. The CRE then announced that it would undertake its own formal investigation, specifically into race relations at the Croydon branch (CRE, 2001)[2]. This investigation found that managers had allowed a situation to persist in which staff teams in the branch were segregated on racial lines.

Among the other main findings of the Denman Inquiry were significant workforce under-representation of black and minority ethnic (BME) staff, particularly at senior lawyer and administrative grades, weaknesses in management practice, and poor management training on equality and diversity, which were seen as underlying causes of many of the problems highlighted. Existing equality and diversity plans and structures were found to lack strategic coherence, and there was unwarranted complacency about the possibility of discrimination in the prosecution process in areas such as the handling of racist crimes. Performance on race equality was found to vary markedly across the 42 CPS areas. Devising mechanisms to hold areas accountable for performance on equality and diversity was seen as key to securing improvements. The concept of institutional racism was not generally

---

[2]The CRE's decision to go to formal investigation on this specific issue did not supersede the wider decision to suspend a formal investigation.

understood or acknowledged, and many staff who considered they had been discriminated against did not complain, partly because they lacked confidence in the complaints procedure. There were fewer positive points to emerge from the Denman Inquiry. They included the fact that senior management had demonstrated a clear commitment to effect change on equality and diversity. Also, there was emerging evidence of change to the culture of the CPS, to one that positively embraced all sections of the community. In the three years following the Denman Inquiry, the CPS made significant progress in addressing its recommendations on structures, staffing, and awareness raising. Committees to take forward equality and diversity issues were established, a strategic Equality and Diversity Unit was embedded in Headquarters structures and a number of awareness raising conferences and other events were held (CPS, 2004).

Meanwhile, the CPS moved towards a more transparent staffing and recruitment process, based on job profiles, person specifications, and work-based assessment. Most managers had equality and diversity training, but there were mixed views on the quality of what was provided according to an unpublished internal evaluation of training. Specifically, the training was seen as having raised awareness without consistently enhancing competence. The CPS has more recently focused on including equalities modules in mainstream training. An equality and diversity staff complaints procedure was also implemented, though significant issues remain in terms of delays in completing investigations on time and to standard. A revised procedure was implemented in 2007–08.

There has been no formal positive action to address under-representation in middle and senior levels. However, the CPS already has one of the more ethnically diverse workforces across Whitehall (see below). In recent years, the Service has appointed its first black or minority ethnic staff at the Chief Crown Prosecutor level. It has also introduced a law scholarship scheme; while this is not a positive action scheme in the strict legal sense, in reality it is an equalizing measure, which significantly benefits women and black and minority ethnic employees.

In terms of performance management, the CPS Equality and Diversity Unit (EDU) oversaw the introduction of an initial equalities performance reporting system for areas. This contributed to the development of a more performance management focus to achieve improvement on equalities and was significantly enhanced in 2005–06 when the Service moved to an outcome-based approach linked to the CPS Area Performance Review System. This involves all 42 CPS areas reporting quarterly their performance on such business issues as outcomes in hate crime cases and the nature, extent, and impact of community engagement alongside other key performance measures.

The CPS was recognized in the years following the Denman Inquiry for its success in beginning to engage diverse communities in framing key policies on domestic violence, racist, and religious and homophobic crimes. Community stakeholders were also engaged in framing its first statutory race equality scheme through an interactive workshop where the draft Scheme was critically appraised and significantly reshaped. The CPS also conducted a comprehensive race impact assessment of the prosecution process, through the Race for Justice (Diversity Monitoring Project) launched in November 2003, which addressed a key issue raised by Denman about potential racial bias in prosecutors' decision making.

The CRE lifted its threatened formal investigation in 2002 and entered a voluntary formal monitoring partnership focused on continuous race equality improvements, with particular emphasis on employment. This agreement ran from 2002 to 2007, with the CRE and CPS meeting every six months for monitoring purposes; prior to these meetings, the CPS submitted a report on its performance on equalities in employment, with a particular focus on race equality in employment. This period was marked by a focus on sensitizing the organization to the importance of race equality and wider equality and diversity issues to CPS business. To its credit, the CPS not only largely delivered on Denman's recommendations in less than three years, but went significantly beyond the emphasis on infrastructure to set agendas and undertake innovative policy development and review. On the transition of the CRE into the new Equality and Human Rights Commission (EHRC), the CRE commended the extent of progress made by the CPS and recommended that the EHRC just keep a watching brief on the CPS annual equalities in employment reports and other key developments (CRE, 2007).

Post Delivery of Denman – Taking Race Equality Towards an Outcomes Focus

The CPS equality and diversity stocktake (CPS, 2004) concluded that the key priority from 2004 to 2008 had to be to move equalities and issues of race equality into their logical second phase, namely the delivery of outcomes and results. A number of broad outcome measures were set, with a particular focus on hate crime outcomes, community engagement, and workforce representation. These included, for example, reducing unsuccessful outcomes in hate crime cases, achieving prosecution decisions free from discrimination, increasing levels of public confidence, and increasing employee satisfaction across all groups.

In order to help achieve these outcomes, the CPS vision for equality is based on the premise that crime affects all communities, which must see the CPS as their prosecution service, and trust it to make fair decisions. For both the public and the CPS, equality and diversity in employment and in the prosecution process appear firmly linked (CPS, 2005).

Race, Race Equality, and Employment

A small number of race and sex discrimination cases in employment in the late 1990s and early 2000s provided the impetus for serious management action on race equality in the CPS. A fundamental challenge was posed by these cases; if the Service could not be trusted to treat its employees fairly, it could hardly be trusted to conduct its prosecution business fairly. In 2000, there also emerged a new staff network, the National Black Crown Prosecution Association (NBCPA), which aimed to challenge and help develop the organization and its own membership on issues impacting on black and minority ethnic staff. It is fair to say that, against the backdrop outlined above, its early years were often marked by considerable challenge to the Service and less focus on development and education. Faced with this degree of challenge internally and significant external monitoring by the CRE, the CPS demonstrated a leadership commitment to responding positively to the challenges raised. Sir David Calvert-Smith, the previous DPP, provided that leadership, and this has been significantly built on by Sir Ken Macdonald QC, the current DPP. Calvert-Smith went on public record as saying he accepted that the CPS, like many public sector institutions, was institutionally racist. Views differed at the time regarding his identification of the Service in this way, but it had a powerful galvanizing effect.

In terms of race equality and employment in the CPS, I would identify three main ongoing areas of concern. These are employee representation, employee satisfaction, and employee experiences, and engagement.

Firstly, the CPS workforce profile in terms of ethnicity as in March 2005 (latest available data) showed 14.6% black and minority ethnic staff overall. This compares with 12% in 2003 and situates the CPS as one of the more ethnically diverse workforces in the criminal justice system. At more senior levels, the CPS has made some of its most significant progress in securing a diverse workforce: 13.3% of Chief Crown Prosecutors (CCPs) were of black or minority ethnic origin in 2005, compared with 7.5% in 2003. This has increased further to over 15% since 2003, although published data is not yet available. This contrasts with the Police Service, for example, where there was (in 2007) just one black or minority ethnic Chief Constable. Within the senior civil service, 10.5% of staff (excluding CCPs) were of black and minority ethnic origin in March 2005. This progress on workforce representation is also evidenced at what are termed 'feeder grades' for senior levels in the Service, that is Grades 7 and 6 in civil service terms. At Grade 6, the black and minority ethnic workforce profile was 7.1% overall, and at Grade 7, the black and minority ethnic profile is 9.9% overall. This compares with a Grade 7 and Grade 6 workforce profile of 0% in 2000 (CPS, 2006; HMCPSI, 2006).

There is, however, no room for complacency. In many instances, at senior levels, there are very small numbers of senior posts and a move of one or two people can have a significant impact. Further, whilst significant progress has been made, there are areas of the country where the workforce is not yet representative of local communities. In line with a Cabinet Office initiative, the 'Diversity 10 point plan', and in order to meet senior level targets, a diversity delivery plan was put in place in 2005–06. The Service also undertook a thematic review of workforce representation in all 42 CPS areas, which involved workforce representation targets up to 2008 and an action plan of supporting actions. A progress check followed by good practice guidance will follow in 2008–09.

Secondly, with regard to employee satisfaction and perceptions, the Service undertakes a staff survey every two years, which includes a number of questions on equality and diversity themes. The results are also analysed by ethnicity. The most recent survey was conducted in early 2006, with results produced in May 2006. It had a 60% response rate (5,103 completed surveys), and 10% of respondents identified themselves as being of black or minority ethnic origin. The results revealed a mixed picture. For example, black or minority ethnic staff tended to be slightly less satisfied with their job, but more likely to recommend the CPS as an employer. Black staff were most likely to recommend the CPS as a good place to work (63%) compared to 45% of Asian staff and an overall figure of 43%.

On specific measures of equality and diversity, and dignity at work, 32% of black or minority ethnic staff respondents felt that the CPS valued its staff compared to 28% of other staff. These are overall low percentages across all groups. In terms of treatment with fairness and respect, 67% of black respondents indicated that they were treated with fairness and respect. This compares with 69% of Asian staff and 64% of CPS staff overall. In terms of belief that the CPS is working towards equality and diversity, 72% of black respondents felt this to be the case, compared to 64% of Asian staff and 66% of CPS staff overall. Notwithstanding what appear in significant respects to be quite positive results in relation to black staff satisfaction levels and perceptions in particular, 76% of black respondents and 68% of Asian respondents believed that the CPS could do more to ensure dignity at work. This is significantly higher than the figure of 48% for all ethnic groups (CPS Staff Survey, 2006).

Thirdly, with regard to employee experiences, the CPS monitors a range of employee experiences by ethnicity and reports on these as part of its Annual Equalities in Employment Report. Analysis of the available ethnicity data for 2005–06 again indicates mixed results. For example, in relation to two key in-house legal training programmes important to progression, black or minority ethnic staff comprised 8.7% of trainees on the Proactive Prosecutor programme and 12.5% of trainees on the Higher Court Advocacy programme. They have been less well represented on the generic management development programme, 'Transform', on which 6.8% of participants were of black or minority ethnic origin. In 2005–06, black and minority ethnic staff comprised 34% of participants on the Law Scholarship Scheme mentioned above.

The CPS has operated an employee complaints procedure involving internal and external investigators, introduced following the Denman Inquiry. A more recent review highlighted an enduring lack of confidence in the handling of complaints, and a time-consuming and costly procedure (CPS, 2006a). It recommended that employee complaints should be brought back in house over a two-year period, during which confidence and competence would be built within the organization. The total number of employee complaints made in 2005–06 (40) was similar to the previous year (39). At the year's end, two complaints had been upheld, nine not upheld, two were withdrawn, five did not identify sufficient reason for complaint, and the remainder were ongoing. Of the 40 complaints, three cited racial discrimination or racial harassment as part of the complaint, and at the year's end one of these was not upheld and two were ongoing.

The data for 2005–06 indicates that there were 18 disciplinaries in total, four related to gross and four to serious misconduct. Seven involved black and minority ethnic staff (38.8%), which is significantly higher than the black and minority ethnic workforce profile. In recent years, there have been fluctuations in terms of black and minority ethnic representation in disciplinaries. As a result, the service is undertaking an equality and diversity impact assessment, which involves both data analysis and consultation with staff and unions, including the National Black Crown Prosecutors Association. When published, this will inform the revised disciplinary procedure.

In terms of leavers, based on limited available data, 9% of all leavers were of black and minority ethnic origin, which is relatively low compared to a workforce profile of 14.6% BME staff. The main reasons stated were change of career, followed by improved career prospects.

Nine complaints were lodged with an employment tribunal in 2005–06, compared with 15 in 2004–05. Three alleged race discrimination, and all three also alleged sex discrimination. During the 2005–06 year, there was also one employment appeal tribunal, which made an adverse finding of racial discrimination against the Service. Whilst overall numbers of tribunal cases are small, black and minority ethnic origin staff comprise approximately 30% of those who took tribunal cases whilst comprising 14.6% of the workforce overall. This disproportionality needs to be kept under review.

More recently, the CPS has undergone an external inspection on equality and diversity in employment, which found that:

... the necessary commitment to change and leadership ... at the highest levels within the CPS. Commitment has been backed up by changes to governance structures, the development of a strong Equality and Diversity Unit and a good level of engagement with both internal and external stakeholders to support change. However, the clear link made at the highest levels between equality and diversity in employment and the prosecution process is not always made at operational management level. (HMCPSI, 2006: 4)

The inspectorate concluded that:

> The CPS .... sees itself as having successfully journeyed through its first phase, that of agenda setting and awareness raising, and is now moving towards its second phase – the delivery of outcomes. The review has confirmed that this is the position and that significant progress is being made, despite the need for improvement in some aspects. Overall, the CPS has sought to ... move the Service forward into a position where there are no differences in employees' experiences that cannot be justified. It is working hard to achieve this objective. (HMCPSI, 2006: 4)

Race, Race Equality, and Prosecutions

Whilst it was issues of race equality in employment that provided the impetus for the first serious focus on equality and diversity in the CPS, concerns about race equality in prosecutions were raised by community organizations at roughly the same time. This was outside the specific remit of the Denman Inquiry but was later picked up by a number of studies, some external to the service and some commissioned by the CPS itself. These tended to show mixed results, partly because they looked at different aspects of the prosecution process, and partly because they took place at different times, allowing for limited comparisons.

The first studies to look at potential variations in the treatment of suspects by ethnicity were conducted by Mhlanga (1999) and Barclay and Mhlanga (2000). They looked at CPS decisions in a study of 6,100 cases of young defendants during September and October 1996. They found that termination of cases on grounds of insufficiency of evidence was more common for black and minority ethnic than white defendants. They had access to data about each case, and the study was carried out using a multivariate analysis to get into the case details behind the raw data. They were able to boost the sample from black and minority ethnic defendants, and within the 6,100 cases they concentrated on, there were 5,500 cases where ethnicity was recorded.

The second significant study to look at race and the prosecution process was the CPS-commissioned and independently conducted research by Gus John (Gus John Partnership, 2003). This study analysed the charging process with regard to offence group and found a number of different patterns by offences and ethnicity. For example, half of all men and two-thirds of all white and African-Caribbean women received a dishonesty charge; and a grievous bodily harm charge was twice as common among white male suspects as among African Caribbean suspects. As far as the charging process is concerned, John found that percentage differences between ethnic groups were too small to be statistically significant but there was a greater tendency towards no further action on evidential and public interest grounds in relation to African Caribbean suspects than those from other ethnic groups.

HMCPSI has twice conducted thematic inspections of cases with a minority ethnic dimension (HMCPSI, 2002 and 2004). The Inspectorate identified inappropriate police overcharging on both occasions and found evidence that the CPS significantly corrected for police overcharging but did not eliminate it. In approximately 120 cases where overcharging of minority ethnic defendants occurred, it found that the CPS rectified the position at initial review in 61.8% of cases in 2002, and this had improved further to 68% in 2004.

The key development since these earlier studies of race and the prosecution process and the earlier inspections has been the introduction of statutory charging across the CPS. Up to 2002, charging decisions were taken by the police, although in many cases they consulted with the CPS. A review by Lord Justice Auld (2001) recommended that the CPS be given greater legal powers to determine the decision to charge in all but minor cases. A pilot of CPS charging was conducted over 6 months in 2002 and found to be very encouraging; subsequently, statutory charging was delivered in all CPS areas, by March 2007.

The CPS commissioned an independent ethnic and gender impact assessment of charging decisions for the 42 CPS areas (Lewis, 2005). It covered the six-month period from September 2004 and involved an analysis of approximately 225,000 charging decisions. The study was based on a statistical report of data produced from the CPS case management system, COMPASS. Over 99% of all records included a gender code, but an ethnicity code was available for only 65%; in 17% of cases, the suspect chose not to provide his/her ethnicity; and this left 18% of cases where ethnicity was not recorded. The main results on ethnicity were:

- There were no significant differences across different ethnic groups in the proportion of cases finalized by a charge.
- There were some differences by ethnicity in cases finalized by no further action (NFA) on evidential grounds, that is, cases where the lawyer's decision was that no further action should be taken against the suspect on the basis of the available evidence. Just over a quarter (25.4%) of cases nationally with white suspects were so finalized; black, mixed, and other suspects were less likely to have their cases finalized NFA on evidential grounds (all significantly lower than white at 19–20%). There were some other differences within the wider ethnic classification system such as that cases with other white, mixed white/black African, or mixed other suspects were much less likely to have their cases finalized NFA on evidential grounds (all below 18%).

The main results when looking at ethnicity and gender together were:

- There was considerable variation in patterns of charging for females by ethnic category, though much of this could be attributed to the small numbers involved. On average, 40.3% of white British females were charged, compared with 26.4% of Pakistani females and compared to 48% for mixed other females, 46.7% for black Caribbean females and

45.6% for white Irish females. It is not clear why Pakistani females had such a low charge rate and mixed other females had such a high rate. This requires further consideration in future impact assessments.

- The proportion of females for whom no further action on evidence grounds was taken also varied and is in need of more investigation. This was 30% for white British females, 25% for mixed (other) females, 22% for Asian other females, and 42% for Pakistani females.

The CPS will continue to undertake annual equality and diversity impact assessments of charging decisions for a number of years to establish if significant differences exist over time, and to inform strategies to address any such significant differences. A more recent impact assessment for 2005–06 confirms the findings set out above.

Racist Crimes

The CPS launched a Public Policy Statement on the Prosecution of Racist and Religious Crimes in July 2003, which was informed by extensive community consultation and engagement with black and minority ethnic community organizations. This has been supported by a training programme on racist and religious crimes, with over 1,600 prosecutors trained to date. The community consultation was commended by the National Audit Office (2004) in its first study on equality and diversity in Whitehall.

Data on the performance of CPS handling of racist crimes comes from two sources, namely from an annual racist incidents monitoring scheme report (RIMS) and from a hate crime measure which is one of the top 15 measures in the CPS Area Performance Review system since April 2005. The RIMS shows that, in the year 2005–06, prosecutions for racially aggravated offences rose by 28% from the previous year with 7,430 defendants; 71% of defendants pleaded guilty, with a further 16% found guilty after trial so that convictions accounted for 87% of 8,114 charges prosecuted. This is an increase of 3% on the previous year's figure.

Since April 2005, a hate crime measure has been in place across all 42 areas, which records performance in reducing unsuccessful outcomes in hate crime cases, including racist, religious, homophobic, and domestic violence crimes. In April 2005, unsuccessful outcome across the three categories of hate crime combined was 42%. This had reduced to 38% by April 06 (against a target of 36%). However, by the third quarter of 2006–07, this had reduced to 32.5%. A new stretching target across the three hate crime categories has been set for March 2008 of 28%.

A direct comparison is not possible between the data set out in the annual RIMS report cited above and the data on performance against the hate crime measure as the RIMS data is based on defendants, and the Hate Crime Measure is based on charges.

Religious Crimes

The RIMS report also includes data on religiously aggravated crimes. Religiously aggravated cases rose by 26.5% in 2005–06, with 43 defendants, 41 of whom were prosecuted. The overall conviction rate for religiously aggravated offences was very high at 98%, with a significant rise in the number of guilty pleas from 46.5% in 2004–05 to 70.5% in 2005–06. However, compared to racist crimes (7,430 defendants in the same year), few religious crimes are referred to the CPS.

The actual or perceived religion of the victim was not known in 21 of the 43 cases. In the 22 cases where the religion was known, 18 victims were identified as Muslim, three as Christian, and one as Sikh. The data covers the period following the 7 July 2005 London bombings, and the number of victims identified as Muslims throughout the whole of 2005–06 was 81.8%, a rise of 5% on the previous year. There were more religious crime cases in July 2005 than for any other month. The CPS had 12 such cases in this month, and in 6 of these cases the defendants referred specifically to the London bombings. However, the rise experienced in July 2005 did not continue into August or during the rest of 2005–06.

The CPS has, since January 2006, held a series of 'Listening, Reassurance, and Information' events with Muslim communities across England and Wales, partly to explain how the CPS prosecutes religious crimes and to encourage people to report such incidents. These events have helped the CPS to reach over 350 Muslim community organizations and individuals and have provided information on three topics identified by them: the prosecution of racist and religiously aggravated crimes, the prosecution of incitement to hatred crimes, and the prosecution of terrorism-related crimes. The feedback on these events has been positive, although in terms of reach, women and younger people have so far been under-represented.

Incitement to Racial Hatred Crimes

Few cases of incitement to racial hatred are referred to the CPS. However, as with a single tribunal case on the employment side, they are often high profile and can have a significant impact on community perceptions, trust, and confidence. Such cases are referred to specialist lawyers at CPS HQ, reflecting the seriousness with which they are considered. Furthermore the Attorney General has to give consent for such cases to be prosecuted.

Although very few in number (29 were recorded between 1997 and 2007), such cases raise important issues of the balance to be struck between free speech and hate speech in open societies. They can also raise key issues about the expectations gap between communities' desire to see such cases brought to justice and the parameters of the existing legislation, which allow for people to be seriously offended and insulted without such offending behaviour constituting a prosecutable offence. The Government has recently agreed to introduce legal provisions to cover incitement to religious hatred.

Engaging Diverse Communities, Addressing Public Confidence, and Community-Informed Policy Making

Public confidence in the criminal justice system and in the CPS in particular is central to creating an effective and legitimate prosecution service. Despite significant public policy attention in recent years, it is fair to say that the CPS and other parts of the criminal justice system are still developing an understanding of what drives public confidence. We know that communication and people's direct experience of the Service and the wider criminal justice system are important. We also know that community and staff engagement have roles to play in discussing and responding to the real concerns of local communities, including those of black and minority ethnic communities with historic low levels of trust and confidence. The CPS has increasingly recognized that it will not acquire the stature of a respected world class public prosecution service without clear engagement with and accountability to different communities.

A Little History on Engagement and Lack of Engagement

Prior to considering more recent developments on community engagement in the CPS, it is worth recapping on a little wider context and history. The CPS had, to put it mildly, something of a difficult birth in 1986. The Service was given a narrow, modest remit from the outset – essentially receiving files of cases investigated and charged at their discretion by the police. Prosecutors would review those files in accordance with the appropriate tests. If these tests were passed, the case would more often than not be handed to an external barrister to prosecute in court. The Service was in part sandwiched between the police and the Bar.

As a result, it largely internalized the view that it had no role in engaging with the public. Constraints on its remit and narrow internal responses fused to result in a service that was viewed and experienced as remote, weak, and lacking in public awareness and confidence. There was historically a prevalent false view within the CPS that contact with the public could contaminate prosecutors' professional decision making. Independence and distance from the public were confused in the organizational mindset, and this was manifested by the fact that many CPS offices were in the early years ex-directory and therefore hard for the public to contact.

It is untenable to have a public prosecution service that is not engaged and respected by the public, because prosecuting without engagement risks prosecution without consent. This becomes more challenging but no less important when prosecuting in the context of an ethnically diverse society. The challenges the CPS faced in the late 1990s, described above, were arguably amongst the best things to have happened to the CPS in the past ten years. Such community challenges shook CPS complacency and blew open the door to engagement and wider modernization.

The CPS has journeyed a long way in the past ten years. Community-informed policy making and area-level engagement are now much more routine. In recent years, the CPS has, for example, produced a 'How to Handbook' on community engagement and implemented a programme of community engagement in all 42 CPS areas. It has also piloted a range of approaches to community engagement, including public scrutiny on hate crimes performance. But, perhaps most significantly, the CPS has developed a number of community-informed policies, initially in the areas of hate crime but extending more widely in recent years. The CPS progress in this area was noted and commended by the Cabinet Office–led Capability Review of CPS (June 2007), which noted that community stakeholders, including black and minority ethnic groups, positively commended CPS engagement in framing policies (Cabinet Office, 2007).

Community-Informed Policy Making

Diverse communities have been consulted in the framing of a range of public policies, including those on racist and religious crimes, domestic violence, and homophobic crime, as well as in the framing of the previous race equality schemes and more recent single equality scheme. Community-informed policy work also includes that on deaths in custody, and more recent work on so called honour crimes, forced marriage, and sexually transmitted infections. There have been a range of models of engagement. For example, the racist and religious crimes policy involved a project board including black and minority ethnic and faith community partners working alongside CPS staff. This was then the subject of wider consultation with over 120 community organizations, many working specifically with minority communities. The Single Equality Scheme had a project board and a wider reference group involving black and minority ethnic community partners, as well as an interactive workshop involving a range of black and minority ethnic groups.

Public confidence in the CPS is part of the measurement of public confidence in the criminal justice system overall. There are two key measures: the first considers confidence in bringing offences to justice. On this measure, BME communities are more confident than white communities. The second measures BME communities' confidence as to whether they will be treated fairly by a range of criminal justice agencies on the basis of their ethnicity. Table 4.1 sets out the position in relation to this measure as at 2005.

The data above shows that the CPS has achieved a small but statistically significant decrease in the percentage of black and minority ethnic people who

Table 4.1 Percentage of black and minority ethnic people who feel they would be treated worse as a result of their ethnicity

Agency	2001 HOCS	2003 HOCS	2005 HOCS	% Required for a statistically significant fall from 2001 baseline
Police	27%	23%	24%	24.5%
CPS	14%	12%	11%	11.8%
Courts	14%	13%	12%	12.4%
Probation	11%	10%	10%	9.2%
Prisons	21%	17%	17%	18.4%

feel they would be treated worse by the Service over the period 2001–05. Notwithstanding such progress against external measures, the CPS recognizes, in the words of its Director, that 'it is only in the foothills' on community engagement (Directorate of Public Prosecutions, keynote speech to CPS Community Engagement Conference, November 2006). That is why the Service is embarking on a programme to implement hate crime scrutiny panels in all areas, as well as community involvement panels during 2007–08 and into 2008–09. In this way, the CPS aims to move community engagement with diverse communities on from the level of simply *sharing* information, to encouraging active community *scrutiny* of performance.

Concluding Thoughts: Where Now and What of the Future?

As a large public sector organization, the CPS was a 'late starter' on the equality and diversity agenda, and some serious shortcomings needed to be addressed. However, while there is still much to do, the evidence points to considerable achievements in race equality in employment, prosecution policies and practice, and in community engagement. The current emphasis is on an outcomes- and measurement-based approach to making progress on race equality – an approach suited to the CPS's phase in a journey to equality and diversity, building on an earlier agenda-setting period with the current results-based approach. This progress has been independently assessed and confirmed by the recent HMCPSI thematic review (HMCPSI, 2006).

There are and will continue to be new and emerging challenges that test the CPS's race equality policies and ethos. Current challenges, for instance, include the issue of prosecuting the transmission of serious sexual infection. There have been very few cases to date, but concerns have been expressed about potential disproportionality in prosecutions in terms of ethnicity and sexuality. Specifically, there is a concern that black or minority ethnic and gay men are disproportionately represented amongst the few prosecutions to date. There is a risk in this policy initiative of the CPS wittingly or unwittingly contributing to racializing sex, sexualizing race, and at the same time inadvertently 'recriminalizing' aspects of gay sexuality. The CPS is acutely alert to these challenges, recognizing the current uneven social distribution of infections such as HIV. The CPS's policy response will in part be a test of the maturity of its race equality approach and there are clear indications to be confident in its response. Other current challenges include the prosecution response to so-called honour crimes and forced marriage. This raises the attendant challenges of potentially problematizing minority cultures, whilst perceived to be protecting transcendent human rights. The CPS is currently piloting the monitoring of these crimes in a number of areas of the country with a view to informing future handling of such cases. These pilots will run until summer 2008. Again, the CPS policy response will be a test of the maturity of its overall approach.

Looking to the future, issues of race and race equality will remain central to the further development of an independent, respected, and trusted public prosecution service. These issues are likely to grow in salience, not least because of the consequences of globalization and the attendant risks of racialized responses from powerful institutions such as the CPS, as society becomes increasingly diverse.

Summary

In the mid–late 1990s, prompted by findings against the CPS from a small number of employment tribunals brought by black and minority ethnic staff, by community concerns about potential racial bias in CPS decision-making, and by the Stephen Lawrence Inquiry (Macpherson, 1999), the CPS's historic 'race neutral' approach to its business was fundamentally challenged. The Denman Inquiry into race discrimination in the CPS (CPS, 2001) found evidence of segregated working in one office, weaknesses in management practice, and poor management training on equality and diversity. The CPS responded positively to the recommendations of the Denman Inquiry and has made progress in securing a more diverse workforce at all levels, and in improving perceptions amongst black and minority ethnic employees.

Concerns about potential race bias in prosecutions has generated several studies, which have, amongst other things, found no significant variation of charging decision by the main ethnic group of the suspect, except that non-white suspects were slightly less likely to receive a decision to no prosecution on evidential grounds. A recent report (Lewis, 2005) found variations in patterns of charging for women by ethnic category. Data on CPS handling of racist crimes shows that prosecutions for racially aggravated offences have risen markedly and that unsuccessful outcomes in hate crime cases are reducing significantly.

At its inception, the CPS had largely internalized the view that it had no role in engaging with the public and was experienced as remote, weak, and lacking

(Continued)

in public awareness and confidence. However, community-informed policy making and area-level engagement have improved significantly. Diverse communities have been consulted in the framing of a range of public policies, including those on racist and religious crimes. Public confidence measures also show that black and minority ethnic people have increased confidence in the CPS's ability to bring offences to justice and in fair treatment by the CPS.

Overall, though a 'late starter', there has been significantly tangible progress towards race equality in various areas, although there is scope to build further understanding of potential ethnic disproportionality in the prosecution process.

Key Texts

Her Majesty's Crown Prosecution Service Inspectorate (HMCPSI) (2006) Review of equality and diversity in employment practice in the CPS: Equalities driving justice. London: HMSO.

Spalek, B. (2008) *Communities, Identities and Crime*. Bristol: The Policy Press.

Crown Prosecution Service (CPS) (2006) Single Equality Scheme 2006–10. www.cps.gsi.gov.uk

References

Auld, Lord Justice (2001) Review of the Criminal Courts of England and Wales. London: HMSO.

Barclay, G and Mhlanga, B (2000) Ethnic Differences in Decisions on Young Defendants Dealt with by the Crown Prosecution Service. London: Home Office.

Cabinet Office (2007) Capability Review Report on the Crown Prosecution Service. London: Cabinet Office.

Commission for Racial Equality (2001) The Crown Prosecution Service, Croydon Branch: Report of a Formal Investigation. London: CRE.

Commission for Racial Equality (2007) A Lot Done, a Lot To Do: Our Vision for an Integrated Britain. London: CRE.

Crown Prosecution Service (2001) Report of an Independent Inquiry into Race Discrimination in the Crown Prosecution Service (The 'Denman Report'). London: CPS.

Crown Prosecution Service (2004) Addressing Equality and Diversity in the Crown Prosecution Service – a Stocktake Report. London: CPS.

Crown Prosecution Service (2005) Equality and Diversity Policy. London: CPS.

Crown Prosecution Service (2005) Equality and Diversity Strategy 2005–08. London: CPS.

Crown Prosecution Service (2006) Annual Equalities in Employment Report 2005–06. London: CPS.

Crown Prosecution Service (2006a) Review of Equality and Diversity Complaints Procedure, Anjali Arya Consultancy for the CPS. London: CPS.

Her Majesty's Crown Prosecution Service Inspectorate (HMCPSI) (2002) Review of CPS Casework Having a Minority Ethnic Dimension. London: HMSO.

Her Majesty's Crown Prosecution Service Inspectorate (HMCPSI) (2004) Follow up Review of CPS Casework Having a Minority Ethnic Dimension. London: HMSO.

Her Majesty's Crown Prosecution Service Inspectorate (HMCPSI) (2006) Review of Equality and Diversity in Employment Practice in the CPS: Equalities Driving Justice. London: HMSO.

Gus John Partnership (2003) Race for Justice: A Review of CPS Decision-Making for Possible Racial Bias at Each Stage of the Prosecution Process. London: CPS.

Lewis, C (2005) Equality and Diversity Impact Assessment of CPS Statutory Charging: England and Wales Sept 2004–Feb 2005. London: CPS.

Macpherson, W. (1999) *The Stephen Lawrence Inquiry. Report of an Inquiry by Sir William Macpherson of Cluny* (Cm 4262). London: HMSO.

Mhlanga, B. (1999) Race and CPS discussions: Report for the CPS 1999. London: CPS.

National Audit Office (2004) Delivering Public Service in a Diverse Society. London: NAO.

FIVE

Prisons and Race Equality

Hindpal Singh Bhui

Over twenty thousand prisoners in England and Wales identified themselves as being from a black or minority ethnic group[1]. This equates to just over a quarter (26%) of the male and 28% of the female prison population (Ministry of Justice, 2007a)[2]. The over-representation of black and minority ethnic people, particularly black African Caribbeans, at earlier stages of the criminal justice process (Ministry of Justice, 2007a) makes it virtually inevitable that they will figure disproportionately in the prison system (Edgar, 2007). The reasons for disproportionality throughout the criminal justice process have been long debated. Discussion has tended to centre on two main contentions: that social exclusion, deprivation, and demographics produce genuinely higher rates of offending in minority ethnic communities; or alternatively, that racist treatment and discrimination within the system create overrepresentation and a false impression of criminality in minority ethnic communities (see Bhui, 1999). However, little consensus has emerged, partly because of the lack of reliable research evidence, leading some to argue, convincingly, that there is a need for the debate to move beyond these parameters, and towards the development of minority ethnic perspectives on criminal justice (Phillips and Bowling, 2003). This chapter is written in that spirit and focuses on research specifically about the racism experienced and perpetrated by prisoners and prison staff, and the efforts that have been made to address it within the prison system.

While 'race' and racism in prisons is an under-researched subject, recent years have seen increased attention on this area, driven largely by one tragic and seminal event: the murder of a young Asian man, Zahid Mubarek, by his violent racist cell-mate in Feltham Young Offenders Institution (YOI) in 2000.

---

[1]The terms 'minority ethnic' or 'black and minority ethnic' (which emphasizes visible minorities) will be used in this chapter to refer to all minority groups (see Smith, Chapter 1 for more discussion on terminology).

[2]The breakdown for the male population was 15% black, 7% Asian, 3% mixed, and 1% Chinese or 'other'; for women, it was 20% black, 2% Asian, 4% mixed, and 2% Chinese or other.

This was shortly after the publication of the Stephen Lawrence Inquiry (Macpherson, 1999; see also the chapters by Rowe and Hall in this volume). Mubarek's murder prompted Commission for Racial Equality (CRE, 2003a) and public (Keith, 2006) inquiries into the circumstances of his death. It was also followed by a further CRE investigation (CRE, 2003b), and a Prison Inspectorate thematic review into race relations in prisons (HMIP, 2005b).

These reports, supported by the other research discussed below, paint a complex picture, with evidence of both improvements and setbacks in the prison system's race equality journey. However, the common theme of all of the available evidence is a persistence of sometimes direct, though increasingly more 'subtle' and often unwitting, racism; this has fuelled alienation amongst black and minority ethnic prisoners, resulting in poorer relationships with staff and therefore potentially less stable prisons. Such alienation has become particularly apparent amongst Muslim prisoners (HMIP, 2008b, 2008c), most of whom are black or Asian, and whose experiences have yet to be examined in any detail (see also Spalek, Lambert, and Baker in this volume).

This chapter will consider the messages of the limited existing research on racism in prisons, giving particular attention to the Prison Inspectorate's (HMIP, 2005b) wide-ranging thematic investigation, and to more recent inspection data[3]. It will examine evidence on the specific experiences of Muslim prisoners and black and minority ethnic prison staff. The efforts made to improve the situation are then discussed, along with an exploration of the prison service's difficult journey towards race equality. The chapter concludes with a consideration of issues which, it is argued, are key to progress towards race equality in prisons[4].

Existing Research on Racism in Prisons

The Home Office–funded study by Genders and Player (1989) was the first substantial research on racism in prisons in the UK. It was followed by Burnett and Farrall's (1994) study and, together, they remained the only extensive considerations of race relations issues in prisons until Zahid Mubarek's murder. Both studies presented evidence of verbal and physical abuse, discriminatory use of discretion by prison officers, resulting, for example, in excessive use of disciplinary procedures, and poorer access to prison education and employment for minority ethnic prisoners.

---

[3]This chapter makes use of Inspectorate data, not all of which has previously been published.

[4]The circumstances of foreign national prisoners, who contribute substantially to both the minority ethnic prison population and to the higher number of Muslims, is not specifically discussed here, as a whole chapter is devoted to this issue in this volume (see Bhui's chapter 9).

Genders and Player's study was based on interviews, observation, and data analysis in five prisons in the mid-1980s. It uncovered anecdotal evidence of prison officers placing black and racist white prisoners in cells together to 'stir up' trouble, more than a decade before Mubarek was killed after being placed in a cell with a man known to be a violent racist[5]. Genders and Player found that prison officers often did not regard racism as a problem or think there was a need for a race equality policy. African Caribbean black prisoners were characterized as noisy and unintelligent 'control' problems, and Asian prisoners were seen as devious. Officers unashamedly gave the researchers a number of damning quotes, including: 'They remind me of a monkey colony', '… we're infested with West Indians', and 'Negroes are lazy … like music and leaping and dancing around'. A suggested solution to such 'problems' was to limit the numbers of black prisoners in any one prison.

Burnett and Farrall's (1994) later research, conducted in eight prisons, was commissioned as a result of concern over the very low numbers of racial incidents being reported by prisons[6]. Out of their sample of 373 minority ethnic prisoners, the researchers found that nearly half of black prisoners, a third of Asians, and nearly a quarter of 'others' (which included mixed-heritage and Chinese prisoners) said they had been racially victimized by staff. Black prisoners were much less likely to perceive relationships with staff positively than white prisoners, and all prisoners were less likely than staff to consider relationships as positive.

The main messages of this early research were reinforced by the CRE's two reports (CRE, 2003a, 2003b); these investigations started in 2000, though they were not completed and published until three years later. The first of these reports stated that the prevalence of racism in Feltham YOI had desensitized staff to such an extent that signs of racism by Robert Stewart, the young man who murdered Zahid Mubarek, were not registered. Both investigations demonstrated the complexity of understanding, assessing, and responding to racism in the closed world of prisons, particularly when, as was the case with Robert Stewart, it is combined with mental disorder.

A number of other useful studies have been published since 2000. Edgar and Martin (2004) considered situations of conflict in prisons, and how perceptions of racial differences could influence staff and prisoner interactions. They recommended increasing the number of black and minority ethnic staff and more sophisticated training. However, their main recommendation was that there

---

[5] Allegations during the Mubarek public inquiry (Keith, 2006) of Feltham prison officers playing 'Gladiators', i.e., placing BME and racist white prisoners in the same cell to encourage fights, were never substantiated in this specific case; however, the Mubarek Inquiry did not rule out the possibility of it having happened in other cases.

[6] The Prison Service definition of a racial incident was used during this study. It was very similar to the Macpherson (1999) definition, and its criteria were satisfied if 'any of the parties involved … alleges that a racial motivation is present or is perceived' (quoted in Burnett and Farrall, 1994: 1). In 1990–91, only 22 such incidents were recorded across the whole prison estate, a number that many prisons today exceed in a single month.

should be a fundamental rethink of the 'legalistic and punitive disciplinary' (p. 36) approach to the investigation of racial complaints lacking evidence of blatant racism, and in which officers had generally acted unwittingly – that is, in an *institutionally* racist way (Macpherson, 1999). They argued that, to promote communication and minimize defensiveness from accused officers, there should be a mediation approach focusing on 'explanations and mutual understanding rather than guilt and punishment' (p. vi). A trained and independent race equality adviser from outside the prison service – which would be potentially costly – was seen as crucial to this model.

Cheliotis and Liebling's (2006) study, which drew on surveys of 4,860 prisoners' perceptions of the quality of prison life, showed that minority ethnic prisoners consistently rated the quality of race relations in prison more poorly than their white counterparts, something that also emerged from the HM Inspectorate of Prisons (2005b) thematic review. They concluded that the perceived quality of race relations was significantly associated with prisoners' views on other aspects of their treatment, such as relationships with staff and safety. Their research illustrates the multiple and complex issues that need to be taken into account when developing explanatory frameworks for prisoners' experiences of racism.

Haslewood-Pócsik, Smith and Spencer (2006) examined the experiences of black and minority ethnic prisoners in a number of establishments in the North West of England, with a view to establishing how race relations policy was implemented. They concluded that the policy did not provide 'a sufficient framework for practice' (p. 6) on its own and highlighted the importance of a respectful prison context (see below). Wilson and Moore's (2003) research on the perceptions of young black men in three young offender institutions concluded that young black people were using two distinct strategies to deal with the emotional and practical implications of racism in prison: 'keeping quiet' and assuming a low profile that might minimize victimization; or 'going nuts' when the stress became too great. All of these studies have found evidence of enduring, sometimes extreme, but often more subtle, racism and discrimination within the prison system. A discernible shift from overt to more 'covert' racism was also a prominent finding of the Prison Inspectorate's thematic review of race relations (HMIP, 2005b), which is now considered in more detail along with other, more recent Inspectorate data.

The Race Thematic Review

The review was based on analysis of inspectorate survey responses from 5,500 prisoners of all ethnic backgrounds; group interviews in 18 fieldwork prisons with 265 minority ethnic prisoners; semi-structured individual interviews with over 200 white and minority ethnic prison staff; analysis of race relations data in the fieldwork prisons, including ethnic monitoring[7] and racist complaints; and a national survey of governors and race equality officers. Many of its findings are echoed in other research (e.g., Haslewood Pócsik, Smith, and Spencer, 2006; Edgar and Roberts, 2005).

In answer to survey questions, about 14% of black and minority ethnic prisoners (all of them from visible minorities) said they had been racially 'victimized' by staff and 11% that they had been racially victimized by other prisoners. These figures are a cause for concern, but are considerably lower than those reported by Burnett and Farrall in 1994. Key areas of general prisoner dissatisfaction included the slow response of staff to emergency cell call bells, the quality of healthcare, the poor quality and range of food, ineffective complaints systems, unfair incentives and earned privileges (IEP) schemes, and lack of respect from staff. The review broke down its findings by ethnic group and found considerable differences between the experiences of black, Asian, and mixed-heritage prisoners, though all tended to have worse perceptions and experiences than white prisoners. In prisoner surveys, significantly more black than Asian or mixed-heritage adult men reported that they had experienced racist victimization by staff and that they had felt unsafe, while Asian men reported slightly more racist bullying by other prisoners. Additional negative comments in group interviews were made about religious provision and a general lack of respect for different religious beliefs. Prisoners' comments included: 'Because I'm Palestinian, the officers accuse me of being a terrorist. When they open my door, they call me "Jihad"'; 'One officer said G wing is becoming planet of the apes'; 'White staff take the mickey out of black and Asian names, e.g., when officers call a prisoner called Mr. Singh 'they go "la, la, la"'; and 'Black people are kicked off enhanced (i.e., the top level of the incentives and earned privileges scheme) for suspicions rather than evidence' (HMIP, 2005b: 13).

A similar overall pattern of experience emerged for women, male juveniles, and young adults, though there were some notable differences in emphasis. In group interviews, women from visible minorities were highly critical of the extent to which their specific needs were overlooked, citing examples such as the lack of black hair and beauty products in the prison shop, the high cost of international phone calls, the lack of variety in food, and poor healthcare provision. They were also vociferous about poor treatment by staff; black women in particular said they often did not feel able to approach staff when something was wrong, and only did so when they were at 'boiling point'. This contributed to a view that they were 'aggressive' and bullies. One black

---

[7]Ethnic monitoring in prison uses a range-setting formula to interpret, with 95% confidence, whether prisoners from black and minority ethnic groups are fairly represented within the activity in question. This is interpreted by calculating whether the proportions of minority ethnic prisoners in any activity are within the range expected for the size of activity and the size of the population in the prison.

woman prisoner summed up a widespread perception that prisoners were only treated well 'if your face fits, your hair flicks, and you have blue eyes' (HMIP, 2005b: 15). Asian women were three times more likely to report being bullied by other prisoners than black or mixed-heritage women. However, more Asian women than black or mixed-heritage women reported that most staff respected them, and no Asian women reported being segregated or physically restrained by staff.

In the surveys, black and minority ethnic male juveniles (age under 18) reported worse experiences than white male juveniles across a range of key areas, including the likelihood of being insulted, assaulted, or restrained by staff. Black juveniles were the least positive of all groups about the prison regime and their relationships with staff, and more reported being picked on or insulted by staff, or being disciplined, restrained, or segregated. Young adults (18–21-year-olds) also described a similar range of negative experiences. Notably, far more Asian than black young adult prisoners said that they had felt unsafe, and that they had been the victims of bullying, particularly racist bullying, both by other prisoners and by staff.

The review found that many of the official processes for addressing racism and discrimination were in place, such as race relations officers, and more effective systems for making and investigating racial complaints than those found by Burnett and Farrall. However, the next step of implementation was not being taken consistently, something that is routinely found in the course of ongoing prison inspections (HMIP, 2006a). Notwithstanding the quotes given above, the overt racism highlighted by Genders and Player (1989) had certainly diminished, and prisoners acknowledged that some progress had been made, particularly in provision for different faiths and in the inclusion of products for minority ethnic groups in prison shops. However, there was little shared understanding of race issues within prisons or of the distance yet to be travelled; while governors (all white) and white race relations officers generally believed that their regimes operated without discrimination, minority ethnic staff and prisoners usually felt the opposite. White staff were far more likely than black and minority ethnic staff to identify racism between prisoners than to recognize the existence of staff on prisoner racism, and similarly more likely to say that BME prisoners 'played the race card' rather than acknowledging genuine grievance.

The ethnic monitoring that could have helped to uncover any disparities was often incomplete; in only 7 of the 18 prisons (39%) was it accurate over a period of a full six months. Even where it was accurate, it was generally seen more as a procedure to be completed rather than a tool to drive change. Low numbers of black and minority ethnic staff and a consequent lack of cultural understanding were also widely referred to as barriers to progress.

The Picture in 2006–07

The most recent available inspectorate evidence, taken from an analysis of prisons inspected between September 2006 and August 2007 (HMIP, 2008), suggested more procedural improvements, but some enduring problems in terms of outcomes. Survey results from black and minority ethnic prisoners were generally negative and, as in previous years, the only area where they consistently reported more positive experiences than white prisoners was in their appreciation of education and training provision. More governors were providing unequivocal leadership on tackling race discrimination, and helping to create an atmosphere of intolerance towards racism; prisoners rarely reported overt racist behaviour. If it was reported, robust action was usually taken by prison managers. However, they continued to report covert discrimination, described as 'inconsistency', 'favouritism', 'ignorance', and 'subtle prejudice'.

There was a lack of both the kind of sophisticated training needed to help staff to understand and tackle such behaviours, and of the direct communication necessary to address any prisoner distrust, misinterpretations, and misconceptions. While there was new and relatively extensive training for the sub-group of the senior management team known as the 'race equality action team' (see Prison Service Order 2800, http://www.hmprisonservice.gov.uk/resourcecentre/psispsos/listpsos/), most staff were considered to be 'in date' with diversity training if they had completed a generic three-hour diversity course within the previous three years. Even this training had been delivered to only 58% of staff according to the most recent published statistics (Prison Service, 2007a).

More 'race equality officers', whose main task is to lead on the implementation of prison race equality policies, were full time and therefore able to put greater energy into the role. However, they also often lacked specialist training, and many found that almost all of their time could be taken up with the racist incident investigations. The quality of such investigations remained variable. Prison race equality action teams were routinely examining ethnic monitoring figures, but staff did not always understand the results or investigate the reasons for identified discrepancies. Prisoners' confidence in staff commitment to race equality was low; inconsistent staff treatment, or perceptions of inconsistent treatment, were interpreted as being racially motivated, and positive engagement between staff and black and minority ethnic prisoners was still much less evident than it was for white prisoners.

One notable difference from the 2005 thematic findings was the shift in the relative experiences of black and Asian prisoners. While the thematic review replicated earlier findings (Burnett and Farrall, 1994), that Asian prisoners were less likely than black prisoners to feel safe but more likely to feel respected, the 2006–07 data shows almost identical (and negative) findings on both safety and respect from both groups, who now had a similar tendency to fear victimization from staff more than from prisoners. The difficulty of building and sustaining confidence amongst black and minority ethnic prisoners is evident from these results.

Muslim Prisoners

The most recent statistics show that about 11% of the prison population were Muslims in 2006, compared to 6% ten years earlier (Ministry of Justice, 2007b). There is evidence of a strong link between ethnic and religious identities: the 2001 Home Office citizenship survey (Attwood *et al.*, 2003) revealed that religion played an important role in the self-identity of Asian respondents (61%)[8] and black respondents (44%), compared to only 17% of white respondents. At the same time, the terrorist attacks of September 2001 and July 2005 have substantially increased the spotlight on Islam and Muslims in prisons, particularly those of Asian appearance. Consequently, religious affiliation needs to be included in any realistic consideration of race issues in prisons, particularly in light of the mounting evidence of dissatisfaction amongst, and discrimination against, Muslim prisoners (Weller *et al.*, 2001; Spalek and Wilson, 2002; HMIP, 2005a, 2006a).

In 2006–07, when the Prison Inspectorate analysed the prisoner surveys conducted at every full inspection, 103 out of 163 responses from Muslim prisoners were significantly worse, and in some cases dramatically so, than those of non-Muslims, and also worse than those of black and minority ethnic prisoners in general. Forty per cent of Muslims, compared to 22% of non-Muslims, said they had been victimized by staff; 28% said that they felt unsafe at that moment, compared to 17% of non-Muslims. In some prisons, these discrepancies were even greater: in Portland Young Offenders Institution, 58% of Muslims, compared to 24% of non-Muslims, had felt unsafe; at Birmingham, the comparable figures were 53% and 18%. In general, prisons were more sensitive to the religious needs of Muslims: all observed religious festivals, and most (but not all) had acceptable rooms for worship and a regular, sometimes full-time, Muslim chaplain. However, it was apparent that this did not percolate into Muslim prisoners' day-to-day dealings with staff, and that there was considerable distance, and a high degree of mutual mistrust in many prisons.

Identifying and engaging with prisoners who may feel inclined towards extremism is a growing policy concern, and in 2007, the Prison Service embarked on a programme of training to help staff to identify and respond to signs of radicalization. In his introduction to the annual report on the

---

[8]The most recent available statistics show that 71% of Asian prisoners defined themselves as Muslims (Ministry of Justice, 2007b).

prison service's race equality scheme (Prison Service, 2007a), the then Director General of the Prison Service stated that:

> ... tackling extremism and radicalisation ... is crucial for national security. It is equally crucial that it is carried out in a way that is consistent with our duty to promote race equality, and I am determined to ensure that this is achieved, through building awareness amongst staff and implementing the necessary measures in a sensitive way. (Prison Service, 2007a: 2)

The degree to which this dual aim is being and can be achieved is a moot point. The identification of potentially extremist Muslim prisoners is an easily understood security-driven objective in a system where security is the most legitimate task. It is therefore unsurprising that achieving widespread staff 'buy in' to this function has been relatively straightforward. It has traditionally proven far harder to achieve such understanding, legitimacy, or enthusiasm for the task of promoting and upholding race equality in prisons. At the Prison Service's 2007 'Race Equality Action Group' Conference, one of the questions put to a 'question-time' panel suggested that concern over the commitment to tackling extremism might indeed have been taking priority over the Service's commitment to race equality. This would be a profoundly dangerous development for the future of race relations in prisons, not least because good relationships between staff and prisoners underpin information flow and contribute to the 'dynamic security' that helps to keep prisons safe and secure. The same principle applies to policing, where intelligence from local communities is often the police service's most valuable mechanism of crime detection and prevention. If Muslim prisoners feel they are no longer subject to the basic protections of a race equality–focused approach in prisons, and feel they are being seen primarily as potential terrorists, this will do little to create the right conditions to maintain the information flow that might help staff to identify and tackle extremism, and may instead create the conditions to exacerbate alienation and encourage poor relations. Race equality must be seen as a basic and irreducible foundation for any work to tackle extremism, and to reduce its importance in theory or in practice would surely be extremely unwise. As general progress towards race equality has been shown to be at best faltering, it is perhaps not surprising that the evidence suggests a considerable and developing problem with tackling extremism (e.g., see HMIP, 2008b, 2008c).

The Experience of Black and Minority Ethnic Staff in Prisons

The CRE investigations (2003a, 2003b) and the Zahid Mubarek public inquiry (Keith, 2006) were extremely critical of some prison staff for racism, collusion, or incompetence, but it was not part of their specific remits to examine the experiences of black and minority ethnic staff. This gap has been addressed to some extent by Edgar and Roberts (2005) and the race thematic review (HMIP, 2005b) and by some other recent studies, including Haslewood-Pócsik, Smith, and Spencer's (2006) research.

The thematic review found that the main source of racism for black and minority ethnic staff was not prisoners, but colleagues. Staff who identified as black were especially likely to have experienced some form of racism in their work. Overall, 20 out of 28 minority ethnic staff (71%) who identified themselves as black reported such experiences, compared to 8 out of 14 Asian staff (57%) and 7 out of 11 mixed-heritage staff (64%). More than two-thirds of the minority ethnic staff interviewed (38, 68%) said they had experienced racism in their establishments, and almost half (24, 41%) said they had experienced racism from colleagues[9]. This usually manifested in offensive statements dressed up as 'banter' rather than in blatant racism. The emotional impact of racism from colleagues was far greater than the distress experienced as a result of prisoner racism.

Less than a third of minority staff who had encountered racism said they had submitted racist incident reporting forms about their experiences, and only three staff said they had submitted forms complaining about the behaviour of colleagues. Lack of confidence in the complaints system, and it 'backfiring' on them were the main reasons. Most minority ethnic staff said they dealt differently with black and Asian prisoners, usually citing the fact that such prisoners were more likely to approach them. This was perceived as something that could increase the vulnerability of staff to suspicion and malicious allegations, and some expressed concern over alienating white colleagues, suggested that they were under pressure to distance themselves from black and minority ethnic prisoners. There is a significant association between attrition rates of prison staff and ethnicity, and there remains a dearth of senior prisons managers from black and minority ethnic backgrounds (Bhui and Fossi, 2007). Given this under-representation, it was concerning that some minority ethnic staff said they were not motivated towards promotion because of suspicions of collusion, and the feeling that 'they will be targeted on trumped up charges and get dismissed, because there seems to be a history of this' (Bhui and Fossi, 2007: 57).

Edgar's and Roberts' (2005) study on 'RESPECT' – the black and minority ethnic prison staff support network – broadly supported the findings of this study. They found that members of RESPECT felt that 'direct and blatant forms of racism have become less frequent, and that covert and structural forms are the main concern' (p. iv). A prominent form of perceived 'structural' discrimination was in relation to promotion and job prospects, and the first four recommendations made by the authors were about promotion. They included the prison service making public ethnic monitoring data on career progression,

---

[9]The RESPECT study (Edgar and Roberts, 2005) showed that 153 out of 220 (70%) staff had experienced racial discrimination at work, 76 (35%) of whom were BME.

and RESPECT providing a mentoring scheme for full members. Over 60% of full members[10] interviewed said they had experienced some form of racism. They were more likely to report racism or discrimination from colleagues than associate members, and were less likely than associate members to identify prisoners as a source of racism. However, only 40% of those who said they had experienced racial discrimination reported it, leading Edgar and Roberts to conclude that their 'working environment does not enable people to be open about their perceptions of racism' (p. 60). (See Bhui and Fossi, 2007, for more discussion).

There is an emerging sense from the limited research of the multi-faceted role that black and minority staff must perform in the prison environment. They are forced to balance their identities as black, Asian, or mixed-heritage people, with cultural similarities and sympathies with prisoners, with their identities as prison officers who needed to establish and maintain clear professional boundaries. The establishment of a 'Black and minority ethnic senior managers forum' and attempts to establish reasons for minority ethnic staff leaving the prison service are recent steps forward (see HM Prison Service, 2007b), though the results of such initiatives have yet to be evaluated.

Responding to Race Inequality and Discrimination

The major aim of the prison service's race relations policy in the 1980s and 1990s was to tackle extreme and overt racism, for example, by dismissing openly racist staff (Bhui, 2006). In that respect, it has been reasonably successful, and over the last 25 years, more stringent management, lines of accountability, reduced discretion, and use of disciplinary procedures have all contributed to progress. At a strategic level, there is no doubt that the prison service now has a genuine commitment to tackling racism, even if it took Mubarek's murder for it to take centre stage. Martin Narey, director general between 1998 and 2003, announced his belief that the prison service was institutionally racist and launched what became known as the 'decency agenda'. This was intended to signal an absolute intolerance of abuse and racism within prisons and was the context for the much publicized ban on members of the far-right British National Party joining the service in 2002. Narey's appointment of a race advisor in 1998 and the launch of RESPECT and RESPOND (Racial Equality for Staff and Prisoners) were also significant and progressive steps. The decency agenda was supported by his successor, Phil Wheatley, who also signed up to a CRE/Prison Service 5-year joint action plan to promote race equality following publication of the CRE's damning reports (2003a, 2003b). The prison service also has a

---

[10]'Full' members are BME staff, and 'associate' members are white staff who support the aims of RESPECT.

substantial dedicated 'race equality action group' based at its headquarters to advise the director general, and to help drive forward change in prisons. The recently instituted 'race scrutiny panel' (HM Prison Service, 2007b), chaired by the minister for prisons, is a good indicator of the commitment to change and gives an insight into the current challenges facing the prison service.

The Challenge of Culture Change

Although Narey identified the need to move beyond the 'tick box' approach to race equality (Keith, 2006), the evidence discussed above shows how difficult this has been to achieve. Deeper reasons for this situation have to be sought and addressed, and one of those reasons may be that the 'underpinnings' of anti-racist practice in the prison service are relatively fragile. The *culture* of the prison service has certainly been less supportive of the efforts of committed individual staff, leading to the lack of implementation of good policies, which in any event cannot make a genuine difference to prisoners' lived experiences, unless sustained and strengthened by the general prison culture. This is summed up well by Haslewood-Pócsik, Smith, and Spencer:

> ... race relations in prisons are deeply embedded in the overall functioning of the establishments, and particularly the general quality of interpersonal relationships, as manifested in the day to day interactions within and between prisoners and staff ... positive race relations are unlikely to be achieved by the conscientious application of the relevant policy alone. (2006: 6)

It is important to recognize the inherent difficulties of achieving general culture change and linked race relations progress in prisons. The prison service task does not stress the uniqueness of the individual, but rather the importance of security and the effective management of prisoners. It encourages suspicion and defensiveness. However, anti-racism is, to a degree, tied up with recognition of individuality and of the diversity of people. This is actively discouraged by institutions designed to maintain order, and where attempts at reform and change are compromised by 'carceral clawback' (Carlen, 2002), that is, the tendency of the prison system to confound genuine attempts at reform by reverting back to its most basic purpose of containment, and the perceived requirements of control and security. Alongside these intrinsic characteristics of the prison environment, there are other factors discouraging the development of anti-racist practices – the prison estate is dangerously close to its absolute capacity (HMIP, 2008: 5–9), and this promotes a focus on security, above all else. It does not encourage prison cultures where we can consistently expect to see respect for individual rights or promotion of race equality.

Prisoner Perceptions

It is important to note the apparently disproportionate impact of inconsistent treatment on prisoners' perceptions of racism, which is a recurring theme of the research. For example, Edgar and Martin (2004) argued that 'informal partiality' by prison officers was often construed as discriminatory. That is, with previous experience of staff racism, there may be an understandable tendency to interpret *inconsistent* treatment by prison staff as being racially motivated in all circumstances. Barnett-Page's (2005) exploration of the nature and impact of institutional racism also provides a fascinating insight into possible reasons for both the negative perceptions of minority ethnic prisoners, and for their frequent overrepresentation in prison disciplinary figures. He describes an 'amplification spiral' emanating from a prison officer's unconscious prejudice:

> ... a prison officer ... may be a little less comfortable and confident around black prisoners ... A black prisoner notices that he is being treated slightly differently. This compounds his previous experiences of racism in the wider society – at school and from the criminal justice system ... the two, unconsciously, avoid each other ... No relationship develops between the two ... Weeks or months later an issue of conflict arises and the prisoner gets angry. There is no shared history and empathy available to be drawn on to defuse it. Instead of humour and under-enforcement of the rules, the prisoner is met by the threat of disciplinary action from the defensive officer, and the situation escalates into physical confrontation...
> (Barnett-Page, 2005: 28)

Training

There is little doubt that the eight-week prison officer course is insufficient to enable prison staff to do the complex interpersonal work with which they are presented, in sometimes highly stressful environments where immediate and instinctive decisions are needed. In-service diversity training is inadequate, as noted above, and the now non-mandatory race relations training which preceded it was often delivered by staff who themselves had an imperfect understanding of the issues, and a lack of the skills necessary to challenge stereotypes (HMIP, 2004a). The prison service acknowledged the need to rethink training on race and diversity in the action plan agreed with the CRE (CRE/Prison Service, 2003), though many prison staff have yet to see substantive outcomes from this commitment. This is a concern in light of the complex psychological processes described by Barnett-Page (2005) and Edgar and Martin (2004), and the reminder from the Mubarek inquiry (Keith, 2006), which talked of need for prison officers to be able to 'notice what is happening on the wing' (p. 648) and to receive training that helps them to put themselves 'in the shoes of BME prisoners' (p. 512). It was also notable during the thematic review that that many white staff described feelings of defensiveness and of being victimized by a race relations agenda which they perceived as casting them in the role of 'bad guys'. This is clearly something that needs recognition in skilfully delivered training courses if it is not ultimately to undermine progress towards race equality. In short, prison officers rarely have enough time to reflect on and develop their own views and values, or to consider the complex genesis of complaints of racism. This is despite the fact that reflective time is critical to the development of anti-racist attitudes and practice (Bhui and Fossi, 2007; Barnett-Page, 2005). In the short term, in view of the funding cuts (3% in 2008–09) that the prison service is facing, it seems unlikely that such time can be built into initial or ongoing training.

Diverse Staff

Although a more diverse prison staff group can increase communication and the legitimacy of prison amongst different groups of prisoners and is desirable for that reason alone (e.g., HMIP, 2004b), increasing black and minority ethnic prison staff is in itself no guarantee that discrimination will not take place. Interestingly, in Cheliotis and Liebling's (2006) study, neither the ethnic composition of each prison's population, nor the respective ratio of white to ethnic minority staff had a significant impact on how prisoners viewed the quality of race relations. This easily understood aim, which is amenable to simple numerical targets, has too often been seen as a panacea for promoting positive race relations. The complexity of the findings discussed above demonstrates the importance of more sophisticated, inter-dependent strategies.

Private Prisons

A further complication that deserves mention is the difference between the public and private sector prisons. Without the entrenched and inherited culture of poor race relations evident in many public sector establishments, private prisons in theory have a head start over the prison service and should be better at providing an environment where respectful relationships between prisoners and staff from different ethnic groups can develop. However, the development of race relations systems, which can help establishments to identify and grapple with race issues, has tended to be relatively weak in private establishments to date (CRE, 2007; HMIP, 2006a; HMIP, 2007b), though there are signs of improvement (e.g., HMIP, 2006b; HMIP, 2006c). Private prisons do not have the sophisticated and centralized support provided to the public sector prisons by the Race Equality and Action Group, although they are subject to Prison Service Order 2800 which sets out a series of requirements on race equality. High staff turnover amongst lower-paid private-sector prison staff also appears to affect prisoner perceptions: in one prison, feelings of discrimination were linked by black and minority ethnic prisoners both to perceived inconsistency and favouritism, and to 'the relatively high turnover of staff, the resultant difficulties in building relationships and new staff who were less aware of procedures and policies' (HMIP, 2006b: 28). While the good structures put in place by the prison service have their limitations, their value is clearly illustrated by this contrast. At the time of writing (April 2008), the former director general of public sector prisons, Phil Wheatley, has just been appointed as the Chief Executive of the National Offender Management Service, and has consequently assumed responsibility for private as well as public prisons. This is a significant change that should help to bring about greater sharing of expertise and knowledge across the public and private sectors, though it remains to be seen how quickly and how effectively this happens.

Conclusion

There has clearly been considerable progress towards decency and fairness in prisons over the last 25 years, and there is a greater focus on outcomes and action in prison race relations strategies. However, the prison system currently has to negotiate a number of substantial difficulties, not least a severe overcrowding problem that threatens to undermine prison cultures where individuality and difference is respected to the degree necessary to embed a commitment to race equality. In this context, prisons are struggling to move from the development and implementation of policies and procedures to a change in what the CRE (2003a and 2003b) termed the 'general atmosphere' in prisons. While the specific focus and conclusions of the research studies and investigations discussed above have differed to some degree, most have highlighted the importance of a multi-faceted response, which goes beyond the creation or even implementation of discrete race relations policies. In other words, improving race relations is inextricably tied to improving communication and culture.

One tangible reform that can help communication and cultural change is to promote the idea of prisons as genuine communities where dialogue within and between staff and prisoners is seen as paramount. Consultation groups are in place in many establishments, but few use them to their optimum potential, to challenge misperceptions and promote cooperation and positive communication (See Bhui, 2005, for more evidence of the value of such groups). While use of black and minority ethnic peer representatives is widespread, the effectiveness of such posts also varies widely from prison to prison, and their potential is as yet generally untapped. Prisoners who are working for each other can also provide staff with intelligence about race relations issues on the ground. Such intelligence can of course include information about potential radicalization, and about the way that such concerns are impacting on the wider goal of race equality.

Along with improving training and professionalization of prison officers, addressing radicalization without undermining race relations is an interconnected challenge. The way that Muslim prisoners are managed in a hostile wider climate will be a key test of the prison service's commitment to and capacity to improve race relations[11]. Failure to make progress against either of these goals is likely to undermine attempts to promote positive prison cultures, and further reduce the confidence of black and minority ethnic prisoners in the legitimacy of their prison experience. The progress that has been made to date could start to unravel as a result of the pressures described above, and in this respect, the prison service is at crossroads.

Summary

Over a quarter of prisoners in England and Wales are from minority ethnic groups, but until the turn of the century, there had been very little research on this population. The 2000s have seen a number of studies and investigations on race, racism, and prisons, precipitated largely by the murder of a young Asian man, Zahid Mubarek, by his racist cell mate in Feltham Young Offenders Institution in 2000. This tragic event prompted Commission for Racial Equality and public inquiries, and was followed by a small number of empirical research studies examining the experiences of minority ethnic prisoners.

The evidence to date shows a complex picture of both improvements and setbacks in the prison system's journey towards race equality. While overt racism in prisons is less discernible than it was in the 1970s and 1980s, more 'subtle' and/or unwitting racism persists. This has contributed to a greater sense of alienation of black and minority ethnic groups, and is particularly apparent amongst Muslim prisoners, many of whom are black or Asian. This in turn undermines relationships between staff and prisoners, upon which rest the safety and security of prisons.

There are three major challenges threatening to undermine the development of prison cultures where individuality and difference are respected and a commitment to race equality embedded: addressing severe prison overcrowding, which encourages a stress on security above all else; improving training and professional development of prison officers, who are doing personally challenging work without the complexity of their task being reflected in training; and addressing concerns about radicalization of Muslim prisoners without undermining the progress that has so far been made towards positive prison race relations. Failure to address these key points risks further reducing the confidence of black and minority ethnic prisoners in the legitimacy of prisons.

---

[11] It is notable that a recent investigation into the category A unit for foreign national detainees in Long Lartin (HMIP, 2008b) found that Muslims who wanted to distance themselves from extremism were frustrated at the lack of avenues offered for 'de-radicalisation'.

Key Texts

Genders, E. and Player, E. (1989) *Race in Prisons*. Oxford: Clarendon Press.
HM Inspectorate of Prisons (2005) Parallel Worlds. A Thematic Review of Race Issues in the Prison Service. London: Home Office.
Keith, Justice (2006) Report of the Zahid Mubarek Inquiry, Volumes 1 and 2. London: The Stationary Office.

References

Attwood, C., Singh, G., Prime, D. and Creasey, R. (2003) 2001 Home Office Citizenship Survey: People, Families and Communities. Research Development and Statistics Directorate, Research Study 270. London: Home Office.

Barnett-Page, C. (2005) 'Common sense and institutional racism: blink or think?' *Prison Service Journal*, 163, 26–9.

Bhui, H.S. (1999) 'Race, racism and risk assessment: linking theory to practice with black mentally disordered offenders', *Probation Journal*, 46 (3), 171–81.

Bhui, H.S. (2005) 'Developing Best Practice with Foreign National Prisoners', *Prison Service Journal*, 158: 17–23.

Bhui, H.S. and Fossi, J. (2007) 'The experience of black and minority ethnic prison staff', in Bennett, J., Wahidin, A. and Crewe, B., *Understanding Prison Staff*. London: Willan Publishers.

Burnett, R. and Farrell, G. (1994). Reported and Unreported Racial Incidents in Prisons, Occasional Paper, Number 14, Oxford: University of Oxford Centre for Criminological Research.

Carlen, P. (2002) Women's imprisonment: models of reform and change. *Probation Journal*, 49 (2), 76–87.

Cheliotis, L.K. and Liebling, A. (2006) *'Race matters in British prisons'*, British *Journal of Criminology*, 46 (2), 286–317. Oxford: Oxford University Press.

Commission for Racial Equality (CRE) (2003a) The Murder of Zahid Mubarek: A Formal Investigation by the Commission for Racial Equality into HM Prison Service of England and Wales. Part 1. London: CRE.

Commission for Racial Equality (CRE) (2003b) A Formal Investigation by the Commission for Racial Equality into HM Prison Service of England and Wales. Part 2: Race Equality in Prisons. London: CRE.

Commission for Racial Equality (CRE) and HM Prison Service (2003) *Implementing Race Equality in Prisons: A Shared Agenda for Change*. London: CRE.

Commission for Racial Equality (2007) *A Lot Done, a Lot To Do: Our Vision for an Integrated Britain*. London: CRE.

Edgar, K. and Martin, C. (2004) Perceptions of Race and Conflict: Perspectives of Minority Ethnic Prisoners and of Prison Officers. Home Office On-line Report 11/04.

Edgar, K. and Roberts, L. (2005) RESPECT Five Year On. A Prison Reform Trust Study of the Effectiveness of RESPECT: The Prison Service Minority Ethnic Staff Support Network.

Edgar, K. (2007) 'Black and minority ethnic prisoners', in Y. Jewkes (Ed) *Handbook of Prisons*. Cullompton: Willan.

Genders, E. and Player, E. (1989) *Race in Prisons*, Oxford: Clarendon Press.

Haslewood-Pócsik, I., Smith, E. and Spencer, J. (2006) The Application of National Legislation in Relation to Race and its Application to Prison Service Policy & Practice. Manchester: University of Manchester.

HM Inspectorate of Prisons (HMIP) (2004a) Annual Report. London: Home Office.

HM Inspectorate of Prisons (HMIP) (2004b) Report on an Unannounced Follow Up Inspection of HMP Birmingham. London: Home Office.

HM Inspectorate of Prisons (2005a) Annual Report. London: Home Office.

HM Inspectorate of Prisons (2005b) Parallel Worlds. A Thematic Review of Race Issues in the Prison Service. London: Home Office.

HM Inspectorate of Prisons (HMIP) (2006a) Annual Report. London: Home Office.

HM Inspectorate of Prisons (HMIP) (2006b) Report of an Unannounced Short Follow Up Inspection of HMP Lowdham Grange. London: Home Office.

HM Inspectorate of Prisons (HMIP) (2006c) Report of an Unannounced Full Follow Up Inspection of HMP Dovegate. London: Home Office.

HM Inspectorate of Prisons (2008) Annual Report. London: Ministry of Justice.

HM Inspectorate of Prisons (2008b) An Inspection of the Category A Detainee Unit at HMP Long Lartin. London: Ministry of Justice.

HM Inspectorate of Prisons (2008c) Report of a Full Announced Inspection of HMP Belmarsh. London: Ministry of Justice.

Keith, Justice (2006) Report of the Zahid Mubarek Inquiry, Volumes 1 and 2. London: The Stationary Office.

Macpherson, W. (1999) The Stephen Lawrence Inquiry. London: The Stationery Office.

Ministry of Justice (2007a) Statistics on Race and the Criminal Justice System (Section 95 statistics). London: Ministry of Justice.

Ministry of Justice (2007b) Offender Management Caseload Statistics 2006. London: Ministry of Justice.

Phillips, C. and Bowling, B. (2003) 'Racism, ethnicity and criminology. Developing minority perspectives', *The British Journal of Criminology*, 43 (2), pp. 269–90.

Phillips, C. and Bowling, B. (2005) 'Facing inwards and outwards? Institutional racism, race equality and the role of Black and Asian professional associations', *Criminal Justice*, 5 (4), 357–77.

Prison Service (2007a) Annual report on race equality scheme. London: HMSO.

Prison Service (2007b) Minutes of Race Scrutiny Panel, http:// frontline.cjsonline.gov.uk/_includes/downloads/guidance/race-confidence-justice/Second_panel_meetingv3.doc

Spalek, B. and Wilson, D. (2002) 'Racism and religious discrimination in prison: The marginalisation of imams in their work with prisoners', in B. Spalek (Ed.) *Islam, Crime and Criminal Justice*, pp. 96–112, Devon: Willan.

Weller, P., Feldman, A. and Purdam, K. (2001) Religious Discrimination in England and Wales. Home Office Research Study 220. Research, Development and Statistics Directorate. London: Home Office.

Wilson, D. and Moore, S. (2003) *'Playing the Game' – The Experience of Young Black Men in Custody*. London: The Children's Society.

SIX

The Probation Service and Race Equality

Sam Lewis

Introduction[1,2]

This chapter is concerned primarily with research findings relating to probation practice with minority ethnic offenders, and less with personnel or cultural issues (see Bhui, 2006, for more discussion of these areas). The chapter opens with a brief account of relevant policy initiatives to provide context. It proceeds to review the findings from the largest study of black and Asian men on probation ever conducted in Europe (Calverley *et al.*, 2004; 2006; see also Lewis *et al.*, 2006). Reference is also made to a small study of Irish men on probation (Lewis *et al.*, 2005). This is followed by an overview and critical consideration of current knowledge and debate regarding two key aspects of work with minority ethnic probationers, namely offender assessment and probation programmes.

Anti-Racist Policy Initiatives and the Probation Service

Whilst many probation areas were at the forefront of work to develop anti-discriminatory practice during the 1980s, this impetus was lost during the 1990s (HMIP, 2000, Chapter 3). This was due, in part at least, to poor leadership at the national level, as evidenced by the variable prominence given to race equality in National Standards during this period (Home Office, 1992, 1995, 2000 cited in Vanstone, 2006: 11). The first years of the new

[1]The author is grateful to Hindpal Singh Bhui and Peter Raynor for their comments on an earlier draft and to Patrick Williams (formerly of Greater Manchester Probation Area), Marjorie Harris (formerly of NOMS Directorate of Commissioning and Partnerships), Paul Hindson, and Gareth Mercer (NOMS Offender Assessment and Management Unit) who provided information for this chapter. The author is responsible for any errors.

[2]For consistency, percentages are given in whole numbers throughout the chapter. Thus, they differ slightly from figures given in original sources to one or more decimal places.

millennium saw considerable improvement, which was facilitated by clear leadership, better monitoring, and increased accountability founded on a traditional probation culture rooted in humanitarian concerns (HMIP, 2004; Bhui, 2006: 173).

The documents that heralded the advent of the new National Offender Management Service (NOMS) made little mention of diversity issues, however (Carter, 2003; Home Office, 2004). The introduction of competitive tendering to the provision of probation services met with staunch opposition from the Probation Service, which feared that its role would be usurped by the private and voluntary sectors (see, e.g., NAPO, 2005; NAPO, 2006–07), and that the fragmentation of service provision would undermine traditional probation values, including the commitment to diversity issues (NAPO, 2007). The Commission for Racial Equality[3] (CRE) also expressed concern (CRE, 2006). It noted the failure of several privately run prisons to meet their race equality obligations, which bodes badly for race equality under privately run probation services. It also questioned whether the Home Office and NOMS were meeting their obligations under the Race Relations Act 1976 (as amended) to promote race equality in private prisons and whether the advent of privately run probation services might further undermine the implementation of the Act. Further, it noted evidence of 'a general lack of understanding in NOMS about how race relations legislation applies to them, particularly in relation to the procurement of services from private providers', and suggested that 'there is a lack of guidance from the centre, i.e., NOMS, on what is expected/required' (CRE, 2006: 6).

The now abolished post of National Offender Manager included lead responsibility for diversity matters (Home Office Communication Directorate, 2005), which subsequently passed to the Chief Executive of NOMS. However, at the start of 2008, the promised Equality and Diversity Policy had yet to be published. Equality and Diversity, which should have been central to the development of NOMS from the outset, appears to have been at the periphery. Given the lack of attention paid to diversity issues in the rush to bring NOMS into being, some people fear that the potentially deleterious impact of the changes on work with minority ethnic offenders has not been thought through (see Bhui, 2006).

'Race' and Probation Practice: Messages from Research

Discussions of race and criminal justice practice are constrained by the focus of the Home Office, criminal justice agencies, researchers, and others on

---

[3] In 2007, the CRE ceased to exist and was instead subsumed into the new Equality and Human Rights Commission.

certain racial categories. Garland *et al.* (2006) contend that the focus on 'Asian' and 'Black' groups obscures the often wide and varied experiences of distinct sub-groups; that the myth of homogenous 'white' majority precludes consideration of 'hidden' white minorities such as the Irish and economic migrants from the European Union; and that the distinct experiences of Travellers, refugees, asylum seekers, minority ethnic households in rural areas, people of mixed heritage, and Muslim communities are often overlooked. Further, statistics, research, and theoretical debate tend to centre on minority ethnic men whilst minority ethnic women are paid scant regard (see Farrant's chapter in this book; and Gelsthorpe, 2006). Thus, in the following review of research, we are obliged to view race and probation practice from a particular vantage point and acknowledge that other important perspectives remain out of sight.

There has long been concern that people from minority ethnic groups may be subject to disadvantageous treatment at all stages of the criminal justice process, even if this is not as a result of overt racist discrimination (see Bowling and Phillips, 2002). The report of a Thematic Inspection of Probation, entitled *Towards Race Equality*, highlighted such problems within the Probation Service (HMIP, 2000). In the foreword to the report, Her Majesty's Chief Inspector of Probation professed to being 'particularly disturbed about the disparities found in a number of areas of practice between the approach to work with white offenders compared to minority ethnic offenders'. It was against this backdrop that the Home Office commissioned a national study of black and Asian men on probation (Calverley *et al.*, 2004), which was to address the dearth of knowledge in this area and provide an empirical base for future work with minority ethnic offenders. It is to this study that we now turn.

Black and Asian Men on Probation

The study involved interviews with 483 men on probation or community rehabilitation orders. The 483 interviewees included 241 black, 172 Asian, 57 mixed heritage, and 13 'other' minority ethnic men drawn from areas in England and Wales with varying densities of minority ethnic people on the probation caseload.[4] Of these, 236 were or had been attending a probation programme, whilst the remaining 247 were on an order with no programme requirement. Some categories of offender and types of area were over-sampled to ensure that useful numbers would be available for analysis, and the sample was then weighted to reflect the actual proportions and locations of minority ethnic people in the national caseload of community

---

[4]The Black and Asian categories were sub-divided into 'Black African', 'Black Caribbean', and 'Black Other', and 'Asian Indian', 'Asian Pakistani', 'Asian Bangladeshi', and 'Asian Other', respectively. Ethnicity data were gathered directly from the interviewees.

rehabilitation orders. The findings presented herein are weighted, unless otherwise stated.

A key aim of the study was to assess the criminogenic needs[5] of minority ethnic men on probation using the CRIME-PICS II questionnaire (Frude *et al.*, 1994), which is known to be related to risk of reconviction (Raynor, 1998).[6] CRIME-PICS II is a self-report instrument, and thus not dependent on professional judgement which might reflect assumptions or stereotypes. The assessments were conducted by an ethnically diverse research team to minimize the possibility of racially specific administrator effects. The black, Asian, and mixed heritage groups in the study sample all displayed lower levels of crime-prone attitudes and self-reported problems than the white comparison sample.[7] Whilst acknowledging that the experiences of minority ethnic probationers might differ from those of white probationers in other ways, the researchers concluded that the evidence 'lends no support to the idea that offenders on probation who belong to minority ethnic groups tend to have distinctly different or greater criminogenic needs than white probationers' (Calverley *et al.*, 2004: vi).

Respondents' comments about their supervision were broadly favourable. Eighty-six per cent reported being treated fairly by their supervisor. This positive appraisal echoes findings from other recent studies of white or mainly white groups of probationers (e.g., Mair and May, 1997; Mantle, 1999; Harper, 2000) and from a study of white Irish men on probation in the North of England (Lewis *et al.*, 2005, see below). When asked what makes a good supervisor of a black or Asian person, the most common responses were: someone who is easy to talk to or who listens (27% of the sample); someone who is understanding and sympathetic (27%); and someone who understands the offender's needs, feelings, and experiences as a black or Asian person (20%). Just 3 per cent of interviewees described a good supervisor as being black or Asian, and there was no evidence of a significant relationship between the ethnicity of the supervisor and the perceived helpfulness of supervision or the likelihood of breach. When asked whether having a minority ethnic supervisor had (or would have) been a benefit, 35 per cent of participants said that it had (or would have) made a positive difference, 56 per cent said that a supervisor's ethnicity made no difference, 10 per cent did not know, and 2 per cent preferred not to have a minority ethnic supervisor.[8]

---

[5]Criminogenic needs (or 'dynamic risk factors') are characteristics of people or their circumstances which increase the risk of offending but are capable of change.

[6]Although the original CRIME-PICS II validation sample (Frude *et al.*, 1994) and the subjects of the reconviction research (Raynor, 1998) were mainly white, as a self-report instrument CRIME-PICS II might be expected to have a fairly similar relationship with reconviction for other groups of men.

[7]The original validation sample for CRIME-PICS II (Frude *et al.*, 1994) provided the white comparison sample.

[8]These figures do not add up to 100 because a small number of respondents said that having a minority ethnic supervisor might be good in some ways *and* bad in others.

The programme participants were broadly positive about probation programmes and tutors, although a sizeable minority (22%) reported not liking
anything about their programme. Eighty-six per cent reported fair treatment
by tutors, whilst just three per cent reported unfair treatment. The remaining
programme participants did not know if their treatment was fair, reported
'mixed' treatment, or did not answer the relevant question. When asked
whether the ethnic composition of a programme group is important, most
(66%) respondents said that it is important, of which most (87%, 54% of
the whole programme sample) felt that it should be mixed. There was very
limited support (from 8% of those who said composition is important, 5%
of the whole programme sample) for groups for minority ethnic offenders
only. The authors concluded that the findings support a policy of delivering
programmes to ethnically mixed rather than exclusively minority ethnic groups
(Calverley *et al.*, 2004: 7).

This raises questions about providing offending behaviour programmes to
exclusively minority ethnic groups and empowerment programmes. Empowerment programmes are rooted in the premise that racial victimization is criminogenic and the effects must be addressed (*cf.* Stephens *et al.*, 2004: 14), and
are delivered to exclusively minority ethnic groups. While the research findings
might be thought to justify the cessation of such services, any such conclusion is
premature, as evidence from Greater Manchester Probation Area (GMPA) provides a counter argument (GMPA, 2005; Williams, 2006). In GMPA, in 2003,
of the 177 black and Asian offenders who were referred to offending behaviour
programmes, 80 per cent opted to attend an empowerment programme rather
than a generic offending behaviour programme (Williams, 2006: 152). Also,
feedback questionnaires from attendees on the Think First for Black and Asian
Offenders (TFBAO) programme provided by GMPA as part of the Home
Office–funded black and Asian Offenders Pathfinder Programme (GMPA,
2005, see below) were broadly positive. Further, there is some evidence
to suggest that completion rates for empowerment programmes compare
favourably to those for offending behaviour programmes (Williams, 2006:
152–3). Williams (2006) draws on the desistance literature, including work by
Maruna (2001) and Farrall (2002) that examines the process of desisting from
crime, to suggest that empowerment programmes might help minority ethnic
offenders come to terms with their experiences of racism and discrimination
which may, in turn, be an essential step in the development of a non-offending
identity (see also Lewis, 2006). Perhaps the appropriate conclusion, then, is
that whilst such programmes may be neither needed nor wanted by some
minority ethnic offenders, they may be of real benefit to others. Of course,
the provision of such programmes in areas with few minority ethnic offenders
and staff may be difficult to organize. Areas should not feel obliged to provide
them if it would lead to unacceptable delays, and delivering general offending
behaviour programmes to mixed groups might be the best option in these
circumstances.

Respondents were also asked whether they had been treated fairly by different criminal justice professionals. The police received the most criticism: 62 per cent of respondents reported unfair treatment by the police. Another commonly criticized group was prison officers: two-fifths of those who had been to prison said that staff had treated them unfairly (42%). Magistrates were charged with behaving unfairly by over one-third of respondents (37%). However, probation staff received a generally favourable review. Seventy-eight per cent of respondents said that they had been treated fairly by the probation officer who wrote their pre-sentence report (PSR), 10 per cent reported unfair treatment, whilst the remainder did not know (10%) or the question was not applicable (2%). Fifty-three per cent of respondents said that they had been treated fairly by the probation officer in court, 7 per cent reported unfair treatment, and the rest did not know (16%) or the question was not applicable (24%). Probation service providers might note that experiences of disadvantage alongside unfair treatment at the hands of some criminal justice agencies may reduce confidence in the system as a whole and damage perceptions of the legitimacy of the system which, in turn, may affect motivation and compliance (Cole and Wardak, 2006).

When asked what could be done to improve the treatment of minority ethnic people within the criminal justice system, the most common responses were to eliminate racism and to employ more black and Asian workers, mentioned by 29 per cent and 27 per cent of the sample respectively. A Thematic Review of race relations in prisons found evidence that some minority ethnic staff took a 'tough line' with minority ethnic prisoners to avoid alienating their white colleagues (HM Inspectorate of Prisons, 2005: para. 4.8), casting doubt on the assumption that minority ethnic workers will necessarily provide better treatment to individual offenders. Nonetheless, it seems that the growing body of minority ethnic probation staff has raised the profile of race issues in the Probation Service generally (Vanstone, 2006: 18–19).

Irish Men on Probation

Similar research methods were used in a small study of 48 white Irish men on probation in GMPA ($n = 45$) and Merseyside ($n = 3$) (Lewis et al., 2005). The levels of crime-prone attitudes displayed were comparable to those found amongst black and Asian probationers and substantially lower than those displayed by white British probationers. The Irish probationers reported higher levels of social and personal problems than black, Asian, or white British probationers, however. This was most marked in relation to health, but also notable in relation to self-esteem, anxiety, and relationships. As noted above, respondents were broadly positive about their probation supervision: 92 per cent reported fair treatment by their supervisor. As in the study of black and Asian probationers, the respondents reported unfair treatment at the hands of some criminal justice professionals, most commonly the police.

The interviewees displayed high levels of social disadvantage, comparable to those seen in studies of minority ethnic and white British probationers. It should be noted that many of the interviewees reported prejudicial, discriminatory, and unfair treatment, particularly in relation to education, employment, and housing. The small number of Irish Travellers involved in the study ($n = 9$) reported particularly high levels of prejudice.

Offender Assessment

Offender assessment has long been a key function of the Probation Service (McWilliams, 1983), and this is still the case (Ministry of Justice, 2007). We shall now explore concerns around the completion and use of two key assessments with minority ethnic offenders: pre-sentence reports (PSRs) and the Offender Assessment System (OASys) need and risk assessment.

Research undertaken in the 1980s and early 1990s which compared the preparation and content of PSRs for white and minority ethnic offenders produced mixed findings (see Bowling and Phillips, 2002: 176–80, and Morgan, 2006: 47–50, for summaries). In contrast, *Towards Race Equality*, which included consideration of PSR national policy and local practice guidelines alongside the detailed examination of 484 PSRs for white and minority ethnic offenders from ten local probation services,[9] was unequivocal (HMIP, 2000: Chapter 4). It noted that whilst National Standards (1995) stressed that the work of the Probation Service should be free from discrimination, they said little about how this could be effected in the preparation of PSRs. Whilst the vast majority of local probation services had developed policy and practice guidelines for PSRs, less than half made specific reference to minority ethnic offenders. Moreover, the PSR study found that reports completed on white offenders tended to be of a higher standard than those completed on black offenders. Performance was measured on a range of different variables, and 60 per cent of reports on white offenders and 63 per cent of those on Asian offenders were of a 'satisfactory' or 'very good' standard, compared to just 49 per cent of those on black offenders (para. 4.46).

The report recommended that probation committees and chief probation officers take steps to improve the quality of PSRs. Specifically, they were urged to set an annual target for improvement from 2001; revise policy documents and practice guidance on PSRs to take account of issues pertaining to minority ethnic offenders; collect, collate, and use monitoring (and in particular ethnic monitoring) data; and ensure that quality assurance measures addressed the particular needs of minority ethnic offenders (para. 4.49). A follow-up study, which included an examination of 500 PSRs prepared

---

[9]On 1 April 2001, the 54 local probation services were replaced by the National Probation Service (NPS) for England and Wales. At the time of writing, this comprised the National Probation Directorate (NPD) and 42 local probation boards.

on white and minority ethnic offenders, concluded that the recommendation had been 'partially met' (HMIP, 2004: para. 4.12). It found that all probation areas had set an annual target for improvement from 2001, and many areas had revised policy documents and practice guidance as suggested. Most were routinely collecting and collating monitoring (including ethnic monitoring) data, although fewer areas were using this information to improve practice. The study of PSRs found a notable increase in the overall proportion of a 'satisfactory or better' standard. However, a higher proportion of reports on white offenders than on black, Asian, or mixed heritage offenders were rated 'satisfactory or better' (83%, 79%, 76%, and 71%, respectively) (para. 4.9), and reports on minority ethnic offenders were deemed 'of a slightly poorer quality on virtually every performance variable' (para. 4.11).

Recent research suggests that problems persist. Hudson and Bramhall (2005) compared the PSRs and risk-assessment schedules completed on 144 white and 57 Asian men by probation staff in one area in North West England. They found that the reports on Asian offenders were 'thinner', employed more 'distancing language' (e.g., 'he tells me that…') alongside less direct reporting of information imparted by the offender (e.g., 'he has taken steps…'), and were more likely to include weak, unclear, and no or negative recommendations (pp. 727–28). During the study of Irish men on probation discussed above, the PSRs completed on 30 white Irish offenders were compared with those completed on 30 white non-Irish offenders (Lewis *et al.*, 2005). The PSRs for both groups were judged to be of a comparable quality overall. However, the Irish reports were significantly worse than the comparison sample in their tendency to emphasize background factors unrelated to the offence which can reinforce the negative stereotypes to which the Irish and particularly Irish Travellers are vulnerable. Work to identify and address such problems is vital if the equitable treatment of people from all ethnic groups is to be achieved.

In 1998, the Home Office decided to develop the OASys need and risk assessment instrument, which combines actuarial methods of predicting reconviction with the structured clinical assessment of need and risk. A draft Diversity Impact Assessment (DIA) for Offender Management and OASys was informed by scoping exercises which examined the impact of diversity issues on both areas.[10,11,12] It found that OASys was potentially disadvantageous to minority ethnic groups on certain grounds. Information about OASys is not

---

[10]I hereby acknowledge and thank Gareth Mercer for supplying copies of the draft DIA and the OASys and Offender Management Scoping Exercises. All related information and quotations come from these documents.

[11]Space constraints preclude detailed consideration of Offender Management issues, although it should be stressed that OASys and Offender Management are intricately linked and are best viewed together.

[12]The draft DIA is now obsolete, being superseded by the Equality Impact Assessment (EIA) of Offender Management that is due to be published in 2008, whilst OASys is to be considered separately. Nonetheless, the issues raised remain relevant.

readily available in languages besides English, although the self-assessment questionnaire and an information leaflet are available in 38 different languages. Because actuarial scales are based on group data, reconviction predictions may be less accurate for minority groups. This echoes concerns raised by many critics of need and risk assessments (see below). It was stated that, as the OASys Development, Evaluation, and Analysis Team (O-DEAT) gather more data, they might be able to redress this by making 'adjustments to the system, for example, separate weightings for certain groups, such as women offenders' (see also Raynor, 2007: 129–131). Assessors were encouraged to be vigilant 'at every stage of the OASys assessment to avoid stereotyping and prejudiced attitudes towards any individual or group'. The overall conclusion of the draft DIA was that, having considered 'the potential impact on different racial groups, examined all the available sources of information for evidence of previous racial discrimination, and consulted relevant stakeholders to assess whether the function, policy, or practice is meeting the needs of different racial groups', OASys is 'fit for purpose'.

Nonetheless, there may still be cause for concern. Evidence suggests that the differential quality of PSRs completed on white and minority ethnic offenders may also be a problem for OASys. An evaluation of OASys in three pilots included, in the second pilot, the scrutiny of 2,031 assessments completed on white (82%), black (9%), and Asian[13] (4%) offenders and some of other (2%) or unspecified (3%) ethnic origin (Howard et al., 2006). The male (84%) and female (16%) subjects were drawn from both Prison (37%) and Probation (63%) settings.[14] The authors found that 68 per cent of all assessments were 'completed well enough to be used in section-by-section criminogenic need profiles and reconviction analysis' and thus 'valid' for research purposes (p. 37). Table 6.1 shows how the proportion of 'valid' assessments varied between ethnic groups.

The difference in the proportion valid for black as compared to white and to Asian offenders was 'highly statistically significant' (p. 41). Invalid assessments

Table 6.1 Proportion of offenders with 'valid' OASys assessments by ethnicity

Ethnicity	Percentage of offenders with 'valid' assessments (n)		
	Prison	Probation	All offenders
White	72 (627)	68 (1033)	70 (1662)
Black	59 (68)	53 (111)	55 (180)
Asian	74 (23)	68 (60)	70 (83)
Other	53 (15)	60 (25)	58 (40)

Source: Howard et al., 2006: 42, Table 3.2.

---

[13]Whilst Howard et al. (2006) refer to the 'South Asian' ethnic group, the term 'Asian' is used throughout this chapter for consistency.

[14]The site of assessment was missing in four cases.

on black offenders tended to be missing information in relation to financial management and income, relationships, and lifestyle and associates. Howard *et al.* (2006) suggested that 'an unwillingness to make "value-based" judgements when assessing offenders of different ethnicity to the assessor' may have contributed to this outcome (p. 55). Unless many of the assessors were Asian, however, this does not explain why higher proportions of white *and Asian* offenders had a valid assessment.

Moreover, the authors' validity rules were more stringent than those contained in the OASys Manual. According to the Manual's rules, 96 per cent of assessments were valid, and this high figure may be an underestimation as the research required a police national computer (PNC) match to obtain data for some parts of the study (pp. 42, 43). It seems, then, that a higher proportion of assessments completed on black offenders were 'valid' according to the OASys Manual's criteria despite containing a notable amount of missing data.

The evaluation also compared the accuracy with which various versions of OASys and the Offender Group Reconviction Scale (OGRS) predicted reconviction.[15] It was only possible to include the assessments completed on 728 white (86%), black (6%), and Asian (6%) offenders and a small number of 'other' ethnicity (2%) in this part of the evaluation. All of the assessment tools revealed poor predictions for black offenders, although the differences in accuracy of prediction between the white, black, and Asian groups were not statistically significant. Howard *et al.* (2006) stressed that the findings 'should be interpreted cautiously given that the sample included only 46 black offenders' (p. 141).

Two of the ten probation services visited as part of the Thematic Inspection of Probation (HMIP, 2000) were pilot services for OASys. Neither service felt that the tool, in its then form, paid enough attention to work with racially motivated offenders or with minority ethnic offenders (HMIP, 2000: 79). These views were echoed in a study by Mair *et al.* (2006) of 180 probation officers' views of OASys, which included questions about the tool's adequacy in relation to diversity issues. The majority of respondents felt that OASys dealt inadequately with ethnicity (51%), whilst the remainder felt that it did so adequately (33%), partly (4%), did not know (12%), or did not respond (1%). The interviewees criticized the lack of specific detail about diversity issues generally, saying that the extent to which ethnicity, gender, sexual orientation, and disability matters were pursued was left to their professional judgement. The desire for more detailed guidance may reflect a lack of confidence to make judgements about anyone from a different ethnic group or a lack of knowledge about how to explore cultural issues with anyone of different ethnic origin.

---

[15]The versions of OASys examined were the second pilot version and the shorter OASys One and standard OASys Two versions that were available from the third pilot. OGRS is an actuarial risk of reconviction predictor devised by the Home Office which relies on the following static risk factors: age, sex, criminal history, past sentences, and current offence (Copas and Marshall, 1998).

There may be other obstacles to the use of OASys with minority ethnic groups. A study of the impact of the Prison Service Sex Offender Treatment Programme (SOTP) on minority ethnic offenders found black and Asian offenders had higher mean scores on all of the denial measures used pre-treatment (denial of premeditation, denial of repetition, and denial of offence) and the black offenders had a significantly higher level of denial of repetition after treatment compared to a matched sample of white offenders (Webster et al., 2004). The authors argue that 'denial is often related to the level of perceived social disapproval' and that lower levels of tolerance in some minority ethnic communities for sexual behaviour which departs from community norms may have precipitated higher levels of denial amongst minority ethnic offenders (p. 122). Similarly, researchers involved in a study of the needs of minority ethnic people with drug and alcohol problems, noting the low uptake of services by minority ethnic groups, stated that 'the stigma of drug use, shame and guilt, and the pressure of keeping up appearances within the community were found to have a huge impact on the ability to seek professional help' (Luger and Sookhoo, 2005: 172).

The qualities of empathy, concern, genuineness, and concreteness have long been recognized as the cornerstones of effective helping relationships and resonate with traditional probation values and casework skills (Truax and Carkhuff, 1967). Displaying such qualities alongside cultural sensitivity can only be beneficial. However, whilst some believe that the effective completion of OASys relies on traditional casework skills, there is concern that the OASys tool itself, coupled with time pressures and an absence of traditional casework skills training in a changing and pressurized service, may reduce the use of such skills as assessments become routine, mechanical, and informed by 'all manner of subjective judgements' (Fitzgibbon, 2007: 94; see also Robinson, 2006).

A further concern is that the apparently objective and scientific nature of need and risk assessment instruments obscures a different reality. Some have argued that the veneer of scientific objectivity 'mask[s] the inherently moralis-tic/normative elements of this penal exercise ... The risk/need assessments and prescribed interventions are predicated on middle class normative assumptions that are highly gendered and racialized' (Hannah-Moffat, 2005: 37, italics in original). Hudson and Bramhall (2005) found that the construction of Muslim/Pakistani in risk-assessment schedules prepared on Muslim/Pakistani offenders was 'uncomfortably close to the popular pejorative stereotype' (2005: 738), demonstrating that the apparently objective and scientific nature of risk assessments does not preclude the possibility of negative stereotyping and cultural assumptions.

Some of the most damning criticism of need and risk assessment tools has come from Canadian academics concerned that the development and use of such tools have ignored the specific needs and experiences of women and minority ethnic groups (Shaw and Hannah-Moffat, 2004). A key argument is that Canadian need and risk assessment tools are predicated on research on the social and personal characteristics of samples of mainly white male offenders, and that the needs of women and minority ethnic groups are substantially different to those of the white male population. As the developers of the prototype OASys (the Offender Assessment Inventory – OAI) drew on research undertaken by the Canadian Correctional Services (Howard *et al.*, 2006: 12), we might ask whether the same charge could be made of OASys. Clearly, these are issues that O-DEAT will need to consider.

Probation Programmes

Programmes to address cognitive–behavioural causes of offending behaviour are a central tenet of the What Works movement (Vanstone, 2000). The dominance of cognitive–behavioural programmes led a former HMCIP to warn against 'programme fetishism' and to stress that other work with offenders is equally important (HMIP, 2002). We shall now turn our attention to the work to tailor such programmes to the needs of minority ethnic offenders that has been undertaken as part of the What Works endeavour.

In June 2000, a survey of locally developed programmes for minority ethnic offenders was conducted for the Home Office (Powis and Walmsley, 2002), to which 45 local probation services responded. Thirteen such programmes had been developed in 10 services, just five of which were still being delivered. There was, then, a paucity of evidence as to what programmes best met the needs of this group.

In May 2001, Probation Circular 76/2001, entitled *What Works, Diversity Issues and Race*, was published. The Circular provided guidance on the use of general offending behaviour programmes with minority ethnic offenders. It stated that, in the absence of counter-evidence, all black and Asian offenders who met the targeting criteria should be placed on general offending behaviour programmes, though these could be run exclusively for black and Asian offenders 'in order to maximise responsivity'[16] (NPD, 2001: 4). The Circular also announced the advent of the black and Asian offender 'Pathfinders' to test different models of offending behaviour programme provision for minority ethnic offenders. Four models were established: 'Preparation Sessions' (a short group-based motivational module) completed prior to Think First for black and Asian only groups (TFBAO) (to be tested in GMPA); Preparation Sessions completed prior to Think First for mixed groups (West Midlands and Thames Valley); volunteer mentors supporting offenders through Think First (Avon and Somerset; Bedfordshire; Cambridgeshire; Essex, and Hertfordshire); and the Drink Impaired Drivers (DIDs) programme delivered to Asian offenders

---

[16]Responsivity concerns matching programme delivery and content to the learning styles of participants.

(Leicestershire) (Stephens *et al.*, 2004). The premise, then, was that general offending behaviour programmes could be adapted for use with minority ethnic groups.

That the preferred approach is one of 'adaptation' and 'adding-on' was confirmed in September 2002 when NPD and the Prison Service published a diversity review report on offending behaviour programmes (NPD, 2002). The review considered the accessibility and effectiveness of three general offending behaviour programmes used with minority ethnic offenders: Reasoning and Rehabilitation, Think First, and Enhanced Thinking Skills. The programmes were all deemed suitable for use with minority ethnic offenders as long as tutors adapted programme materials and their style of delivery to make the programmes meaningful to all participants. Examples of appropriate 'adaptations' included adapting scenarios (e.g., 'using a shop rather than a public house setting, using a culturally relevant setting'), adapting language (e.g., 'using culturally relevant phrases'), and giving some offenders 'additional support during written exercises or enabling them to use drawings to explain a written exercise' (NPD, 2002: 15).

The Pathfinders were intended to throw light on process issues and measure short-term and long-term outcomes, and a reconviction study was planned. However, an interim implementation report revealed problems that were to bedevil the whole enterprise (Stephens *et al.*, 2004; see also Walmsley and Stephens, 2006). Implementation of the Preparation Sessions completed prior to Think First was most successful and produced some positive participant feedback. However, shortages of suitably trained staff and of suitable and eligible offenders limited throughput, whilst variations in implementation between areas rendered any comparison of outcomes meaningless. The mentoring schemes experienced complete implementation failure. A lack of suitable and eligible offenders meant that, by the end of the first year, just three offenders across all five areas had started mentoring. The implementation report recommended abandoning the mentoring strand of the Pathfinder because it was not viable (Stephens *et al.*, 2004: 11). The Asian DIDs programme was dogged by a dearth of suitable and eligible offenders and staff shortages. The implementation report stated that an outcome study was not feasible within a realistic timetable, recommended that plans for any such study be abandoned, and suggested that local managers be allowed to decide whether continuation of the programme was viable (Stephens *et al.*, 2004: 12).

The advent of NOMS led to a restructuring of the Home Office Research, Development and Statistics Directorate (RDS), which was originally to evaluate the Pathfinders, with the result that this task was passed to local areas. To date, to the author's knowledge, no further process information or outcome data have been published by the Home Office, NPD, or NOMS. However, the three areas providing the Preparation Sessions alongside the Think First Programme (GMPA, West Midlands, and Thames Valley) continued to do so beyond the publication of the interim implementation report. Subsequently, the areas provided NPD with evaluation reports covering the period April 2003–March 2005. The evaluations were necessarily limited by problems with data recording and throughput. Nonetheless, the report by GMPA showed some interesting results (GMPA, 2005). Two-hundred and eighty-four black and Asian offenders were required to attend the Think First programme during this period. Of these, 111 (39%) elected to attend TFBAO, including the Preparation Sessions, whilst the remainder (173, 61%) opted for the generic Think First programme. Sixty-one per cent of those who started TFBAO went on to complete it, whilst just 47 per cent of the black and Asian offenders who started the generic programme completed it. However, those who chose to attend TFBAO had a markedly lower mean OGRS score (53.47) than those who chose to attend the generic programme (61.06).[17] Further, anyone failing to complete the Preparation Sessions was excluded from TFBAO. In other words, those starting TFBAO (but not the generic programme) had a track record of programme completion. Thus whilst the findings are encouraging, the direct comparison of completion rates is not valid. The report also presented findings from offender feedback questionnaires administered on entry to and exit from the Preparation Sessions and finally on completion of TFBAO.[18] Of those commencing the Preparation Sessions who completed an entry questionnaire, two-fifths (42%) reported that racism was a problem for them. Most respondents felt that the tutors would understand their problems; that having black or Asian tutors would be good for them; and that it was good to be in a group for black and Asian people (77%, 88%, and 86%, respectively). The exit questionnaires produced similar responses. Only a minority of those who completed TFBAO completed a post-programme questionnaire, and they were largely positive about the programme. However, it is interesting to note that whilst 38 per cent agreed that racist comments or behaviour in the group had been challenged, 25 per cent disagreed; the rest (37%) did not respond.

Some writers expressed disappointment with the Pathfinder models at the outset, suggesting that the opportunity to test programmes designed to 'empower' black and Asian offenders had been missed (Durrance and Williams, 2003; Williams, 2006). Although the Pathfinder Preparation Sessions were designed to make limited use of empowerment strategies to secure programme compliance, Durrance and Williams (2003: 217) argued 'for more holistic empowerment programmes that allow black and Asian offenders to explore issues around broad social issues, race, and identity and how

---

[17]NB: OGRS was not calculated for 42% of those who chose to attend TFBAO and for 39% of those who chose to attend the generic programme.

[18]Preparation Sessions: 98 'starters', 78 completed entry questionnaires, response rate 76%. Preparation Sessions: 74 'completers', 59 completed exit questionnaires, response rate 80%. TFBAO: 74 'starters' and 45 'completers', 16 of whom completed exit questionnaires, response rate 36%.

these might relate to their offending as an enterprise in its own right'. Now, probation areas must meet targets for the number of people on offending behaviour programmes. Generic programmes like Think First, whether delivered exclusively to minority ethnic offenders, in conjunction with Preparation Sessions as described above, or otherwise, count towards these targets. Empowerment programmes do not count towards these targets. This might effectively end the delivery of such programmes.

It is difficult not to feel disappointment with the Pathfinder enterprise, which promised so much but produced so little. Problems of implementation, data collection, and throughput meant that the models were never properly tested. The final evaluation reports produced by GMPA, West Midlands, and Thames Valley appear to be gathering dust. It seems that we know little more at the end of the Pathfinder enterprise about what works with black and Asian offenders than we did at the outset.

Some writers have berated the architects of cognitive behavioural approaches for giving little thought to their appropriateness for minority ethnic groups and women, and have suggested that simply tinkering with programme content to make such individuals more responsive fails to recognize the extent to which needs and experiences differ (Shaw and Hannah-Moffat, 2004). Others have criticized the lack of attention paid by programme designers to the social structural causes of offending behaviour (Gorman, 2001; Kendall, 2002, 2004). In response to this last point, however, cognitive behavioural approaches were not designed as an alternative to work to address social structural factors. Rather, they are an additional strategy for use with people who display particular cognitive problems such as impulsiveness, an inability to empathize, or rigid thinking. Efforts to address offending behaviour should combine work to address social structural factors with cognitive behavioural approaches where necessary to enhance a person's capacity to take advantage of the opportunities and resources available.

Conclusion

It is imperative that diversity issues are integral (and seen to be integral) to the development of NOMS. Further, NOMS must take a strong lead on diversity issues to ensure that they remain a priority at the local level. At present, neither appears to be the case.

A key lesson from the study by Calverley et al. (2004) was that a range of views and experiences exists both within and between black, Asian, and mixed heritage groups. The interviewees displayed lower levels of criminogenic needs than their white peers, as measured by CRIME-PICS II. Respondents were generally positive about their experiences of probation, but reported less favourable treatment by some other criminal justice agencies which could diminish their perceptions of legitimacy and levels of compliance. The small study of Irish men on probation found that the subjects displayed lower levels of crime-prone attitudes than white British probationers but higher levels of social problems, particularly in relation to health. They too were generally positive about their experiences of probation whilst being critical of some other criminal justice agencies. They displayed high levels of disadvantage and social exclusion and reported experiencing discriminatory treatment, discrimination being a particular problem for the Irish Travellers.

That assessments completed on some minority ethnic groups do not always meet the standard of those completed on other groups is well documented. The OASys need and risk assessment now forms the backbone of work with offenders. Doubts remain about its suitability for use with minority ethnic groups, however. Further development work and research is needed to ensure that OASys is truly 'fit for purpose'. It seems likely that traditional casework skills and time are needed for OASys to be completed well, both of which appear to be under threat in the Probation Service.

Knowledge as to what offending behaviour programmes work best with minority ethnic offenders is still limited, and questions remain about whether adapting generic offending behaviour programmes for use with minority ethnic offenders will suffice. Some commentators have expressed regret at the demise of empowerment approaches, empirical evidence as to the benefits of which is also in short supply. Well-planned and executed research would shed light on these issues.

The Probation Service's long and distinguished tradition of work rooted in humanitarian concerns affords a strong foundation for the development of anti-racist policies and practice. That the advent of NOMS may be eroding traditional probation culture is a real concern (Bhui, 2006: 178, 79; Vanstone, 2006: 11). Further, the tendency to see the offending population as homogenous is a retrograde step. Probationers have a wide range of views, needs, and experiences, and minority ethnic probationers are an essentially heterogenic group. A 'one-size-fits-all' approach will not suffice. Work with minority ethnic (as with all) offenders must be rooted in a thorough understanding of their particular situation. Anything else would be inequitable.

Summary

This chapter has focused primarily on research findings relating to probation practice with minority ethnic offenders, and less with personnel or cultural issues. It argues that anti-racist practice has been undermined by the fact that diversity issues were not integral to the development or current practices of NOMS. It considers in some detail the results of the largest-ever study of black and

(Continued)

(Continued)

minority ethnic people subject to probation supervision. That study demonstrated a diversity of views and experiences both within and between black, Asian, and mixed heritage groups, who displayed lower levels of criminogenic needs than their white peers, as measured by CRIME-PICS II. They were also more likely to have had a positive experience of probation than of any other criminal justice agency. Assessment practice is considered, and the chapter reflects doubts about whether the OASys need and risk assessment, which now forms the backbone of probation work with offenders, is truly suitable for use with minority ethnic groups. Its effectiveness appears to be undermined by the threat to traditional casework skills and lack of time for probation work. Finally, it discusses the still limited knowledge as to what offending behaviour programmes work best with minority ethnic offenders, and the evidence on whether it is sufficient to adapt generic offending behaviour programmes for use with minority ethnic offenders. It highlights the limitations and failures of research to date and the need for more and better-designed studies on this issue.

Key Texts

Lewis, S., Raynor, P., Smith, D. and Wardak, A. (2006) (Eds.) *Race and Probation.* Cullompton: Willan.
Calverley, A., Cole, B., Kaur, G., Lewis, S., Raynor, P., Sadeghi, S., Smith, D., Vanstone, M. and Wardak, A. (2004) *Black and Asian Offenders on Probation.* Home Office Research Study 277. London: Home Office.
Her Majesty's Inspectorate of Probation (HMIP) (2000) *Towards Race Equality: A Thematic Report.* London: HMIP.

References

Bhui, H.S. (2006) 'Anti-racist practice in NOMS: reconciling managerialist and professional realities', *Howard Journal*, 45(2), 171–90.

Bowling, B. and Phillips, C. (2002) *Racism, Crime and Justice.* London: Longman.

Calverley, A., Cole, B., Kaur, G., Lewis, S., Raynor, P., Sadeghi, S., Smith, D., Vanstone, M. and Wardak, A. (2004) *Black and Asian Offenders on Probation.* Home Office Research Study 277. London: Home Office.

Calverley, A., Cole, B., Kaur, G., Lewis, S., Raynor, P., Sadeghi, S., Smith, D., Vanstone, M. and Wardak, A. (2006) 'Black and Asian probationers: implications of the Home Office study', *Probation Journal*, 53(1), 24–37. Available at: http://prb.sagepub.com/cgi/content/abstract/53/1/24 (Last accessed 10.05.07)

Carter, P. (2003) *Managing Offenders, Reducing Crime: A New Approach*. London: Home Office.

Cole, B. and Wardak, A. (2006) 'Black and Asian men on probation: social exclusion, discrimination and experiences of criminal justice', in S. Lewis, P. Raynor, D. Smith and A. Wardak (eds) *Race and Probation*. Cullompton: Willan.

Commission for Racial Equality (2006) *Offender Management Bill*, House of Commons, Second Reading, December 2006. London: CRE. Available at: http://www.cre.gov.uk/downloads/offender_management_bill_2nd_reading.pdf (Last accessed 19.04.07)

Copas, J. and Marshall, P. (1998) 'The offender group reconviction scale: a statistical reconviction score for use by probation officers', *Applied Statistics*, 47(1), 159–71.

Durrance, P. and Williams, P. (2003) 'Broadening the agenda around what works for Black and Asian offenders', *Probation Journal*, 50(3), 211–24.

Farrall, S. (2002) *Rethinking What Works with Offenders: Probation, Social Context and Desistance from Crime*. Cullompton: Willan.

Fitzgibbon, D.W.M. (2007) 'Risk analysis and the new practitioner: myth or reality?', *Punishment and Society*, 9(1), 87–97.

Frude, N., Honess, T. and Maguire, M. (1994) *CRIME-PICS II Manual*. Cardiff: Michael and Associates.

Garland, J., Spalek, B. and Chakraborti, N. (2006) 'Hearing lost voices: issues in researching "hidden" minority ethnic communities', *British Journal of Criminology*, 47, 423–37.

Gelsthorpe, L. (2006) 'The experiences of female minority ethnic offenders: the other "other"' in S. Lewis, P. Raynor, D. Smith and A. Wardak (eds) *Race and Probation*. Cullompton: Willan.

Gorman, K. (2001) 'Cognitive behaviouralism and the Holy Grail: the quest for a universal means of managing offender risk', *Probation Journal*, 48(3), 3–9.

Greater Manchester Probation Area (GMPA) (2005) Evaluation of the Think First for Black and Asian Offenders (TFBAO) Pathfinder Programme, unpublished report to the National Probation Directorate.

Hannah-Moffat, K. (2005) 'Criminogenic needs and the transformative risk subject: hybridizations of risk/need in penality', *Punishment and Society*, 7, 29–51.

Harper, R. (2000) *Quality of Service Survey*. London: Middlesex Probation Service.

Her Majesty's Inspectorate of Probation (HMIP) (2000) *Towards Race Equality: A Thematic Report*. London: HMIP.

Her Majesty's Inspectorate of Probation (HMIP) (2002) *Annual Report 2001–2002*. London: HMIP.

Her Majesty's Inspectorate of Probation (HMIP) (2004) *Towards Race Equality: Follow-Up Inspection Report*. London: HMIP.

Her Majesty's Inspectorate of Prisons (2005) *Parallel Worlds: A Thematic Review of Race Relations in Prisons*. London: HMIP. Available at: http://inspectorates.homeoffice.gov.uk/hmiprisons/thematic-reports1/ (last accessed 09.05.07).

Home Office (2004) Reducing Crime – Changing Lives: The Government's Plans for Transforming the Management of Offenders. London: Home Office.

Home Office Communication Directorate (2005) NOMS: Special Report. London: Home Office Communication Directorate. Available at: http://www.probation.homeoffice.gov.uk/files/pdf/NOMS%20Special%20Report%20July%202006.pdf (Last accessed 11.05.07)

Howard, P., Clark, D. and Garnham, N. (2006) An Evaluation of the Offender Assessment System (OASys) in Three Pilots 1999–2001. London: Home Office.

Hudson, B. and Bramhall, G. (2005) 'Assessing the "Other": Constructions of "Asianness" in Risk Assessments by Probation Officers', British Journal of Criminology, 45, 721–40.

Kendall, K. (2002) 'Time to think again about cognitive behavioural programmes', in P. Carlen (ed.) Women and Punishment: The Struggle for Justice. Cullompton: Willan.

Kendall, K. (2004) 'Dangerous thinking: a critical history of correctional cognitive behaviouralism', in G. Mair (ed.) What Matters in Probation. Cullompton: Willan.

Lewis, S. (2006) 'Minority ethnic experiences of probation supervision and programmes' in S. Lewis, P. Raynor, D. Smith and A. Wardak (eds) Race and Probation. Cullompton: Willan.

Lewis, S., Lobley, D., Raynor, P. and Smith, D. (2005) 'The Irish on probation in England', Irish Probation Journal, 2(1), 4–19. Available at: http://www.protectnands.org/ipj.asp# (Last accessed 16.04.07).

Lewis, S., Raynor, P., Smith, D. and Wardak, A. (2006) (eds) Race and Probation. Cullompton: Willan.

Luger, L. and Sookhoo, D. (2005) 'Rapid needs assessment and the provision of drug and alcohol services for people from minority ethnic groups with drug and alcohol problems', Diversity in Health and Social Care, 2, 167–76.

Mair, G., Burke, L. and Taylor, S. (2006) '"The worst tax form you've ever seen"? Probation officers' views about OASys', Probation Journal, 53(1), 7–23.

McWilliams, W. (1983) 'The Mission to the English Police Courts 1876–1936', Howard Journal, 22(3), 129–47.

Mair, G. and May, C. (1997) Offenders on Probation. Home Office Research Study 167. London: Home Office.

Mantle, G. (1999) Control, Help and Punishment (Occasional Paper 1). Witham: Essex Probation Service.

Maruna, S. (2001) Making Good: How Ex-Convicts Reform and Rebuild Their Lives. Washington: American Psychological Association.

Ministry of Justice (2007) National Standards for the Management of Offenders: Standards and Implementation Guidance 2007. London: Ministry of Justice.

Morgan, R. (2006) 'Race, Probation and Inspections', in: S. Lewis, P. Raynor, D. Smith and A. Wardak (eds) Race and Probation. Cullompton: Willan.

National Association of Probation Officers (NAPO) (2005) Restructuring Probation: What Works? London: NAPO.

National Association of Probation Officers (NAPO) (2006/2007) Stop the Bill – we can do it! December/January 2007, Issue 185, pp.1–2.

National Association of Probation Officers (NAPO) (2007) 'NOMS and Diversity', *NAPO News*, March 2007, Issue 187, p. 4.

National Probation Directorate (NPD) (2001) *What Works Diversity Issues and Race*. Probation Circular 76/2001. London: Home Office.

National Probation Directorate (NPD) (2002) Offending Behaviour Programmes: Diversity Review Report on Cognitive Skills Programmes. London: NPD.

Powis, B. and Walmsley, R.K. (2002) *Programmes for Black and Asian Offenders on Probation: lessons for Developing Practice*. Home Office Research Study 250. London: Home Office.

Raynor, P. (1998) 'Attitudes, social problems and reconvictions in the STOP probation experiment', *Howard Journal*, 37, 1–15.

Raynor, P. (2007) Risk and need assessment in British probation: the contribution of LSI-R, *Psychology, Crime and Law*, April 2007, 13(2), 125–38.

Robinson, G. (2006) 'Implementing OASys: lessons from research into LSI-R and ACE', *Probation Journal*, 50(1), 30–40.

Shaw, M. and Hannah-Moffat, K. (2004) 'How cognitive skills forgot about gender and diversity', in G. Mair (ed.) *What Matters in Probation*. Cullompton : Willan.

Stephens, K., Coombs, J. and Debedin, M. (2004) Black and Asian offenders pathfinder: implementation report. Home Office Development and Practice Report 24. London: Home Office.

Truax, C.B. and Carkhuff, R.R. (1967) *Towards Effective Counselling and Psychotherapy: Training and Practice*. Chicago: Aldine Books.

Vanstone, M. (2000) 'Cognitive-behavioural work with offenders in the UK: a History of influential endeavour', *Howard Journal*, 39(2), 171–83.

Vanstone, M. (2006) 'Room for improvement: a history of the Probation Service's response to race', in S. Lewis, P. Raynor, D. Smith and A. Wardak (eds) *Race and Probation*. Cullompton: Willan.

Walmsley, R.K. and Stephens, K. (2006) 'What Works with Black and minority ethnic offenders: solutions in search of a problem?', in S. Lewis, P. Raynor, D. Smith and A. Wardak (eds) *Race and Probation*. Cullompton: Willan.

Webster, D.S., Akhtar, S., Bowers, L.E., Mann, R.E., Rallings, M. and Marshall, W.L. (2004) 'The impact of the prison service sex offender treatment programme on minority ethnic offenders: a preliminary study', *Psychology, Crime and Law*, 10(2), 113–24.

Williams, P. (2006) 'Designing and delivering programmes for minority ethnic offenders', in S. Lewis, P. Raynor, D. Smith and A. Wardak (eds) *Race and Probation*. Cullompton: Willan.

SEVEN

Gender, 'Race', and the Criminal Justice Process

Finola Farrant

Introduction

Minority ethnic women[1] experience an amplified version of discrimination when they come into contact with the various institutions and processes of the criminal justice system. However, the magnitude and nature of this experience is insufficiently understood because of analytical and theoretical weaknesses in much of the existing research. This chapter discusses existing evidence and debates, and suggests that in order to move understanding forward, the concept of *intersectionality* should be adopted. Rather than perceiving hierarchies of discrimination, intersectionality allows us to consider how different forms of oppression interrelate with each other to intensify discriminatory experiences.

Interpreting the Evidence Base

To theorize 'race', gender, and crime is to accept the contingent character of each of these constructs: they will vary across spatial and temporal spans (Cheliotis & Liebling, 2006; Weedon, 1997; Winant, 2000). In any society, the prevailing legal system reflects particular values based on class, gender, and racial interests. Assumptions about femininity and 'race' inform and constitute the institutions and processes of the criminal justice system. In making sense of how the legal system frames, interprets, and reinterprets minority ethnic women's experiences, it is necessary to bear in mind the context within which

---

[1]Minority ethnic women is the term used throughout this chapter – however, it is recognized that this is contested terminology which is highly problematic; although the term is used, issues raised by its use are explored. See Garland *et al.* (2006) for a full discussion on issues of 'racial' definition. When studies are referred to the definitions and categories used in the original are maintained.

the legal system operates. Generally, studies on the operations of any of the criminal justice institutions are studies of the socially excluded (Braithwaite, 2003; Rusche & Kirchheimer, 1969)[2]. Furthermore, the concept of justice, rather than being equally applied, serves particular values and interests (Weedon, 1997). Therefore, the operations of racial and gendered power in society are discernible in examining concepts of crime and punishment. For example, prior to 1991 a husband could not be charged with the rape of his wife in England and Wales; and, whilst slavery was abolished in Britain and its colonies in 1838, it would be another quarter of a century before it was abolished in America.

Research suggests that once caught up in the criminal justice process, these values and interests have a significant impact upon the ways in which minority ethnic women are treated, and is manifested in their discriminatory experiences of the justice system. For minority ethnic women in contact with the criminal justice system, racism and sexism affect patterns of offending, victimization, and the experience of justice. Moreover, minority ethnic practitioners in the criminal justice system report having similar experiences to those people of minority ethnic backgrounds who come into contact with the system as suspects, defendants, and prisoners (Bhui & Fossi, 2007; Bowling & Phillips, 2002). Rather than being dealt with primarily on the basis of their offending, it has been argued that women are subject to assessments made about them as wives, mothers, and daughters (Carlen, 1983, 1997; Worrall, 1981). Drawing on her extensive work on women and the criminal justice system, Carlen has concluded that minority ethnic women are subject to a 'series of class-biased, race-biased, and gender-biased negotiations between the various criminal justice personnel' (1997: 152). Other research suggests that minority ethnic women have a markedly different, and inferior, experience from white women. For example, one study reported that two-thirds of black women offenders who had contact with the police had been treated aggressively (Chigwada-Bailey, 2003). In another study (Denney, 1992), probation officers were found to be 'either unable or unwilling' (p. 73) to recognize the structured subordination of black women. Instead, black women offenders were viewed in the context of their biology, to be displaying feminine 'silliness', or to have experienced random misfortune rather than systematic prejudice. Meanwhile, Devlin's (1998) research concluded that black women in prison were routinely regarded as trouble makers, heavily supervised, mishandled, and given the harshest punishments. A recent review of race relations by the Chief Inspector of Prisons also found that Asian women felt significantly more unsafe than other women whilst they were in prison (HMIP, 2005). This would suggest that minority ethnic women experience discrimination at each

---

[2]Corporate or state crimes still largely go undetected, unprosecuted, and unpunished (Green & Ward, 2004).

stage of the criminal justice process, from dealings with the police through to imprisonment.

The Official Statistics

In 1984, the first official statistics relating to the racial and ethnic background of the prison population were produced in England and Wales, although it was not until the introduction of the Criminal Justice Act 1991 that statistical information on race and gender was systematically collected and published from across the criminal justice system. However, it is necessary to issue a note of caution about relying on statistics to inform our understanding. Crime statistics do not provide objective indices of patterns and levels of criminality. This is largely due to variations in the reporting and recording of crime, and the operation of discretion on the part of the various criminal justice agencies. In effect, these statistics demonstrate concerns with only a small proportion of people who have not been diverted from the criminal justice process during one of its various stages (Bowling & Philips, 2002; Cheliotis & Liebling, 2006). In addition, the statistics are themselves problematic.

Section 95 of the Criminal Justice Act 1991 stated that information would be published annually by the government to avoid discriminating against any persons on the grounds of race or sex or any other improper ground. Section 95 publications: *Statistics on Race and the Criminal Justice System* and *Statistics on Women and the Criminal Justice System* concentrate on the statistical differences in relation to being the victim of crime and involvement at different stages of the criminal justice system, such as contact with the police, probation, courts, and prison.

Mapping out the experiences of minority ethnic women in the criminal justice system, based on the information provided by Section 95 publications, highlights a number of definitional and conceptual problems. For example, rather than recognizing the dual impact of sexism and racism, Section 95 publications maintain a sense of separation which fails to adequately detail, or reflect the needs, of those who face discrimination based on both 'race' and gender.

Nevertheless, what we do learn from the official statistics (Ministry of Justice, 2007a) is that minority ethnic women made up 28 per cent of the female prison population in 2006 (according to the 2001 census 7.9 per cent of the UK population is from a minority ethnic group). Black prisoners comprised 20 per cent of the female prison population and 15 per cent of the male population.

The women's prison population is particularly skewed because of the high levels of foreign national women within prison, many of whom are serving long sentences for drug importation. However, even excluding foreign nationals, the proportion of black women serving sentences for drug offences (46 per cent) was still higher than that of white females (26 per cent) and also higher than black males (18 per cent) (Home Office, 2004). Based on such statistics, it should not be surprising that official discourses surrounding minority ethnic women and the criminal justice system resonate with concepts of foreignness, 'blackness', and drug-related offending.

It is not only within official crime statistics that minority ethnic women's presence is partial. Within wider criminological research and theory, these experiences have largely been hidden (Cheliotis & Liebling, 2006; Garland *et al.*, 2006). This is particularly interesting, given that marginalized groups have frequently been the focus of criminological research. A possible reason for this neglect may well be due to the analytical problems in making sense of issues relating to 'race' and 'gender', and the dangers of reductionism, reification, and essentialism (Bowling & Philips, 2002; Cheliotis & Liebling, 2006; Garland *et al.*, 2006; Weedon, 2004). In order to more fully develop criminal justice research, theory, and practice in relation to minority ethnic women, it is necessary to engage with theories relating to gender, 'race', and class.[3] By doing this, it soon becomes clear that a more inclusive theoretical standpoint is required within criminology. This would recognize that experience is shaped in many varied ways which cannot, necessarily, be separated from each other. In addition, the interaction of different forms of oppression can lead to an amplification of discrimination at each stage of the criminal justice system.

Race Without Gender, Gender Without Race

Use of the terms 'gender' and 'race' will, more frequently than not, lead to discussions about women *or* minority ethnic groups. This in turn creates a situation where it appears that gender issues are only pertinent to women, and 'race' issues only relevant to those defined as ethnic minorities (Agozino, 1997; Hooks, 1982). Although gender-related theories have analysed masculinities in a variety of ways and, to a significant extent, gendered the male (Connell, 1995; Kimmel *et al.*, 2005); considering whiteness as part of the discourse on 'race' remains largely absent[4]. Furthermore, when we talk about 'race' the focus tends to be on minority ethnic men, and when we talk about 'women' the focus, tends to be on white women. Indeed, feminist theory has been criticized for largely failing to generate critical analysis of

---

[3] As class-based theories have been an integral part of the British criminological tradition; this chapter will particularly concentrate on theories relating to gender and 'race'. It should not, however, be forgotten that minority ethnic women are frequently amongst the most economically deprived groups in society.

[4] Although not completely neglected – see for example Delgado & Stefancic (1997) or Fine *et al.*, (1997).

the minority ethnic women's experience (Gelsthorpe, 2006; Hooks, 1982; Spivak, 1987).

It is not only theory that has been negligent. Those studies that have taken 'race' or gender as their focus have replicated some of these problems. Examination of minority ethnic women and the criminal justice system is therefore significantly hampered by:

A general failure to consider both race and gender issues in the same piece of research or set of statistics, and by a general failure to clarify concepts and categories of ethnicity. (Gelsthorpe, 2006: 100)

Even in Agozino's (1997) book *Black Women and the Criminal Justice System*, which aims to look at issues relevant to black women and crime within a framework of understanding that criminal justice institutions maintain and reproduce oppression, some of these failures can be found. The chapter on policing, for example, draws heavily upon the experiences of black men. Similarly, in a study on black people's experience of the criminal justice system (Nacro, 1991), a number of conclusions were drawn which did not include the black women's accounts. On policing there was a failure to adequately reflect what the black women in the study reported – instead, their views were subsumed into the 'black' experience. On occasion, the experiences of the women were not included at all, such as when sentencing and imprisonment were discussed. Of the limited criminological writing on minority ethnic women, it appears as though, in an eagerness to present the case for much needed change, there has been a lack of attention to the categories of people included in such studies[5]. Moreover, how best to locate minority ethnic women into criminological theory and research, has been insufficiently considered.

Conceptualising 'Race' and Gender

How knowledge and power is structured and exercised in contemporary Britain has particular bearing upon minority ethnic women in contact with the criminal justice system. Economic, social, and sexual exploitation, and cultural and political imperialism, are all relevant in shaping the criminal justice system's response to minority ethnic women as victims and offenders. Feminist and post-colonial theories offer an opportunity to critically analyse these issues.

Feminist and post-colonial theory have much in common as oppositional discourses which attempt to redress an imbalance in society and culture. Both began with strategies that aimed

---

[5]For example, the uncritical and un-defined use of the term 'black' in the majority of these studies.

to upset dominant hierarchies and recover or reassert marginalized histories and writings. Both have also since turned towards analyses of the construction of those hierarchies, categories, and canons, questioning the systems of thought and forms of critical legitimation behind them. (Hall, 1980: 198)

The importance of language is apparent when considering how feminism is based on examining and changing the oppressions relating to gender; yet challenging the oppressions relating to 'race' does not have a clearly identified theoretical 'name'. There is no 'race' focused theoretical equivalent of 'feminism', although it is possible to identify a number of perspectives that share a commitment to tackling racism. Post-colonialism provides a perspective which challenges the binary nature of more traditional theories, for example, in relation to inferiority/superiority or black/white.

Feminism and post-colonialist theories frequently involve challenging the operation of power systems based on the social meanings given to biological differences. The bodily features of 'race' and 'gender' have become signifiers of certain criminal characteristics[6]. The essentialist notions of 'race' and 'gender' as real, biologically meaningful, fixed, and natural, depends on a biological determinism, which, despite being challenged by a number of theories – feminism, post-structuralism, post-colonialism (as well as within the natural sciences) – retains popular currency. However, as Bowling and Phillips, amongst others, assert, ' "race" is not real, in the sense of discrete, biological or cultural categories' (2002: 31). For Hall (1980) it is the delineation of racial categories based on biology that has allowed the spread of racism. Individuals are forced to view themselves in terms of racialized biological determinants. Feminist theorists, such as Butler, have similarly challenged the concept of a biologically determined gender:

> There is no gender identity behind the expressions of gender; ... identity is performatively constituted by the very 'expressions' that are said to be its results. (Butler, 1990: 25)

Gender, therefore, rather than being a biological given, is a performance: it is what we do, rather than who we are. These approaches do not necessarily have to be viewed as creating some bodiless entity. The corporeal reality of the body is instead recognized and theorized in relation to the way it is transformed by its entry and participation in society (Shilling, 2003, 2005). The body is central to identity, whether that be chosen or imposed, or whether the meaning given to that identity is accepted or is a site of resistance. It is the competing discourses of meanings which seek to define bodies according to gender, skin colour, sexuality, age, physical beauty etc., and how these meanings are used to assert power and control, which is pertinent when considering

---

[6]For example, assumptions about Jamaican women who enter the UK being potential drug mules.

minority ethnic women and the criminal justice system. Uncoupling bodies from the racial and gendered discourses inscribed upon them is one way of challenging many of the racist and sexist assumptions existent within society, which minority ethnic women must contend. Some feminist and post-colonial theories place this uncoupling at the centre of their work. Post-colonialist and feminist theories therefore have a number of shared concerns. Both challenge the dominant modes of thinking within society, both focus on the marginalized and disempowered and, critically, both seek to alter the power systems that structure experience (Ashcroft *et al.*, 2006). Placing this within a criminological perspective, Cheliotis and Liebling convincingly argue that the 'task of criminologists is to decode and eventually unravel existing power relations' (2006: 311).

Feminist theory has had a significant impact upon the criminological discipline. The emergence of feminism in criminology has not, however, always been inclusive of minority ethnic women (Burgess-Proctor, 2006; Rice, 1990). This is despite such an inclusion opening up the possibility for exploring some of the clearest interplay of power in relation to gender, 'race', and class. Although feminist theories are concerned with patriarchal oppression, it is not the case that all feminists, or all feminist theories, share the same philosophical standpoints. Nevertheless, at its core, feminism is a political position directed at changing existing power relations between men and women in society (Weedon, 1997). There are, however, many different types of feminist theories, including liberal, radical, socialist, psychoanalytical, post-structuralist, and black feminism[7]. Although drawing clear distinctions between the various feminist perspectives is not always possible – and may of course not be desirable – one of the main distinctions relates to theories which believe in essentialist differences between 'men' and 'women', and those which regard gender as a socially constructed, rather than biologically determined, category. Bell Hooks, for example, suggests that although poststructuralist critique causes problems for black identity politics it can also be liberating and enabling, allowing women to move beyond 'constricting notions of blackness' (1991: 28).

The idea of biological differences between different 'races' endures today. These divisions, or categorizations, are roughly captured by terms such as black, white, and Asian. Under this thinking, a person's ancestors, skin colour, phenotype, and chromatism, determines membership of a genetically defined racial group. The link between physiology and racial status is fixed. Spivak (1986), however, argues that in ancient Greece there was no sense of racial identity and no racial exclusions. Although claims to cultural superiority were made, they were not based on biological differences. A similar situation could also be found in Europe before the 1400s when the term 'race' tended

---

[7]See Weedon (1997) for a full discussion on the various feminist theories. See Burgess-Proctor (2006) for a discussion on feminist criminology.

to designate the 'human race' rather than separate 'races'. By the fifteenth century, however, the concept of 'race' began to enter social discourse. By the nineteenth century serious scientific theories about 'race' were being widely developed. Philosophical explanations of 'race' proliferated in tandem with scientific theories. Understandings of 'race' were used to exclude and denigrate, to condition thought, feeling, and anatomy. Bodily differences became the principal site of exploration. Claiming rigorous scientific experimentation, criminological studies at this time focused upon supposed racial and gender differences. For example, Lombroso argued that black people's mental and emotional life was almost entirely determined by biology (Gibson, 2002), whilst in *The Female Offender* it was claimed that 'it will no longer be possible to deny the organicity of crime, its anatomical nature and degenerative source' (Lombroso & Ferrero, 1895: iv).

Most commentators writing on 'race'-related issues today agree that 'race' is not real nor a fact of nature. There are no biological differences that support the notion of distinctly different 'races'. Bhabha (1994) argues, in much the same way that Butler does about gender, that cultural engagement is performative and constructed through the binaries of black/white. 'Race' then is an ideological construct, not an empirical social category, and has no meaning outside of racist discourse (Bowling & Phillips, 2002; Britton, 2000; Calverley *et al.*, 2006; Fields, 1990; Gilroy, 1987/2002; Hall, 1989; Jefferson, 1992; see also Chapters 1 and 2).

Despite this, it has been suggested that 'race' should be retained as an analytical category, not because of any biological absolute, but because it 'refers investigation to the power that collective identities acquire by means of their roots in tradition' (Gilroy, 1987: 247). This potentially creates tension between theory and practice. As long as racism exists then discussions of 'race' issues are necessary. Yet, at the same time, discourses on 'race', as if it has meaning, help create racism (Hall, 1989). It is because of the linguistic meanings given to their 'racial' and gendered status that minority ethnic women who have contact with the criminal justice system experience an amplification of discrimination, based on supposed 'natural' gender and racial hierarchies.

Intersectionality and the Case of Foreign National Women

Intersectionality seeks to provide a tool for analysing the ways in which gender, race, class, and all other forms of identity and distinction, in different contexts, produce situations in which people become vulnerable to discrimination. Rather than viewing the exercise of power as operating in distinct and separate ways – in relation to gender, 'race', or class, etc. – it is seen as operating across all of these distinctions. Power is regarded as cross-cutting and overlapping, operating relationally rather than distinctly. This then results in complex intersections which cause the amplification of discrimination and disempowerment experienced by minority ethnic women in the criminal justice system (Bosworth, 1999; Burgess-Proctor, 2006).

Crenshaw (1989) coined the phrase intersectionality for a set of ideas that increasingly recognized the limiting nature of theories and politics that marginalized minority ethnic women. It was the intersectional identity of minority ethnic women that, Crenshaw argued, led to such neglect within both feminist and anti-racist work. She went on to suggest that feminist efforts to politicize the experiences of women, and anti-racist efforts to politicize minority ethnic groups, were made 'as though the issues and experiences they each detail occur on mutually exclusive terrains' (1991: 1242). Crenshaw's concern about this mirrors the situation in much criminological work on minority ethnic women. In contrast, intersectionality encourages us to account for the multiple elements of identity when considering how the social world is constructed.

In attempting to more adequately understand minority ethnic women's experience of the criminal justice system, these theoretical approaches can be utilized to examine particular issues. For example, the large numbers of foreign national women in prison highlights how power 'inscribes itself onto the body and space of its Others' (Slemon, 1991: 3). Using the concept of intersectionality the case of foreign national women and the criminal justice system will briefly be considered.

Globalization and the uneven distribution of power across national and international systems are of particular interest to post-colonial theories. These types of issues are also relevant to the one in five foreign national women who make up the women's prison population in England and Wales (Ministry of Justice, 2007b). Foreign national women account for the largest proportionate rise in the prison population in the last 5 years. They also serve long sentences. Almost three-quarters of women foreign nationals in prison are serving sentences of more than 4 years, compared to a third of British national women, 63 per cent of foreign national men, and half of UK national men (Allen et al., 2003; see also Bhui in this volume).

The global drug trade has in recent years had an obvious impact on the women's prison population. At the beginning of the 1990s there were a significant number of Nigerian women sentenced for drug offences. But in the past decade Jamaican women have become the largest single group of foreign national prisoners (Prison Reform Trust, 2004). Ninety-six per cent of sentenced Jamaican women were in prison for drug offences of which 90 per cent were first-time offenders. Most are single parents in their mid-thirties with three or four dependent children. A declining economic situation and high levels of poverty have been highlighted as important factors for why women become drug couriers. In the mid-1990s a quarter of Jamaicans were living on less than 2 US dollars a day. There is also evidence to suggest that coercion, violence, abusive, and exploitative relationships, form the backdrop to becoming drug couriers (Allen et al., 2003).

Given this background, of long prison sentences, being held in a foreign country, few visits (if any) from friends and family, along with concerns about what is happening at home, it is unsurprising that the Chief Inspector of Prisons found that women foreign nationals had the highest measures of distress amongst the various prison groupings (HMIP, 2006). Their traumatic and distressing experiences highlight that it is only through the consideration of the uneven distribution of global power, imperialism, sexual and economic exploitation, displacement, and marginality that greater understanding can be reached.

Conclusions

In considering minority ethnic women in the criminal justice system, it is clear that methodologies for research, theoretical developments, and calls for change must be sensitive to all sites of power. The ways in which power is enacted on one site – say in regards to gender – will also have an affect on other areas, such as 'race', class, sexuality, disability, etc. Putting intersectionality at the centre of analysis helps in avoiding essentialism, without ignoring the specificity of the body. It recognizes that 'power and resistance rests, at least in part, on identity' (Bosworth & Carrabine, 2001: 503). By utilizing intersectionality as a mode of analysis, whole new ways of exploring minority ethnic women's experience of the criminal justice apparatus open up. The role of globalization, identity, discourse, locality, and otherness are just some of the possible approaches to the subject. Furthermore, focusing on minority ethnic women shatters the binary nature of much criminological theory and research, on which the criminal justice practice is based. Most research, theory and practice is reliant upon the binaries associated with men/women and black/white but are thrown into disarray when the binaries collide into 'minority ethnic women', or even more confusingly into 'dual heritage/mixed race women' (Garland *et al.*, 2006). Suddenly the neat categorizations on which these ideas are based fall away and their meaningless is exposed. It is not that such research does not or cannot provide usable data or knowledge. Rather, the problem is that being based on erroneous ontological and epistemological presuppositions, it is embroiled in contradictions and is inherently partial or one-sided.

In moving criminological theory and criminal justice practice forward, we need to get beyond simply looking for overt forms of discrimination or relying on official monitoring statistics to inform debate (Gelsthorpe, 1992). Instead, the processes and constructions of 'race', 'gender', and the binary notions of 'otherness' should inform how we explore and examine the issue. Recognizing the political aspects of this work is crucial if real change is to be achieved. Furthermore, without analysis, change may be ill-founded and counter-productive, based less on real understanding and more on generalized versions of experience. Analysis is necessary in order to challenge some of the most ingrained and entrenched views about 'race' and 'women'. We should, as Weedon (1997) states, think in terms of transforming the social relations of knowledge production as well as the types of knowledge produced. However, the issue is further complicated by the strategic need to claim racial, gendered, sexual, and class identities as meaningful in specific ways. We should not deny the existence of the structures of domination within the criminal justice system but recognize that 'race' and gender have resonance because racist and sexist discourses still shape our experiences.

Within criminology both 'race' and 'gender' have attracted significant attention. However, that attention has largely been directed at minority ethnic men and white women. What has been missing from these analyses is an investigation of the various intersections relevant in the construction of 'crime', 'criminals', 'victims', and 'justice'; within which 'race' and gender, amongst other areas of identity, are all relevant (Gelstorpe, 2006). It is nonsensical to deny that those currently defined as 'minority ethnic women' face specific and real discrimination within the contemporary criminal justice system. Minority ethnic women experience harassment, abusive, and unequal treatment within the criminal justice process which is amplified because of the combination of 'race', gender, and class identities (Bowling & Phillips, 2002; Chigwada-Bailey, 2003; Devlin, 1998).

If we start to deconstruct the negative meanings given to these terms we can begin to challenge the powerful structures that shape the minority ethnic women's experience of the criminal justice process. Intersectionality provides us with the opportunity to recognize and understand the various sites of domination. Post-colonialism and feminism names a politics and philosophy of activism that contests the disparities found in society and each seeks to change the way people think and behave in order to produce more just and equitable relations between different peoples. Adopting these approaches can provide a significant step forward in criminological thinking and criminal justice practice on issues relating to all aspects of social identity.

Summary

This chapter explores minority ethnic women's experiences of the criminal justice system. There is significant evidence to suggest that minority ethnic women experience an amplified version of discrimination at every stage of the criminal justice process. Nonetheless, this issue has not been adequately examined in empirical research or criminological theory. It is therefore suggested that in order

(Continued)

(Continued)

to move understanding forward, the concept of intersectionality should be used as this encourages recognition of different forms of oppression and how they link with each other to intensify discriminatory experiences. There are, however, a number of definitional problems in discussing minority ethnic women. Use of the terms 'gender' and 'race' frequently leads to discussions about women or minority ethnic groups, rather than women who are also members of minority groups. Discussions of 'race' tend to focus on minority ethnic men; and when we consider 'women', the focus is generally on white women. This results in minority ethnic women having their racial experiences conceived of through minority ethnic men, and their gender experiences conceived through white women. This is despite minority ethnic women accounting for disproportionate numbers in the criminal justice system, particularly in relation to imprisonment. In 2006, minority ethnic groups made up 28 per cent of the female prison population of which, black prisoners comprised 20 per cent. The women's prison population is particularly skewed because of the high levels of foreign national women, many of whom are serving long sentences for drug importation. However, even excluding foreign nationals, the proportion of black women serving sentences for drug offences (46 per cent) was still higher than that of white females (26 per cent) and also higher than black males (18 per cent).

Of the somewhat limited research that exists on minority ethnic women, it appears that once caught up in the criminal justice system assumptions about femininity and 'race' result in discriminatory treatment – whether they are victims, offenders, or indeed criminal justice workers. To more fully develop criminological research, policy, and practice a more inclusive theoretical standpoint is required. This would recognize that the interaction of different forms of oppression can lead to the amplification of discrimination at different stages in the criminal justice process.

Intersectionality seeks to provide a tool for analysing the ways in which gender, race, class, and all other forms of identity and distinction, in different contexts, produce situations in which people become vulnerable to discrimination. Rather than viewing the exercise of power as operating in distinct and separate ways it is seen as operating across all of these distinctions. This results in the complex intersections which cause the amplification of discrimination and disempowerment which minority ethnic women in the criminal justice system experience. Using intersectionality opens up new ways of exploring these experiences. For example, the role of globalization, identity, discourse, locality, and otherness can be used to consider the experiences of foreign national women in prison. In moving criminological theory and criminal justice practice forward, we need to get beyond simply looking for overt forms of discrimination or relying on official monitoring statistics to inform debate. Instead, the processes and constructions of 'race', 'gender', and the notion of 'otherness' should inform how we explore and examine this issue.

Key Texts

Burgess-Proctor, A. (2006) 'Intersections of race, class, gender, and crime: future directions for feminist criminology'. *Feminist Criminology*. 1 (1) 27–47.

Gelsthorpe, L. (2006) 'The experience of female minority ethnic offenders: the other 'other'. In: S. Lewis, P. Raynor, D. Smith and A. Wardak (eds) *Race and Probation*. Cullompton: Willan.

Kennedy, H. (1993) *Eve Was Framed: Women and British Justice*. Vintage: London.

References

Agozino, B. (1997) *Black Women and the Criminal Justice System*. Aldershot: Ashgate.

Allen, R., Levenson, J. and Garside, R. (2003) *A Bitter Pill to Swallow: The Sentencing of Foreign National Drug Couriers*. London: Rethinking Crime and Punishment.

Ashcroft, B., Griffiths, G. and Tiffin, H. (2006) *The Post-Colonial Studies Reader*. London: Routledge.

Bhabha, H.K. (1994) *The Location of Culture*. London: Routledge.

Bhui, H.S. and Fossi, J. (2007) 'The experience of black and minority ethnic prison staff', in J. Bennett A. Wahidin and B. Crewe, *Prison Staff*. Willan Publishers.

Bosworth, M. (1999) *Engendering Resistance: Agency and Power in Women's Prisons*. Aldershot: Dartmouth Publishing.

Bosworth, M. and Carrabine, E. (2001) 'Reassessing resistance', *Punishment and Society* 3 (4), 501–15.

Bowling, B. and Phillips, C. (2002) *Racism, Crime and Justice*. Harlow: Pearsons.

Braithwaite, J. (2003) 'What's wrong with the sociology of punishment?' *Theoretical Criminology*. 7 (1), 5–28.

Britton, N.J. (2000) *Black Justice? Race, Criminal Justice and Identity*. Stoke on Trent: Trentham.

Burgess-Proctor, A. (2006) 'Intersections of race, class, gender, and crime: future directions for feminist criminology'. *Feminist Criminology* 1 (1), 27–47.

Butler, J. (1990) *Gender Trouble*. London: Routledge.

Calverley, A., Kaur, G. and Sadeghi, S. (2006) 'Introduction: race, crime and community penalities'. In: S. Lewis, P. Raynor, D. Smith and A. Wardak (eds) *Race and Probation*. Cullompton: Willan.

Carlen, P. (1983) *Women's Imprisonment*. London: Routledge and Kegan Paul.

Carlen, P. (1997) 'Women in the criminal justice system.' In: P. Haralambos (ed.) *Developments in Sociology*. Ormskirk: Causeway Press.

Cheliotis, L.K. and Liebling, A. (2006) 'Race matters in british prisons: *Towards a research agenda'*. *British Journal of Criminology* 46 (2), 286–317.

Chigwada-Bailey, R. (2003) *Black Women's Experiences of Criminal Justice*. Winchester: Waterside Press.

Connell, R.W. (1995) *Masculinities*. California: University of California Press.

Crenshaw, K.W. (1989) 'Demarginalizing the intersection of race and sex: A black feminist critique of antidiscrimination doctrine, feminist theory and antiracist politics'. *The University of Chicago Legal Forum*, pp. 139–67.

Crenshaw, K.W. (1991). 'Mapping the margins: intersectionality, identity politics, and violence against women of color.' *Stanford Law Review* 43 (6), pp. 1241–99.

Delgado, R. and Stefancic, J. (1997) *Critical White Studies: Looking Behind the Mirror*. Philadelphia: Temple UP.

Denney, D. (1992) *Racism and Anti-Racism in Probation*. London: Routledge.

Devlin, A. (1998) *Invisible Women*. Winchester: Waterside Press.

Fine, M., Weis, L., Powell, L.C. and Wong, L.M. (1997) *Off White: Readings on Race, Power, and Society*. New York: Routledge.

Fields, B.J. (1990) 'Slavery, race and ideology in the United States of America'. *New Left Review* 181, pp. 95–118.

Garland, J. Spalek, B. and Chakraborti, N. (2006) Hearing lost voices: issues in researching 'Hidden' minority ethnic communities'. *British Journal of Criminology* 46 (3), 423–37.

Gelsthorpe, L. (1992) *Minority Ethnic Groups in the Criminal Justice System*. Cambridge: University of Cambridge.

Gelsthorpe, L. (2006) 'The experience of female minority ethnic offenders: the other 'other'. In: S. Lewis, P. Raynor, D. Smith and A. Wardak (eds) *Race and Probation*. Cullompton: Willan.

Gibson, M. (2002) *Born to Crime: Cesare Lombroso and the Origins of Biological Criminology*. Westport: Praeger Publishers.

Gilroy, P. (1987/2002) *There Ain't No Black in the Union Jack*. London: Unwin.

Green, P. and Ward, T. (2004) *State Crime: Governments, Violence and Corruption*. London: Pluto Press.

Hall, S. (1980) 'Race, articulation and societies structured in dominance', in UNESCO *Sociological Theories: Race and Colonialism*. Paris: UNESCO.

Hall, S. (1989) 'New ethnicities'. In: K. Mercer (ed.) *Black Film, British Cinema*. London: ICA.

HM Inspector of Prisons (2005) *Parallel Worlds: A Thematic Review of Race Relations in Prisons*. London: Home Office.

HM Inspector of Prisons (2006) *Foreign National Prisoners: A Thematic Review*. London: Home Office.

Home Office (2004) *Statistics on Women and the Criminal Justice System 2003*. London: Home Office.

hooks, B. (1982) *Ain't I a Woman: Black Women and Feminism*. London: Pluto Press.

hooks, B. (1991) *Yearning: Race, Gender and Cultural Politics*. Boston: South End Press.

Jefferson, T. (1992) *The Racism of Criminalization: Policing and the Reproduction of the Criminal Other*. in L. Gelsthorpe (ed.) *Minority Ethnic Groups in the Criminal Justice System*. Cambridge: University of Cambridge.

Kimmel, M.S., Hearn, J. and Connell, R.W. (2005) *Handbook of Studies on Men and Masculinities*. California: Sage.

Lombroso, C. and Ferrero, W. (1895) *The Female Offender*. NY: Appleton.

Ministry of Justice (2007a) *Population in Custody, England and Wales*. London: Ministry of Justice.

Ministry of Justice (2007b) *Statistics on Race and the Criminal Justice System – 2006*. London: Ministry of Justice.

Nacro (1991) *Black People's Experience of Criminal Justice*. London: Nacro.

Prison Reform Trust (2004) *The Plight of Foreign National Prisoners in England and Wales*. London: Prison Reform Trust.

Rice, M. (1990) 'Challenging orthodoxies in feminist theory: a black feminist critique'. in: L. Gelsthorpe and A. Morris (eds), *Feminist Perspectives in Criminology*. Milton Keynes: Open University Press.

Rusche, G. and Kirchheimer, O. (1969) *Punishment and Social Structure*. New York: Columbia University Press.

Shilling, C. (2003) *The Body and Social Control*. London: Sage.

Shilling, C. (2005) *The Body in Culture, Technology and Society*. London: Sage.

Slemon, S. (1991) 'Modernism's last post' in I. Adam and H. Tiffin (eds) *Past the Last Post: Theorizing Post-Colonialism and Post-Modernism*. Hemel Hempstead: Harvester Wheatsheaf.

Spivak, G.C. (1986) 'Three women's texts and a critique of imperialism' in H.L. Gates (ed.) *'Race', Writing, and Difference*. Chicago: University of Chicago Press.

Spivak, G. (1987) *In Other Worlds: Essays in Cultural Politics*. London: Methuen.

Weedon, C. (1997) *Feminist Practice and Poststructuralist Theory*. Oxford: Blackwells.

Weedon, C. (2004) *Identity and Culture: Narratives of Difference and Belonging*. Maidenhead: Open University Press.

Winant, H. (2000), 'The theoretical status of the concept of race'. in: L. Back, and J. Solomos (eds) *Theories of Race and Racism: A Reader*. London: Routledge.

Worrall, A. (1981) 'Out of place: the female offender in court'. *Probation Journal*, 28, 90–3.

EIGHT

Refugees, Asylum Seekers, and Criminal Justice

Claire Cooper

Introduction

Since the British Labour Government came to power in 1997, immigration has become one of its top priorities, driven by public concern about increasing levels of immigration, which has itself been fuelled by often alarmist headlines in the national and local press. Over the last two decades, the numbers of people arriving in, and leaving, the UK has risen sharply. Migration into the UK increased from 265,000 in 1993 to 513,000 in 2002 and out-migration increased from 266,000 in 1993 to 359,000 in 2002 (Office for National Statistics, 2005). In 2006, an estimated 191,000 more people entered than left the UK (Office for National Statistics, 2007). Migrants come in many forms – European Union and European Economic Area (EEA) nationals; tourists, students, diplomats and workers – but it was the rising numbers of claims for asylum in the late 1990s which led to significant media and public attention, much of it negative. In 2003, polls showed that 9 out of 10 voters believed the number of asylum seekers in the UK was a serious problem (Sriskandarajah & Hopwood Road, 2005).

Media reports of overwhelming numbers of refugees and asylum seekers entering the country and placing a burden on public services[1], exacerbated by concerns about global terrorism and national security, has created the sense that they are a threat to the UK, resulting in refugees and asylum

---

[1] http://www.thesun.co.uk/article/0,,2-2002411352,00.html; http://www.dailymail.co.uk/pages/live/articles/health/thehealthnews.html?in_article_id=105119&in_page_id=1797; http://www.mirror.co.uk/news/columnists/carroll/tm_method=full%26objectid=17532512%26siteid=89520-name_page.html

seekers being vulnerable to racial and religious harassment and discrimination. There have been reports of murders and horrific attacks on refugees and asylum seekers[2], of community tensions arising from the dispersal of asylum seekers across the country (Hewitt, 2002), and of the poor treatment and experiences of those detained in immigration removal centres (IRCs) and prisons[3].

Increasing globalization, political and social upheavals across the world and changing patterns of migration have resulted in more refugees and asylum seekers in the UK. The greater ethnic diversity of the population has brought new challenges for society and the criminal justice system. As more diverse groups settle in the UK, whether as migrant workers or those seeking asylum, concepts of racism and race relations have become broader and increasingly complex, stretching beyond the black–white dichotomy (see Smith's Chapter 1 in this volume). Criminological debates in the 1970s and 1980s centred around the issue of 'black criminality' – of whether black people were more likely to offend than white people or whether, in fact, they were treated unfairly, resulting in their disproportionate numbers in the criminal justice system. Although there is now a general recognition that it is impossible to determine 'ethnic differences' in offending in any conclusive way (Bowling & Phillips, 2002), much of the immigration debate in the UK has represented refugees and asylum seekers as 'criminals', and 'harmful to the British people' (Malloch & Stanley, 2005: 55). In the seminal inquiry into the murder of Stephen Lawrence in 1993, Macpherson (1999) warned of the dangers of stereotyping black communities as criminal. However, refugees and asylum seekers appear to have been subjected to a similar labelling process: there seems to have been some displacement of racist attitudes to target these groups, which is unlikely to have been tolerated if directed towards other minority communities. In what is arguably a linked development, although issues relating to refugees and asylum seekers do not technically concern the criminal justice system unless a criminal offence has been committed, this distinction is increasingly blurred by the involvement of criminal justice agencies (mainly the police and prison services) in immigration procedures such as detention and removal.

This chapter examines the issues facing refugees and asylum seekers in contact with the criminal justice system. It considers how criminal justice agencies have sought to understand and address their particular needs and suggests ways of improving policy and practice. But first it is important to set the context and explore the wider issues affecting refugees and asylum seekers in the UK.

---

[2]For example, the murders of Firsat Yildiz in Glasgow (August 2001), Payman Bahmani in Sunderland (August 2002), and Kalan Karim in Swansea (September 2004).

[3]See reports of HM Chief Inspector of Prisons and Prisons and Probation Ombudsman, and chapter 10 in this volume on foreign national offenders.

Refugees and Asylum Seekers in the UK

As signatory to the 1951 United Nations Convention on the Status of Refugees, the UK has a duty to provide protection for persons who flee their country because of persecution. The convention defines refugees as those fleeing across national borders 'owing to a well-founded fear of being persecuted for reasons of race, religion, nationality, membership of a particular social group or political opinion'. Although the term 'asylum seeker' is not defined, it refers to those people who have fled their homeland, applied for refugee status in another country, and are awaiting a decision on their application for asylum. The Refugee Convention makes it clear that *anyone* has the right to apply for asylum in the UK and to remain here until their application has been assessed; therefore, a person cannot be an 'illegal' or 'bogus' asylum seeker (Refugee Council, 2006a).

Whilst the UK has seen rising levels of immigration, the number of applications for asylum has actually been decreasing in years. In the mid-1990s, the number of applications ranged between 20,000 and 40,000 per year but rose to a peak of 84,130 in 2002 (Sriskandarajah & Hopwood Road, 2005: 5). Since then, numbers have been falling and in 2005, 25,710 applications for asylum were made – a fall of 24 per cent compared to 2004 (Heath *et al.*, 2006). In 2006, there was a further drop to 23,610 applications. The highest numbers of applicants came from Eritrea, Afghanistan, Iran, China, and Somalia (Bennett *et al.*, 2007).

The growing numbers of applications in the late 1990s and mounting public hostility resulted in successive government white papers and legislation to reduce the number of applications, speed up the asylum process, and increase removals of failed asylum seekers from the country. Since 1993, there have been six changes to the law on asylum. Key policy initiatives included the creation of the National Asylum Support Service (NASS), which provides asylum seekers with a weekly allowance and/or accommodation[4]; the introduction of a national dispersal policy[5]; no longer allowing asylum seekers to work until they received a positive decision on their asylum application[6]; and the expansion of detention places and wider powers of removal[7]. These are backed by the so-called 'Tipping Point' target to remove more failed asylum seekers every month than those applying to live in Britain [8].

Many of these initiatives have been much criticized by campaigning organizations. For example, the restriction on employment means that those

---

[4]Part VI, Immigration and Asylum Act 1999.

[5]Part VI, Immigration and Asylum Act 1999.

[6]This policy did not require legislation.

[7]Part 4, Nationality, Immigration and Asylum Act 2002 (although the power to detain was first established in the Immigration Act 1971).

[8]See http://www.ind.homeoffice.gov.uk/sitecontent/documents/aboutus/Reports/public performancetarget/.

asylum seekers who do not apply or are ineligible for NASS support are frequently left destitute. There is also evidence that the dispersal policy has often resulted in asylum seekers being housed in poor-quality accommodation, living in poverty and experiencing poor health and hunger (Refugee Council, 2006b). About 37,000 asylum seekers were being supported in dispersal accommodation in the third quarter of 2007 (Home Office, 2007). Glasgow City, Leeds, Birmingham, Manchester, and Newcastle – some of the most deprived local authorities in the country – had the highest numbers of asylum seekers. Dispersal guidelines for local authorities stress that, in choosing an area, caseworkers should ensure there is a 'ready supply of accommodation' (NASS, 2004: 1) and efforts made to house asylum seekers near people from a similar culture and language and with a community structure which can support them. However, unpublished research for the Home Office warned that asylum seekers had been dispersed to 'highly volatile environments' where they were subject to hostility and prejudice. Researchers argued that the 'procurement of housing in the poorest areas polarises entrenched views held by the host community against the incomers' (reported by Morris, 2007).

It is therefore not surprising that psychological distress appears to be a key issue for refugees and asylum seekers. The considerable length of time it takes to process asylum applications whilst living on an extremely low income, coupled in many cases with past traumatic experiences and social isolation, results in refugees and asylum seekers being more likely to experience poor mental health (Athwal, 2006; Burnett & Peel, 2001). Frequently, hostile media headlines also serve to either engender or perpetuate negative feelings towards those seeking asylum. A report on asylum attitudes (Coe *et al.*, 2005) found that levels of self-reported racial prejudice correlate more closely with the number of media articles than with immigration figures. Similarly, research (ICAR, 2004) showed clear evidence of negative, unbalanced, and inaccurate reporting, which was likely to promote fear and tension within communities, notwithstanding the fact that there has been an overall improvement in press coverage of asylum since the Press Complaints Commission published a guidance note for journalists in 2003 (ICAR, 2007).

Media reports often suggest that the country is 'swamped' with asylum seekers who have entered the UK illegally and are involved in criminal activity[9]. The following section explores this claim, looks at refugee and asylum seeker involvement with the criminal justice system, and at how agencies are responding to their needs.

---

[9]http://www.dailymail.co.uk/pages/live/articles/news/news.html?in_article_id=112979&in_page_id=1770; http://www.thesun.co.uk/article/0,,2001340002-2003031435,00.html; http://www.telegraph.co.uk/news/main.jhtml?xml=/news/2006/04/03/nimm03.xml; http://www.timesonline.co.uk/tol/news/uk/article811080.ece

Refugees and Asylum Seekers and the Criminal Justice System

Refugees, Asylum Seekers, and Offending

The association between refugees, asylum seekers, and crime[10] has been the subject of much media and public attention. Asylum seekers have been implicated in 'gang warfare', drug trafficking, kidnapping, corruption, and people trafficking (Malloch & Stanley, 2005: 57). Recent reports in the press suggest that research by the Metropolitan Police highlights an increase in young people with significant post-traumatic stress resulting from witnessing and being involved in significant violent situations prior to arrival in the UK, which, in turn, has led to their involvement in gangs[11]. However, despite much speculation about the disproportionate involvement of refugees and asylum seekers in criminal activity, there is no data or research available to either confirm or deny this. Only the Prison Service collects information on the nationality of the offenders they come into contact with, but it does not record the number of failed asylum seekers or those who seek asylum while in its establishments. No other criminal justice agency collects any nationality data and, importantly, none collects information on immigration status. In addition, official crime data only captures those crimes reported to, and recorded by, the police – it does not provide a complete picture of levels of crime in the UK, which the British Crime Survey estimated to be around 10.9 million in 2004–05 (Walker *et al.*, 2006). This, compounded by a lack of data on convictions of refugees and asylum seekers, makes it impossible to know what proportion of crimes is committed by them. While a Public Accounts Committee report on returning failed asylum applicants (House of Commons Committee of Public Accounts, 2006) contained some data, showing that failed asylum seekers were convicted of 203 offences in 2004–05, and 168 in 2005–06, it only referred to deportations and convictions. It did not, for example, capture those who were committing offences but whose application for asylum was ongoing.

Living in some of the most deprived local authorities, with little or no support networks or educational and employment opportunities, places refugees and asylum seekers in a vulnerable position. Solomon (2006) argues that asylum seekers are at greater risk of committing acquisitive offences because of their experiences of poverty, marginalization, and personal insecurity. Delays in processing applications for support have often left people without money or housing and the number of destitute asylum seekers is thought to be growing (Joint Committee on Human Rights, 2007). Evidence suggests that some

---

[10]This chapter focuses on crime either committed by or against refugees and asylum seekers once they arrive in the UK, it does not discuss serious and organized transnational crime. For information on organised crime, see http://www.soca.gov.uk/

[11]The Metropolitan Police report was unavailable at the time of writing. See http://news.bbc.co.uk/1/hi/england/london/6612817.stm and http://www.amren.com/mtnews/archives/2007/05/immigrants_from.php

asylum seekers feel they are forced to work illegally or to commit minor offences to get a bed for the night, albeit in a cell (Refugee Action, 2006):

I was so hungry that I went into a police station and asked them if I could spend a night in a cell. They said no as I had not done anything wrong. I was so desperate that on the way out I deliberately smashed a police car headlight so that they would have to arrest me. I spend a week in jail. (Man from Zimbabwe, ibid. 2006: 80)

The Criminalization of Refugees and Asylum Seekers

Despite a lack of robust and meaningful data to support the claims, suggestions of links between refugees and asylum seekers and crime – and even terrorism – as well as references to 'illegal' and 'bogus' asylum seekers in the press have effectively led to their 'criminalization'. Participants in research by the Refugee Council (Rudiger, 2007) frequently cited feelings of criminalization and stigmatization:

You expect freedom but you are tagged like a criminal, told you are illegal but you're not, you have registered as an asylum seeker, you are not bogus. (ibid. 2007:27)

The term refugee is nearly equated with the term criminal. ... There's some stigma that's attached to the term refugee, which criminalizes a huge segment of the population. (ibid. 2007:27)

The language used by government has often fuelled this criminalization. For example, the 1971 Immigration Act uses the words 'detention' and 'imprisonment' interchangeably to refer to people sentenced for criminal offences. The 1998 White Paper – *Faster, Fairer and Firmer* – also talks of 'immigration offenders', implying that asylum seekers and other immigrants are breaking laws. Using the words 'detention' and 'offenders' to refer to two different things – punishment of criminals and immigration control – has established a link between the two (Malmberg, 2004). In addition, comparative research across seven nations found that the more restrictive a nation's immigration policy the greater the incarceration rates of foreigners and the greater the public's belief that immigrants increase crime rates in their country (Lynch & Simon, 1999). The use of detention as well as electronic monitoring[12] – both of which have only been used previously in criminal cases – has further strengthened the association between refugees and asylum seekers and criminality. Banks (2008) argues that policies on crime control and on asylum have much in common, with the emphasis being on 'retribution and deterrence' and on 'identifying and managing unruly groups'. The active construction of the image of 'deviant' asylum seekers serves as the justification

---

[12]Section 36, Asylum and Immigration (Treatment of Claimants, etc.) Act 2004.

for increasingly punitive measures and takes the emphasis away from a focus on protection to one of control and containment.

The increased use of detention to aid the faster processing of asylum seekers (Home Office, 2005a) has been fiercely criticized by those who feel that imprisoning individuals who have not been tried before a court for a criminal offence is unjustifiable (United for Intercultural Action, n.d.). On 29 September 2007, there were 1,625 detainees who had claimed asylum at some stage in the UK (Home Office, 2007); 1,580 were being held at IRCs and 50 at Short Term Holding Facilities[13].

Detention is an important area into which the Prison Service is being drawn, blurring the boundaries between asylum and immigration and criminality. Although the 'routine practice of holding asylum seekers in prison who have not committed a criminal offence ended at the beginning of 2002' (*Hansard*, volume 417, column 605w, January 30, 2004), prison accommodation has been used for 'reasons of security and control' such as following disturbances in IRCs[14]. In addition, the holding of foreign national former prisoners either across the detention estate or in prisons used as IRCs is an issue that has been frequently highlighted by campaigners and other key organizations (Prison Reform Trust, 2004; Her Majesty's Chief Inspector of Prisons, 2007a). The revelation in April 2006 that 1,023 foreign nationals convicted of serious crimes, who should have been considered for deportation, had been freed from prison resulted in individuals being returned to closed prisons, including some British citizens. Prisoners were held in prisons and IRCs well beyond their sentence end date whilst the Border and Immigration Agency (BIA, which was known until 2 April 2007 as the Immigration and Nationality Directorate) made decisions about what action should be taken[15] (Her Majesty's Chief Inspector of Prisons, 2007b). However, as reliable statistics on those detained in prison establishments under sole Immigration Act powers are not available (Home Office, 2006), it is impossible to ascertain just how many refugees or asylum seekers this affects.

Electronic monitoring has been used as an alternative to detention. On 31 December 2005, 71 asylum claimants were wearing an electronic tag and funding had been allocated for 200 new inductions in 2005–06, increasing to 800 in 2006–07. Although no data is available on who is subject to electronic monitoring, an assessment of a tagging exercise carried out in Croydon and Liverpool in December 2005 found a 'disproportionate negative impact on

---

[13] Data on asylum detainees only provides a snapshot of numbers on that particular day – it does not capture how long those people remain in detention or give a complete picture of numbers throughout the year.

[14] This was the case following the fire at Yarl's Wood removal centre in 2002 and in 2004, following riots at Harmondsworth.

[15] Her Majesty's Inspectorate of Prisons found that, in their foreign nationals follow-up investigation, 55% of their interviewees were detained following completion of a custodial sentence (Her Majesty's Chief Inspector of Prisons, 2007b: 10).

Zimbabwean and Somali applicants' (IND, 2007). Critics have argued that electronic monitoring, like detention, is simply another means of criminalizing people who have committed no crime and is a disproportionate response to the risk of asylum seekers failing to report to the BIA (Beynon, 2004).

Refugees and Asylum Seekers as Victims

Immigration status is not recorded in official crime statistics, including those published under Section 95 of the Criminal Justice Act 1991 on race and the criminal justice system (Ministry of Justice, 2008), and annual Crown Prosecution Service (CPS) data on racist incidents (CPS, 2007). While it is impossible to obtain an accurate picture of the extent to which refugees and asylum seekers are victims, they undoubtedly experience significant economic, social and psychological vulnerability. Research for the Mayor of London found that low-level harassment and abuse was a 'persistent problem of significant but unmeasured dimensions' (ICAR, 2004: 8). Refugee Action research also reported that 83 per cent of female refugees and asylum seekers said they did not go out at night because they feared abuse and harassment (Refugee Action, 2002, cited in Refugee Council, 2006b).

The Commission for Racial Equality's monitoring of local racial tensions shows that hostility towards, and attacks on, refugees and asylum seekers occur regularly, particularly in deprived neighbourhoods where there is competition for scarce resources. Far right political parties have capitalized on these tensions and, during the May 2006 local elections, exploited this for electoral gains (CRE memorandum to the Joint Committee on Human Rights, 2007). Refugees and asylum seekers remain unlikely to report racist or other offences committed against them, possibly owing to fear of deportation or of jeopardizing their asylum application, which leaves them vulnerable to victimization and exploitation. Police involvement in immigration enforcement – by assisting in the removal of failed asylum seekers – may also reduce the willingness of refugees and asylum seekers to come forward. There have been horrific media reports of dawn raids on families, with accusations of the use of heavy-handed tactics[16]. None more so than the case of Joy Gardner – a Jamaican woman who died in 1993 following a struggle with police who arrived at her home in London to deport her. During the struggle, Joy was gagged with 13 feet of tape and bound with a leather belt – she died 4 days later[17]. The inherent conflict between police assistance in these operations and their community support role may well result in the loss of trust and confidence amongst asylum-seeking communities and their subsequent reluctance to report crime. It is also likely

---

[16]See http://news.bbc.co.uk/1/hi/scotland/4293600.stm and http://news.bbc.co.uk/1/hi/england/2150645.stm

[17]http://news.bbc.co.uk/1/hi/uk/279922.stm. Also see the case of Ghanaian Joseph Crentsil who fell to his death following a raid by immigration and police officers, http://www.irr.org.uk/2003/march/ak000007.html

that such reports will have an impact on the perceptions and confidence of other minority ethnic communities in the state and in criminal justice agencies in particular.

As well as racial violence, their experiences of deprivation and social exclusion mean that refugees and asylum seekers are also vulnerable to victimization. The Association of Chief Police Officers (ACPO) has pointed out that they may be forced to pay 'protection money' to criminal gangs within their own communities; women may be exploited for the sex trade; and others may work for a minimal wage for gang masters. The majority of these crimes do not appear in crime statistics (ACPO, 2001).

The Response of Criminal Justice Agencies

Their community safety role, as well as their involvement in assisting the immigration service, means that the police service is *the* criminal justice agency that the majority of refugees and asylum seekers are most likely to come into contact with. ACPO has produced a guide for police forces on meeting the needs of refugees and asylum seekers (ACPO, 2001), highlighting the significant role that the service plays in the management of dispersed communities. Although some forces have undertaken training on refugee diversity issues and others have published welcome packs or leaflets (Clark, 2004), the most recent available evidence suggests that implementation of the guide is patchy (Hewitt, 2002)[18].

For those found guilty of offences, criminal justice agencies need an understanding of how their immigration status impacts on offending. For example, there may be a need to send money home or to pay traffickers (London Probation Area, 2006b). Insecurity of residency, lack of social networks, restrictions on access to benefits and work, discrimination and vulnerability to exploitation, and victimization are all issues that need to be considered. London Probation Area has undertaken work to ensure probation officers understand how immigration status impacts on offending behaviour. It offers a comprehensive training course for probation staff working with refugees and asylum seekers and has produced a 3-year strategy to provide 'equitable services to people of all nationalities who are subject to proceedings in the criminal justice system' (London Probation Area, 2006a). Similarly, Hampshire Probation Area published a practice manual (Hampshire Probation Area, 2004) containing guidance on the use of interpreters, assessment and report writing, and the importance of cultural understanding in community supervision. However, there is little mention of these communities in any

---

[18]At the time of writing, a review of the guide was being undertaken by the National Policing Improvement Agency and was to include an up-to-date assessment of its use by forces (S. Owens, 2007, pers. comm., 27 April)

national policy documents and strategies produced by the Probation Service or other criminal justice agencies. For example, the CPS received considerable praise for its policy on the prosecution of racist and religious crime (CPS, 2003a, b), which makes only a brief reference to refugees and asylum seekers in the context of defining a racial group. Any documentation that is available focuses on immigration enforcement issues, such as how to deal with those individuals working or remaining in the UK illegally[19], or considers the wider group of foreign nationals whose needs can be very different to those who have sought or are seeking asylum.

This lack of attention to the needs of refugees and asylum seekers is reinforced by little focus on outcomes for these groups in inspection regimes. Although all criminal justice inspectorates have undertaken thematic reviews or inspections on issues relating to race and diversity, little is reported on how criminal justice agencies are meeting the needs of, or treating, refugees and asylum seekers. The only inspectorate to have made any inroads in this area is Her Majesty's Inspectorate of Prisons, whose remit was extended by the Immigration and Asylum Act 1999 to include a statutory responsibility to inspect all IRCs and holding facilities on behalf of the BIA (e.g., see HM Chief Inspector of Prisons, 2006a, b, 2007b, and Chapter 10 in this book).

The Way Forward

The lack of data collection, monitoring, and research makes for a weak evidence base. However, given that official police recorded crime data only captures a fraction of crime in the UK, monitoring of immigration status by criminal justice agencies alone is not enough to gain a true picture of the extent to which refugees and asylum seekers are either perpetrators or victims of crime. Areas for future research should include qualitative studies of the nature and extent of refugee and asylum seeker involvement in the criminal justice system; their experiences of hate crime, victimization, and discrimination; the impact of dispersal on community and race relations; and evaluations of criminal justice agencies' responses to the needs of refugees and asylum seekers. Improvements in data and research, as well as in policies and procedures in criminal justice agencies, will only lead to better practice where practitioners are given appropriate training, support, and guidance. However, with the exception of the police service, none of the criminal justice agencies currently publishes specific national guidance on meeting the needs of refugees and asylum seekers, which in turn means there is no coordinated national approach. Whilst issues relating to refugees and asylum seekers will be of greater significance in parts of the country where these groups are most concentrated,

---

[19]See, for example, CPS legal guidance on Immigration offences and protocol (http://www.cps.gov.uk/legal/section12/chapter_j.html)

core guidance and training at a national level are vital, with scope to adapt them to local circumstances. Implementation in all areas will encourage consistency of service. The common national occupational standards for the justice sector on equality and diversity[20] could be developed further to specifically include issues of asylum and immigration and help ensure that refugees and asylum seekers do indeed receive the same level of treatment and service across the country.

Criminal justice inspectorates and other bodies responsible for overseeing the criminal justice system – such as Independent Monitoring Boards, Independent Custody Visitors, and police authorities – have a key role to play in ensuring that policy and practice relating to refugees and asylum seekers is adhered to on the ground. The Prisons Inspectorate has a statutory duty to inspect all IRCs and immigration-holding facilities, but none of the other inspectorates monitor how criminal justice agencies deal specifically with refugees and asylum seekers. In relation to detention, annual reports of Independent Monitoring Boards of IRCs make almost no reference to issues of race and diversity, other than to report the existence of a race relations policy, training, or committee. There is no real analysis of whether detainees are suffering any racial discrimination or being treated unfairly on the basis of their ethnic or national origin. Similarly, Independent Custody Visitors need to tackle the new challenges faced by the holding of immigration detainees in police custody by ensuring that visitors have the knowledge and understanding necessary to enable them to recognize and address the needs of this group.

Implementation of the Race Relations Act 1976

The Race Relations Act 1976, as amended by the Race Relations (Amendment) Act 2000, gives public authorities a general statutory duty to promote race equality. In carrying out their functions, public authorities must have due regard to the need to eliminate unlawful racial discrimination; and to promote equality of opportunity and good relations between people from different racial groups. To help meet the duty, certain listed public authorities must publish a race equality scheme setting out their arrangements for meeting the duty, including undertaking race equality impact assessments, monitoring policies for adverse impact, consultation on proposed policies, and training staff.

The race equality schemes of the Home Office (Home Office, 2005b; IND, 2005; Prison Service, 2005), CPS (CPS, 2005), and the former DCA[21] (Department for Constitutional Affairs, 2006) make very little reference to refugees and asylum seekers. Where they are mentioned, it is again primarily

---

[20]http://www.skillsforjustice.com/template01.asp?PageID=57 AA1 - Promote equality and value diversity and AA2 - Develop a culture and systems that promote equality and value diversity.

[21]In May 2007, the Ministry of Justice (MoJ) took over the responsibilities of the DCA and some responsibilities of the Home Office. At the time of writing, a MoJ Equality Scheme was being developed.

in relation to immigration control rather than any recognition that government departments and criminal justice agencies must ensure that refugees and asylum seekers do not suffer unlawful racial discrimination. This may be because an assumption is made that 'race' does not encompass migration status and nationality. Asylum issues must be conceptualized in terms of race relations in order for criminal justice agencies to meet their statutory duty. Implementation of the Race Relations Act will help to ensure that criminal justice agencies identify and address the specific needs of asylum seekers and refugees, and that the implications of policies and procedures have been thoroughly considered. Government departments and those criminal justice agencies required to publish race equality schemes – namely, police forces and authorities – should ensure that their schemes identify the issues affecting refugees and asylum seekers and take steps to address these.

Community safety and community relations are also areas where progress is needed. Currently it is only possible to estimate the extent to which refugees and asylum seekers are subject to racial harassment and abuse, and it is therefore difficult for agencies with an interest in community safety to construct responses to the problem. It is important that the probable under-reporting is taken into account when local Crime and Disorder Reduction Partnerships (CDRPs) develop their community safety strategies. Mechanisms are needed to enable third-party reporting of hate crime and for the concerns of refugees and asylum seekers to be built into local strategies. Increasing the range of available reporting methods and improving the recording and monitoring of hate crime should help the police service, and its community safety partners, through the CDRP, target areas where community tensions may develop and, in turn, gain the confidence of asylum seeking and refugee communities.

Finally, there are many issues relating to refugees and asylum seekers that have a direct effect on the criminal justice system, yet are outside its control. The dispersal and detention of asylum seekers and negative media reporting are probably the most significant. The dispersal of asylum seekers to particular parts of the country and unbalanced and emotive reports in the press can give rise to community prejudices and tensions which the police service must then deal with. Asylum is in this respect clearly a race relations issue. Similarly, increases in the number of immigration detainees place an additional pressure on police and prison custody. Partnership working is therefore important in the context of rapidly changing asylum and immigration policy, to establish mechanisms for working in partnership at a local level to improve information flow.

Conclusion

This chapter has highlighted the hostile and racialized nature of debates around asylum, immigration, and crime. Gaps in data, knowledge, and understanding make it impossible to obtain a clear picture of the nature and extent of refugees and asylum seekers' involvement in the criminal justice system, whether as offenders, victims, or witnesses. National policy on asylum and immigration, with the increased emphasis on detention and removal, has drawn criminal justice agencies into areas previously outside their scope. Despite the absence of such information, some criminal justice agencies at a local level have made efforts to meet the needs of refugees and asylum seekers and to promote anti-discriminatory practice. However, much more work is needed at a national level to ensure consistency of treatment and service across all criminal justice agencies throughout the country.

Refugees and asylum seekers remain one of the most vulnerable groups in society today – victimized because of their ethnicity and/or nationality and excluded from mainstream society. The focus of the criminal justice system since the Macpherson inquiry has been on improving trust and confidence amongst ethnic minority communities. The experiences of refugees and asylum seekers in the UK today suggest that there is still a long way to go before this aim is fully realized.

Summary

The arrival of refugees and asylum seekers to the UK over the last two decades has brought new challenges for the criminal justice system. Their experiences of deprivation, poverty, and poor housing in run-down areas, along with public concerns about global terrorism and national security, mean that these are socially isolated groups, frequently subject to racial harassment and discrimination. Hostile media reports have fuelled public fear and led to tensions within local communities, whilst references to 'illegal' and 'bogus' asylum seekers in public discourse have implied a relationship between refugees and asylum seekers and criminality, which is not based on evidence. In addition, the increasing involvement of criminal justice agencies in immigration procedures, such as detention and removal, means that the boundaries between immigration and the criminal justice system are gradually being eroded.

This chapter argues that refugees and asylum seekers have been subjected to a process of 'criminalization'. Yet, the lack of data on immigration status in official crime recording makes it impossible to determine the precise nature and extent of refugee and asylum seeker involvement in the criminal justice system, whether as offenders, victims, or witnesses. Whilst their experiences of marginalization, poverty, and insecurity of residence may well put these groups at a greater risk of offending behaviour, this cannot currently be either confirmed or denied. Similarly, the failure of criminal justice agencies to collect or monitor data by immigration status of those subject to racial harassment means that we simply do not know the extent to which asylum seekers and refugees are the victims of hate crime.

(Continued)

Whilst some criminal justice agencies, primarily in those areas with the largest numbers of asylum seekers and refugees, have made considerable efforts to ensure that their staff are equipped to deal sensitively and competently with these groups, there is much work still to be done to engender the trust and confidence of asylum seeking and refugee communities. It is argued that asylum is a race relations issue and that policy in this area has an impact on the perceptions and confidence of settled minority ethnic communities.

It is concluded that improvements are required in a number of areas, including: data collection, monitoring and research, training and guidance, inspection regimes, implementation of race equality legislation, community safety, and partnership working.

Key Texts

Banks, J. (2008) 'The criminalisation of asylum seekers and asylum policy'. *Prison Service Journal*, Issue 175, 43–9.
Joint Committee on Human Rights (2007) *The Treatment of Asylum Seekers. Tenth Report of Session 2006–07*. London: The Stationery Office.
Malloch, M.S. and Stanley, E. (2005) 'The detention of asylum seekers in the UK: Representing risk, managing the dangerous'. *Punishment & Society*, vol.7(1), 53–71.

References

Association of Chief Police Officers (ACPO) (2001) *ACPO Guide to Meeting the Policing Needs of Asylum Seekers and Refugees*. Association of Chief Police Officers.

Athwal, H. (2006) Demands for Better Asylum Seeker Mental Health Care. Retrieved on 23 October 2006, from http://www.irr.org.uk/2006/june/ha000024.html

Banks, J. (2008) 'The criminalisation of asylum seekers and asylum policy'. *Prison Service Journal*, Issue 175, 43–9.

Bennett, K., Heath, T. and Jeffries R. (2007) *Asylum Statistics United Kingdom 2006. Home Office Statistical Bulletin 14/07*. London: Home Office.

Beynon, R. (2004) Electronic Monitoring of Asylum Seekers. Joint Council for the Welfare of Immigrants.

Bowling, B. and Phillips, C. (2002) *Racism, Crime and Justice*. Harlow: Longman.

Burnett, A. and Peel, M. (2001) 'Health needs of asylum seekers and refugees'. *British Medical Journal* , 322, 544–47.

Clark, A. (2004) The Reporting and Recording of Racist Incidents Against Asylum Seekers in the North East of England. A Report for The North East Consortium for Asylum and Refugee Support (NECARS) (formerly known as the North East Consortium for Asylum Support Services). Northumbria University.

Coe, J., Fricke, H.J. and Kingham, T. (2005) Asylum Attitudes: A Report for the Commission for Racial Equality on Public Attitude Campaigning. A Research Study. London: Commission for Racial Equality.

Commission for Racial Equality (2007) Memorandum from the commission for Racial Equality. Written evidence to the Joint Committee on Human Rights inquiry into the Treatment of Asylum Seekers.

Crown Prosecution Service (CPS) (2003a) *Guidance on Prosecuting Cases of Racist and Religious Crime*. London: Crown Prosecution Service.

Crown Prosecution Service (2003b) *Racist and Religious Crime – CPS Prosecution Policy*. London: Crown Prosecution Service.

Crown Prosecution Service (2005) *Race Equality Scheme 2005–08. Building on Success – Delivering Race Equality*. London: Crown Prosecution Service.

Crown Prosecution Service (2007) *Racist and Religious Incident Monitoring Annual Report 2006–07*. London: Crown Prosecution Service.

Department for Constitutional Affairs (2006) *Race Equality Scheme 2006–09. England, Wales and the Scotland Office*. London: Department for Constitutional Affairs.

Hampshire Probation Service (2004) *Practice Manual for Working with Asylum Seekers and Refugees*. Hampshire Probation.

Heath, T., Jeffries, R. and Pearce, S. (2006) *Asylum Statistics United Kingdom 2005. Home Office Statistical Bulletin 14/06*. London: Home Office.

Hewitt, R. L. (2002) *Asylum –Seeker Dispersal and Community Relations – An Analysis of Developmental Strategies*. London: Goldsmith's College, University of London.

HM Chief Inspector of Prisons (2006a) Foreign National Prisoners: A Thematic Review. London: Her Majesty's Inspectorate of Prisons.

HM Chief Inspector of Prisons (2006b) Report on an Unannounced Inspection of Harmondsworth Immigration Removal Centre. 17–21 July 2006. London: Her Majesty's Inspectorate of Prisons.

HM Chief Inspector of Prisons (2007a) Annual Report. 2005/2006. London: The Stationery Office.

HM Chief Inspector of Prisons (2007b) Foreign National Prisoners: A Follow-up Report. January 2007. London: Her Majesty's Inspectorate of Prisons.

Home Office (2005a) Controlling Our Borders: Making Migration Work for Britain. Five Year Strategy for Asylum and Immigration. London: The Stationery Office.

Home Office (2005b) The Core (non-IND) Home Office Associate Race Equality Scheme. London: Home Office.

Home Office (2006) *Asylum Statistics: 3rdQuarter 2006. United Kingdom*. Home Office and Office of National Statistics.

Home Office (2007) *Asylum Statistics: 3rd Quarter 2007. United Kingdom*. Home Office and Office of National Statistics.

House of Commons Committee of Public Accounts (2006) *Returning Failed Asylum Applicants. Thirty–fourth Report of Session 2005–06*. London: The Stationery Office.

Immigration and Nationality Directorate (IND) (2005) *Immigration and Nationality Directorate Associate Race Equality Scheme*. London: Home Office.

Immigration and Nationality Directorate (2007) *Race Equality Impact Assessment on Electronic Monitoring (EM) – Review of tagging at the Asylum Screening Units (ASU)*.

Information Centre about Asylum and Refugees (ICAR) (2004) *Media Image, Community Impact: Assessing the Impact of Media and Political Images of Refugees and Asylum Seekers on Community Relations in London. Report of a Pilot Research Study*. Executive Summary. London: ICAR.

Information Centre about Asylum and Refugees (2007) *Reporting Asylum – The UK Press and the Effectiveness of PCC Guidelines*. London: ICAR.

Joint Committee on Human Rights (2007) *The Treatment of Asylum Seekers. Tenth Report of Session 2006–07*. London: The Stationery Office.

London Probation Area (2006a) *London Probation Foreign Nationals Strategy 2005–08*. London Probation.

London Probation Area (2006b) *Working with Foreign National Offenders and Victims. A Training Resource Pack Developed by London Probation, Diversity Directorate*. London Probation.

Lynch, J. P. and Simon, R. J. (1999) 'A comparative assessment of criminal involvement among immigrants and natives across seven nations'. *International Criminal Justice Review*, 9, pp. 1–17.

Macpherson, W. (1999) The Stephen Lawrence inquiry, report of an inquiry by Sir William Macpherson of cluny. London: Home Office.

Malloch, M.S. and Stanley, E. (2005) 'The detention of asylum seekers in the UK: Representing risk, managing the dangerous'. *Punishment & Society*, 7(1), 53–71.

Malmberg, M. (2004) *Control and Deterrence: Discourses of detention of asylum-seekers. Sussex Migration Working Paper No.20*. Sussex Centre for Migration Research, University of Sussex.

Ministry of Justice. (2008) Statistics on Race and Criminal Justice System – 2007. A ministry of Justice Publication Under Section 95 of the Criminal Justice Act 1991. London: Ministry of Justice.

Morris, N. (2007) *Dispersal policy 'put asylum-seekers at risk'*. The Independent, 16 March 2007.

National Asylum Support Service (NASS) (2004) *Dispersal Guidelines. NASS Policy Bulletin 31*.

Office for National Statistics (2005) *International Migration*. Retrieved 3 January 2007, from http://www.statistics.gov.uk/cci/nugget_print.asp?ID=766

Office for National Statistics (2007) *Migration*. Retrieved 23 January 2008, from http://www.statistics.gov.uk/CCI/nugget.asp?ID=260&Pos=3&ColRank=1&Rank=310

Prison Reform Trust (2004) *Forgotten Prisoners – The Plight of Foreign National Prisoners in England and Wales*. London: Prison Reform Trust.

Prison Service (2005) *The Prison Service Associate Race Equality Scheme*. London: Home Office.

Refugee Action (2006) *The Destitution Trap: Research into destitution among refused asylum seekers in the UK*. London: Refugee Action.

Refugee Council (2006a) *Tell it like it is. The truth about asylum*. London: Refugee Council.

Refugee Council (2006b) *The facts about asylum*. Retrieved 26 September 2006, from http://www.refugeecouncil.org.uk/practice/basics/facts.htm

Rudiger, A. (2007) *Prisoners of Terrorism? The impact of anti-terrorism measures on refugees and asylum seekers in Britain*. London: Refugee Council.

Solomon, E. (2006) *Asylum and Criminality. Unpublished presentation to ICAR and Chatham House Asylum and Security Seminar, 27th March 2006*.

Sriskandarajah, D. and Hopwood Road, F. (2005) *United Kingdom: Rising Numbers, Rising Anxieties*. Migration Information Source. Retrieved on 5 January 2007, from http://www.migrationinformation.org/Feature/display.cfm?ID=306

United for Intercultural Action n.d, (2004) *Detention in Europe: Take Action Against the Imprisonment of Refugees*. Retrieved 7 August 2006, from www.united.non-profit.nl/pages/info22.htm

Walker, A., Kershaw, C. and Nicholas, S. (2006) *Crime in England and Wales 2005/06. Home Office Statistical Bulletin 12/06*. London: Home Office.

NINE

Foreign National Prisoners: Issues and Debates

Hindpal Singh Bhui

Introduction

Although foreign nationals make up 14 per cent of the prison population, until recently they received little attention in operational practice or policy development. This relative anonymity disappeared in dramatic circumstances in April 2006, when it was discovered that over a thousand foreign national prisoners had been released before the immigration authorities[1] had considered whether or not they should be deported. A group that had previously been labelled by some commentators as 'the forgotten prisoners' (PRT, 2004; Cheney, 1993) suddenly came to the fore of national consciousness and debate. Fear and anger were two dominant public and political reactions to these releases and led, it is argued here, to damaging outcomes for what had already been identified as a disadvantaged group in the prison population (HMIP, 2006b; PRT, 2004; Bhui, 2004a; Cheney, 1993).

This chapter explores possible explanations for the high foreign national prison population as well as the genesis and the consequences of the events of April 2006. It puts the debate into context by examining the key messages of the research on foreign national prisoners' experiences of imprisonment and the response of the prison system to their needs[2]. Over 70 per cent of foreign nationals are from an ethnic group other than 'white' (MoJ, 2007a) and they constitute around 40 per cent of the overall black and minority ethnic prison population (MoJ, 2007b). Consequently, they are also central to any consideration of race issues in prisons (see Bhui's Chapter 5 in this volume).

---

[1]The 'Immigration and Nationality Directorate' changed its name to the 'Border and Immigration Agency' in 2007 and then changed it again to the UK Border Agency (UKBA) in 2008.

[2]There is very little empirical research on foreign nationals at other stages of the criminal justice process, though many will have experience of the police and immigration authorities as a result of immigration enforcement action (see Cooper's chapter in this volume).

The interplay between ethnic, cultural, and national identities, and the impact on prisoner experiences of gender and country of normal residency, is examined, drawing largely on the Prison Inspectorate's thematic review of foreign national prisoners (HMIP, 2006b), the most extensive research on foreign national prisoners to date. Emerging evidence about the way that the specific resettlement needs of foreign nationals are addressed in prison and in the community is also discussed.

The Growth of the Foreign National Prisoner Population

In December 2007 foreign nationals made up 14 per cent of the prison population, amounting to 11,300 prisoners, an increase of 250 per cent since 1997, when there were 4,500 foreign nationals in custody (prison statistics quoted in *Hansard*, 26 Feb 2008, Column 646). There are a number of possible explanations for such a rise in numbers. These include a larger migrant population in the UK, especially as foreign nationals seeking work are more likely to be young and to live in urban areas, both of which are greater predictors of offending. A major contributor is the disproportionate number of foreign nationals imprisoned for drugs offences. While this group has started to reduce, particularly amongst the female prison population, it is still substantial: in December 2006, 35 per cent of all sentenced foreign national prisoners were convicted of drug-related offences, compared to only 14 per cent of British prisoners[3]. Drug couriers are particularly prevalent amongst the female foreign national prisoner population, and about a third of all sentenced female drug offenders in 2006 were foreign nationals, overwhelmingly drug couriers (MoJ, 2007a; see also HMIP, 2006c). The long deterrent sentences for female drug couriers have, for some time, been criticized by campaigning groups, partly because poverty has been shown to be an overriding motivation for many female couriers at the bottom of a criminal chain, and partly because deterrent sentencing is unlikely to have an impact in the context of minimal awareness in home countries of how seriously the offence is being viewed in Britain (PRT, 2004; Allen, Levenson, & Garside, 2003; Green, 1998). The recent reductions in the numbers of female drug importers may be a result of better international communications and targeted campaigns in Jamaica and West Africa by the voluntary group Hibiscus (see below).

An increasing number of foreign nationals are also imprisoned for fraud and forgery offences (typically possession of false documents to gain entry to the UK). The prevalence of this offence has risen dramatically in recent years as immigration controls have become tighter. In December 2006, 883 serving foreign national prisoners were convicted of fraud or forgery offences, amounting to 12 per cent of all of those sentenced. This compared to

---

[3] Figures supplied by Home Office Research Development and Statistics Directorate.

838 British prisoners, amounting to only 1.5 per cent of all sentenced British nationals (figures taken from *Hansard*, written answers, 14 March 2007, columns 399W–402W). This figure can be substantially boosted by numbers remanded in custody: prison statistics (quoted in HMIP, 2006b) show that in 2005, nearly 2,000 foreign national prisoners (21 per cent of the foreign national population at the time) were charged with fraud or forgery offences.

Other reasons for the larger numbers in foreign nationals in custody include the fact that they are very unlikely to be given home detention curfew, release on temporary licence, or D-category status if subject to a deportation recommendation, and if that recommendation eventually becomes a definite decision to deport, they have virtually no chance of getting any of these things, regardless of the fact that they often have good prison records (HMIP, 2006b).

The rising population has not yet been significantly checked by government measures to speed up deportations; these include the 'early removal scheme', which since April 2008 has allowed for deportation up to 270 days before the usual release date (it was previously 135 days) and the 'facilitated removals scheme', which provides foreign national prisoners with some resettlement assistance under the auspices of the International Organisation for Migration if they accept and cooperate with deportation[4]. The implementation of these schemes has so far been inconsistent (HMIP, 2008b, c, 2007b). Furthermore, although attempts are being made to negotiate more repatriation agreements, only 111 prisoners were repatriated to serve the remainder of their sentences in their home countries in 2007 (*Hansard*, 26 Feb 2008: Column 646).

Detention of Time-Served Prisoners

There are significant numbers of foreign national ex-prisoners detained under immigration powers in prisons or in immigration detention centres following sentence completion. In 2007, 1,300 'time served' foreign nationals were so detained (*Hansard*, 29 Oct 2007: Column 809W). This may be for a number of reasons, including poor practice by immigration caseworkers responsible for completing paperwork before someone can be deported or their release authorized (Home Office, 2007; HMIP, 2005, 2006b, 2007c); problems with obtaining travel documentation from home embassies; deportation recommendations made on people who have been remanded in custody, which means they have little time left to serve once finally sentenced; foreign nationals appealing against deportation shortly before the end of their sentences, which means that the appeal process cannot be finished in time; or applications for asylum status which similarly take a long time to resolve. The likelihood of post-sentence detention has risen since April 2006, when the immigration

---

[4]Since its inception in October 2006 to 28 January 2008, approximately 1,200 prisoners had been removed under the FRS, receiving a cash discharge grant of £46 and reintegration assistance to values up to £3,000 once in their home country (http://www.parliament.uk/deposits/depositedpapers/2008/DEP2008-0651.pdf).

authorities became understandably reluctant to take any chances with risk assessment and release of foreign nationals in the face of public scrutiny and political interest. Consequently, those foreign nationals already in prison in April 2006 experienced longer periods of post sentence detention while immigration staff decided on what, if any, action was to be taken in their cases (HMIP, 2007c). At the same time, the prison service recalled foreign nationals held in open prisons to closed conditions with no warning and without individual risk assessment (ibid).

The rising numbers of ex-prisoners transferred to immigration removal centres[5] (IRCs) after April 2006 left a problematic legacy for IRCs struggling to maintain more relaxed regimes in centres where the population mix includes people who have never transgressed criminal law and, in three centres[6], where children are held with their parents. It is notable that serious deficiencies have been identified in the standard of immigration casework relating to ex-prisoners (Home Office, 2007), and these contributed to some of the many disturbances that have taken place in IRCs in the last few years (Whalley, 2007).

Are Foreign National Prisoners More Dangerous?

There is no evidence to support the view that foreign nationals are in prison for longer because they are a more dangerous population than British nationals. While there are many possible reasons for the intensity of the public outcry following April 2006, the main reason seems to have been that it combined concerns about two areas that elicit heightened public angst and therefore political sensitivity: crime and immigration. Opinion polls demonstrate the strength of feeling in this regard; the most recent research from Ipsos Mori shows that 'race relations, immigration and immigrants' are the top public concern, while crime, law and order, violence, and vandalism are close behind. These separate issues are combined to a significant extent in the public imagination (see Cooper's chapter in this volume for more discussion; also Malloch and Stanley, 2005, and Amnesty International, 2005). In this case, they appear to have fuelled and heightened concerns about public protection, although there is no evidence that foreign nationals are any more dangerous than the thousands of British citizens released at the end of sentence. Home Office offence type statistics can provide only a blunt measure of offence seriousness, but the December 2006 figures suggest that rates of violent and sexual offences for sentenced foreign and British nationals are either comparable or lower amongst foreign nationals. For example, 10 per cent of sentenced foreign nationals were imprisoned for sexual offences against 11 per cent of British nationals, and 18 per cent of

---

[5] In April 2006, about half of the IRC population were foreign national prisoners.

[6] Yarl's Wood is the main immigration removal centre holding children, while Tinsley House near Gatwick Airport and Dungavel, the only Scottish IRC, hold children and families for short periods only.

foreign nationals were imprisoned for 'violence against the person' compared to 28 per cent of British nationals. Interestingly, in April 2008, the Association of Chief Police Officers also announced that an internal study had found no evidence of higher levels of offending by migrant communities (see http://www.acpo.police.uk/default.asp). It is evident, therefore, that the anger at the releases was not simply because of valid concerns about public protection or because foreign nationals were unusually dangerous. Latent prejudice against foreign nationals and, for politicians, the need to avoid further political embarrassment, and to buttress public confidence in the immigration system were at least as important. However, the impact of these changes on foreign national prisoners was considerable, as is discussed below.

Experiences of Foreign National Prisoners

Prior to the thematic review of foreign national prisoners (HMIP, 2006b), a number of smaller studies and reports (Bhui, 1995, 2004a, b; PRT, 2004; Tarzi & Hedge, 1990, 1993; Cheney, 1993) had consistently identified several key problem areas, including: immigration-related problems, language problems, and a lack of information about and understanding of the prison and criminal justice systems, isolation, limited family contact and associated psychological distress, a lack of preparation for release, and racism within prisons. The need for broader and better resourced research was met by the two investigations by HM Inspectorate of Prisons (2006b, 2007c). The main review (2006b) was based on semi-structured interviews with 85 prison staff and over 170 foreign national prisoners across 10 prisons holding varied populations. Probation service foreign national specialists investigated resettlement provision in detail and immigration legal advisors examined the quality of immigration casework, and liaison between prisons and the immigration authorities[7]. The fieldwork for the follow-up report (HMIP, 2007c) was conducted between September and November 2006, some 6 months after the concerns over foreign national prisoners first became headline news and at a time when the immigration authorities had taken action to resolve the problems that had led to the earlier crisis. Evidence was obtained from Inspectors' interviews with 17 people detained following sentence solely under immigration powers, and five serving foreign national prisoners known to have immigration problems, with supplementary evidence obtained from members of the Independent Monitoring Boards in 86 prisons.

---

[7]The review also involved a health questionnaire administered to the main interviewees and to a control group of 12 British prisoners, as well as a national survey of prison foreign national coordinators and analysis of Inspectorate survey results from almost 6,000 prisoners collected over a period of 18 months. The responses of British and foreign nationals who filled out the surveys were separated, compared, and then tested for significance.

The main review (2006b) concluded that there were three major problems to which nearly all others were linked: family contact, immigration, and language. Resettlement problems were closely linked to immigration difficulties, and these two areas are therefore considered together below. It is notable that staff identified the same three primary problems as prisoners and scored them very highly in terms of prevalence – family contact (79 per cent compared to 55 per cent by prisoners), immigration (60 per cent compared to 47 per cent by prisoners), and language (81 per cent compared to 41 per cent by prisoners). However, staff perceived the seriousness of problems faced by foreign nationals as being less intense. They also judged lack of information about the prison, isolation, racism, and cultural issues as more prevalent but less serious problems than did the prisoners themselves.

Language Problems

Language problems have been identified by previous research as exacerbating all other difficulties faced by foreign nationals. Bhui (2004a) found that prisoners were frustrated at not being understood by staff, at having little to read in their own languages, and missing out on basic provisions such as showers and association because they had not understood instructions. In the thematic review (HMIP, 2006b) prisoners who mentioned language difficulties were also likely to mention difficulties in almost every other area that the interview schedule examined. The links between language and issues such as isolation, mental health, self-harm, and immigration cases became clear when prisoners' comments were examined in detail. They showed how reliant many foreign national prisoners were on the assistance that could be provided within the prison. For example, two prisoners stated:

> I am very depressed; there are no other Kurdish people here. There is no common language, so I communicate with Indian and Pakistani prisoners by sign language.

> I didn't understand the time-scale for my appeal and so I think I missed the deadline. There is a language barrier – so I can't talk to staff.

Family Contact

The problem of family contact is also strongly reflected in other research (e.g., Richards *et al.*, 1995; Cheney, 1993) and has implications for mental health and well-being, as well as for resettlement and reintegration of prisoners returning to the community and to their families after release. Foreign national interviewees for the thematic review (HMIP, 2006b) had significantly greater difficulties in keeping in touch with families than British nationals, and over a third said they had not had a visit since arriving at their establishment. These problems emerged even though most prisons offer what is known as an 'accumulated visits' scheme, which means that prisoners with families coming from a distance can save up and add together their allotted visiting time. Most further comments made by prisoners about family contact (58 per cent of the 79 comments made) related to difficulties with phones, usually about the expense of calls or not having enough time on the phone. For example, one commented:

My family is in Pakistan, I have had no contact at all with them [because of the expense of calling home] – I am beside myself with worry as they will be wondering what has happened to me.

Women were particularly likely to report difficulties with family contact, reflecting the greater likelihood of them being the primary carers for children: 71 per cent of women considered family contact a problem compared to 59 per cent of adult men and only 32 per cent of young people (all rating it as a 'big problem', 4 on a 1–5 scale). Similarly, 63 per cent of women considered immigration to be a problem, compared to 49 per cent of men and only 28 per cent of young people. As immigration detention delays the return to family, it is possible that for many women the two issues were connected.

Immigration and Resettlement

Anyone without a British passport is at risk of deportation or removal[8]. Of the 65 comments made about immigration during the thematic review, most (54 per cent) were about not knowing what was happening with regard to immigration. This was for a variety of reasons, including a lack of English and poor understanding of immigration paperwork:

I was sent a letter [by immigration] a year ago, I am not sure what it was about.

There is a general lack of information and progress. No advice and legal officers[9] are unsure about immigration.

In relation to immigration practices, the review found that both staff and prisoners were frustrated because of a lack of support and contact from the immigration authorities. Cases were often acted on at the last minute, with little or no warning of deportation proceedings or detention. This made it extremely difficult for prisoners to prepare for release or removal

---

[8]Deportation and administrative removal both entail foreign nationals being taken back to home countries, but deportation is a more formal process used for more serious offences. It requires the Minister of State to sign a deportation order and means that people are barred from returning to the UK unless they have obtained permission to do so. Administrative removal is a far quicker procedure used for those who do not have permission to be in the UK. It is often used in relation to people serving short sentences for relatively minor offences. There is no appeal allowed against a decision to remove.

[9]This prisoner was referring to prison legal services officers whose main role it is to help prisoners access legal services.

from the country, and affected the ability of prison and probation staff to provide them with appropriate sentence planning and support. Specialist resettlement staff indicated that foreign nationals were less likely to be given assistance with education, training, housing, and employment advice, because limited resources were targeted on those who were certain to be resettling in the UK. There was a reluctance to obtain housing or employment opportunities for foreign nationals who might be informed of deportation proceedings on or near their day of expected release and therefore detained.

In terms of risk assessment and management, the unavailability of previous convictions and other information about foreign national resident abroad was also a hindrance to effective sentence planning and raised important public protection issues. The risk and needs assessment tool used in the National Offender Management Service (NOMS), the Offender Assessment System (OASys), was less reliable because of the absence of information on previous offence history, and it was difficult to set realistic offending related or other targets. In fact, staff noted that it was quicker and easier to do an OASys with foreign nationals because there was rarely any verifiable information to enter. In several cases, prison resettlement staff expressed concern that there was no mechanism for them to relay concerns about vulnerable and high-risk people to home country authorities (see also Bhui, 2004b). Some foreign nationals were unable to access offending behaviour programmes because of language, but more concerning was that they had in some cases been excluded from local programme completion targets and were therefore considered low priority referrals (see HMIP, 2006b: 49). Only 18 per cent of the interviewees had had any probation contact.

Many of these general thematic findings were confirmed by inspections of the two wholly foreign national prisons in 2007 (HMIP, 2008b, c). Both prisons, along with NOMS, were manifestly failing to meet or even properly to recognize the resettlement needs of foreign national prisoners, although in most other respects they were well run, safe, and decent establishments. Underlying everything was the lack of certainty about immigration status, which affected the ability of the prisons to provide effective resettlement planning and provision, and deterred external agencies from becoming involved. Taking the example of HMP Canterbury, which was providing the slightly better resettlement service of the two, the overall approach lacked coherence and clarity. Resettlement services had not been planned to respond to the needs of a complex population, that included people discharged under the facilitated returns scheme, the early removal scheme, those deported or removed at the end of sentence and a substantial number – about 14 per cent – who were eventually released into the community. There had been no guidance or support from NOMS, and the prison had not conducted its own internal resettlement needs analysis to help inform and drive progress.

A key issue was the impossibility of prison staff or offender managers identifying which 14 per cent were to be released and to direct resources accordingly, mainly because they often did not know until the last stages of sentence, about whether or not someone was to be deported. Probation staff were reluctant to engage with prisoners until immigration status was confirmed and so had little or no contact with them. The default assumption was that prisoners would be deported. A team of immigration liaison staff had recently been provided in the prison, but they did not hold the cases of prisoners in the establishment and had trouble obtaining timely information from immigration colleagues who were remotely managing them. Risk was difficult to assess for the foreign national population because of a lack of pre-sentence reports and information on previous convictions, particularly for prisoners who had previously been resident abroad. Some limited accommodation casework was undertaken with around 30 people, but there was a lack of specialist provision that could take account of the needs of the population, particularly prisoners returning to live outside the UK.

A main recommendation of that inspection was that there should be a national policy for the management and support of foreign national prisoners, which provides clear practice guidelines to establishments, and which is supported by auditable standards, service-level agreements, or contractual requirements. Amongst other recommendations was the need to work on establishing better links with other countries to improve information flow. Neither was original, and had also been made in the thematic report (2006b).

The latter concluded that there was an urgent need for a sustained interest in this group from NOMS and immigration policy makers and managers. It also concluded that the prison service position – that there is no case for a dedicated policy or for seeing foreign nationals as a distinct group – was fundamentally flawed. Although the follow-up report (HMIP, 2007c) recorded some limited improvements in the efficiency of immigration casework, the report was critical of the lack of coordination and communication between the prison and immigration systems, and between the immigration authorities and foreign nationals, as well as the ongoing avoidable delays in processing casework.

Self-harm

Previous research (Pourgourides *et al.*, 1996) has highlighted depression and general mental health needs amongst isolated foreign nationals. This is not surprising given that some may have experienced torture, persecution, and abuse in their homelands, and the fact that the mental health of detainees may be particularly fragile as they can be held with little idea of their eventual release dates. While it found much immigration-related frustration, the main thematic review found little evidence of higher levels of self-harm amongst foreign nationals. However, the follow-up investigation (HMIP, 2007c) found an increase in the mental distress and self-harm attempts reported amongst foreign nationals as a result of immigration action or inaction. While figures taken over a relatively short period should be treated with caution and do not necessarily indicate clear long-term trends, it is concerning that self-inflicted deaths for foreign national prisoners rose markedly between April 2006 and the beginning of 2008. From the second quarter of 2005 to the first quarter of 2006, there were 6 foreign national deaths out of 68 in the total prison population, comprising 6.8 per cent of the total. However, from the second quarter of 2006 (after the deportation furore) to the first quarter of 2007, 9 out of 54 deaths were of foreign nationals, comprising 16.8 per cent of the total. More generally, while foreign national self-inflicted deaths between 2002 and 2005 constituted between 7.4 per cent and 9.5 per cent of all deaths, and were on a downwards trajectory, since 2006 they have started rising again. The figure for 2007 represented a very steep rise: 25 per cent or 23 out of 92 self-inflicted deaths in 2007 were of foreign national prisoners (http://www.justice.gov.uk/news/newsrelease010108a.htm) (see Bhui, 2007, for case studies and further discussion).

Intersections of Different Types of Disadvantage

The thematic review (HMIP, 2006b) identified a range of common problems and needs that justify attention to foreign nationals as a distinct category, despite the persistence of a Prison Service approach that has traditionally rejected the notion that foreign nationals constitute a discrete group. However, it also demonstrated the importance of developing a more sophisticated understanding of the multiple factors that impact on the experiences and treatment of foreign national prisoners. That is, different forms of prejudice and discrimination emanate from static and dynamic characteristics such as skin colour, nationality, language skills, and residency to define the prison experience for foreign nationals, and in many cases to intensify negative experiences. For example, foreign nationals who were also black had a broader range of negative experiences of imprisonment than those who were not visibly different. In the thematic review, black and Asian foreign nationals were the most likely to report problems in the areas of racism, religion, and respect. White foreign nationals made up a third of the foreign national sample and over two-thirds (especially Eastern European groups) felt that foreign nationals were all treated similarly poorly regardless of their skin colour, although conversely a substantial number felt that white foreign nationals had an easier life in prison:

> Whites stand a better chance of survival.

> White people are all treated better; if you are white you are recognized as Europeans - so share the culture of officers.

Black people, or [those] who are more identifiably from a different country are treated much more poorly.

While the overall level of discriminatory treatment reported on the basis of religion was low, amongst those who thought it was an issue, negative perceptions in relation to Muslims and their treatment were prevalent. There was an association between identifying as a Muslim and perceptions of differential treatment, and about two-thirds of further comments about problems regarding religion related to Muslims. Of these, half stated that Muslim prisoners were treated worse than other prisoners or stereotyped as a result of the wider political climate. This was having a direct impact on the way that some Muslims chose to observe their faith:

I would like to grow a beard to be closer to my religion, but I would get judged – called a terrorist, so I don't.

The situation is further complicated by the fact that residency outside of the UK emerged as the single most influential predictor of problems. Just under half of prisoner interviewees said their main country of residence was the UK. Substantially more men (50 per cent) and young people (44 per cent) reported residency in the UK than women (21 per cent). This can partly be explained by the high number of drug couriers amongst the female prison population (discussed above), most of whom enter the country with no intention of staying for more than a few days. Overall, 84 per cent of non-UK residents identified problems or needs, compared to 69 per cent of UK residents. UK residents were almost three times more likely to have English as a main language (40 per cent as opposed to 15 per cent), which appeared to act as a protective factor.

Foreign nationals who had not been resident in the UK before coming into prison reported more problems in all of the primary areas of language, immigration, and family contact. They also reported more problems with legal services and experienced more cultural isolation. They reported less experience of discrimination or disrespect, perhaps because they had different expectations of how they would be treated, and difficulty picking up on expressions of disrespect because of language barriers. In terms of visits, non-residents again had much worse experiences. About 60 per cent of non-UK residents had not had a visit since arriving at their establishment, compared with less than 40 per cent of UK residents.

Individuals from the Middle East emerged as having a particularly wide range of problems and needs. They were most likely to have immigration problems (64 per cent) and to give this problem the highest seriousness score of '5'. They were also more likely than any other group to be ignorant of their immigration status. They had a high likelihood of experiencing language problems and of experiencing prejudice and stereotyping as a result of being Muslim. This group therefore appeared to be particularly vulnerable for a range of reasons, confirming the importance of prison foreign national strategies closely linked to the broader management of race relations and diversity.

Overall, these findings suggest that combinations of faith, language, regional and national identity, and skin colour can create matrixes of vulnerability and protective factors. Sophisticated prison diversity, race equality, and foreign national strategies that are sensitive to these issues offer the best means of identifying those at greatest potential risk and helping to address their specific disadvantages.

Prison Service Responses to the Needs of Foreign National Prisoners

Bhui's (2004a) research in six London prisons found that despite large foreign national populations, none of the research prisons had a coherent strategy to meet their needs. None had established clear and consistent working practices and policies that would allow work with foreign national prisoners to develop and to be sustainable in the longer term. Staff were generally frustrated at their lack of knowledge, the lack of guidance on work with foreign national prisoners, and particularly at the lack of time to develop such knowledge and to work constructively with foreign nationals. 'Sustainability' was identified as the major challenge for effective foreign national prisoner strategies, because so many had faltered on the departure of key individuals, who took with them crucial knowledge and expertise. Such sustainability needs auditable standards and clear practice guidelines so that prison managers are forced to give the issue some priority (Bhui, 2004a; HMIP, 2006b). In the absence of these drivers, progress has been uneven at best. Despite considerable numbers of foreign national prisoners and the high-profile impact of the events of April 2006, there is still no broad Prison Service or NOMS policy addressing the circumstances of foreign national prisoners, and individual prisons have been slow to formulate effective local policies. The result has been frustration amongst front-line staff struggling to work in a policy vacuum, and ongoing criticism of inconsistent practice, as evidenced by numerous Prison Inspectorate reports (e.g., HMIP, 2003, 2006d). In fact, an analysis of all full prison inspection reports published in the year between September 2005 and August 2006 shows that 40 per cent of prisons undergoing full inspections (16 out of 39) had no foreign national prisoner policy. Of those that did, very few were able to demonstrate effective implementation. For example, while foreign national groups and the employment of prisoners themselves as 'orderlies' have been shown to be effective means of promoting communication and addressing concerns (Bhui, 2004a), very few prisons have implemented them (HMIP, 2006a, 2007a, 2008a).

Identification of those liable to deportation and effective liaison with the immigration authorities remains the key focus of prisons, reflecting the Prison Service Order on foreign nationals which gives virtually no attention to anything other than immigration status. The other essential aspects of the care of foreign prisoners, identified in the thematic report, remain marginal and dependent on the energy and commitment of individual prison staff, commonly with little time or dedicated resources (HMIP, 2006a). The main areas of consistent good practice, where the multiple needs of foreign national prisoners are better addressed, are in women's prisons. This is usually driven by the voluntary group 'Hibiscus' (http://www.hibiscuslondon.org.uk/), part of the Female Prisoners Welfare Project, which now has a presence in most women's prisons. Hibiscus has established a strong reputation since its inception in 1990, both for its welfare work in prisons, and for its preventive educational campaigning work in Jamaica, Nigeria, and Ghana.

Conclusion

Foreign national prisoners have many common experiences and needs – usually linked with the primary problems of family contact, immigration difficulties, and language – that make it meaningful to consider them as a distinct group. It is clear, however, that their multiple identities lead to experiences of disadvantage on multiple levels. In line with Garland, Chakraborti, and Spalek's (2006) exhortation to recognize the 'hidden minorities' within broadly defined groupings, the chapter has outlined the distinct experiences of some sub-groups within the foreign national population, which require sophisticated strategies based on needs analyses in individual prisons. These findings support the model for working with foreign national prisoners first proposed in Bhui's (2004a) report, which argues that foreign national strategies should not exist in isolation, but instead be 'embedded' in a wider diversity strategy. This is because:

Insufficient attention to cultures of racism, stereotyping and discrimination in individual prisons will result in foreign national work, like any other initiative which requires respect for diversity, being eroded ....a foreign nationals strategy must be buttressed by, and provide support to, other initiatives that support diversity, cultural change and changes in policy and practice. (Bhui, 2004a: 38)

The deportation furore and its consequences highlight the importance of this point. Foreign nationals, when they did come to prominence, were not seen as the comparatively vulnerable individuals revealed in the research, but as a virtual combined threat (immigrant/criminal) presenting a series of political hazards and operational headaches. It has been argued here that much of the hostile public and media reaction was based on false assumptions and misinformation, and that fears about the dangerousness of those released were fuelled by strong undercurrents of xenophobia and racism. They are still explicitly seen in prison policy mainly as potential deportees rather than individuals with distinct management and welfare needs. While there is no doubt that there is substantial capacity and enthusiasm within the prison estate for effective work with the foreign national prisoner population, there is still little sign of a coherent strategic approach to their needs.

Summary

While foreign nationals make up 14 per cent of the prison population, they were a relatively anonymous group in terms of prison policy and practice until April 2006, when it was discovered that over a thousand had been released before the immigration authorities had considered them for deportation. While there is no single reason for the rise in foreign national prisoners, many receive long sentences for drug offences and an increasing number are imprisoned for fraud or forgery linked to immigration matters. Well over a thousand foreign national ex-prisoners are also indefinitely detained under immigration powers in prisons or in immigration detention centres following sentence completion. There is no evidence that foreign nationals are in prison for longer because they are more dangerous population than British nationals. Political sensitivity about crime and immigration, as well as undercurrents of xenophobia, appear more likely reasons for much of the negative rhetoric about the apparent threat posed by them.

There is a growing amount of research on foreign prisoners, which has consistently identified the problem areas of family contact, language, and immigration. These issues are closely linked to many other 'secondary' problems. For example, resettlement planning is made especially hard by the uncertainty over immigration status. It is also notable that the furore over foreign national prisoners being released before assessment by the immigration authorities was followed by more people being indefinitely detained and a steep rise in the number of foreign national prisoners committing suicide. The recent thematic review of foreign national prisoners (HMIP, 2006b) identified a range of common problems and needs, but also the need for a more sophisticated understanding of the multiple factors that impact on the experiences and treatment of foreign national prisoners, including prejudice and discrimination emanating from skin colour, nationality, language skills, and residency. Despite this evidence base, few prisons have a coherent strategy to meet their discrete needs, due partly to the lack of strategic guidance from prison service or the National Offender Management Service. The chapter concludes that there is a need for more sophisticated strategies – based on existing research evidence and needs analyses in individual prisons – which are 'embedded' within wider prison diversity strategies.

Key Texts

Bhui, H.S. (2004) *Developing Effective Policy and Practice for Work with Foreign National Prisoners.* London: Prison Reform Trust.

HM Inspectorate of Prisons (2006) *Foreign National Prisoners: A Thematic Review.* London. Home Office.

HM Inspectorate of Prisons (2007) *Foreign National Prisoners: A Follow Up Report.* London. Home Office.

References

Allen, R., Levenson, J. and Garside, R. (2003) *A Bitter Pill to Swallow: The Sentencing of Foreign National Drug Couriers.* London: Rethinking Crime and Punishment.

Amnesty International (2005) *Seeking Asylum Is Not a Crime: Detention of People Who Have Sought Asylum.* London: Amnesty International.

Bhui, H.S. (2007) 'Alien experience: Foreign national prisoners after the deportation crisis', *Probation Journal*, 54: 368–382.

Bhui, H.S. (2004a) *Developing Effective Policy and Practice for Work with Foreign National Prisoners.* London: Prison Reform Trust.

Bhui, H.S. (2004b) 'The resettlement needs of foreign national offenders', *Criminal Justice Matters* 56, Summer 2004, pp. 36–37 and p. 44.

Bhui, H.S (1995) 'Foreign National Prisoner Survery', Research note in *Probation Journal* 42(2): 97–99.

Cheney, D. (1993) *Into the Dark Tunnel: Foreign Prisoners in the British Prison System.* London: Prison Reform Trust.

Garland, J., Spalek, B. and Chakraborti, N. (2006) 'Hearing lost voices: issues in researching "hidden" minority ethnic communities', *British Journal of Criminology*, 47, 423–37.

Green, P. (1998) *Drugs, Trafficking and Criminal Policy: The Scapegoat Strategy.* Winchester: Waterside Press.

HM Inspectorate of Prisons (2008a) Annual Report. London: Home Office.

HM Inspectorate of Prisons (2008b) Report on an Announced Inspection of HMP Canterbury. London: Home Office.

HM Inspectorate of Prisons (2008c) Report on an Announced Inspection of HMP Bullwood Hall. London: Home Office.

HM Inspectorate of Prisons (2007a) *Annual Report.* London: Home Office.

HM Inspectorate of Prisons (2007b) Report on an Announced Inspection of HMP Winchester. London: Home Office.

HM Inspectorate of Prisons (2007c) Foreign National Prisoners: A Follow Up Report. London. Home Office.

HM Inspectorate of Prisons (2006a) Annual Report. London: Home Office.

HM Inspectorate of Prisons (2006b) Foreign National Prisoners: A Thematic Review. London. Home Office.

HM Inspectorate of Prisons (2006c) *Women in Prison.* London. Home Office.

HM Inspectorate of Prisons (2006d) *Unannounced Follow up Inspection of Pentonville*. London: Home Office.

HM Inspectorate of Prisons (2005) Annual Report. London: Home Office.

HM Inspectorate of Prisons (2003) Report of an Unannounced Follow-up Inspection of HM Prison Kingston. London: Home Office.

Home Office (2007) A Review of the Failure of the Immigration & Nationality Directorate to Consider Some Foreign National Prisoners for Deportation. London: Home Office.

Malloch, M. and E. Stanley (2005) 'The detention of asylum seekers in the UK: representing risk, managing the dangerous' in *Punishment & Society* 7(1): 53–71.

Ministry of Justice (2007a) Offender Management Caseload Statistics 2006. London: Ministry of Justice.

Ministry of Justice (2007b) Statistics on Race and the Criminal Justice System (Section 95 statistics). London: Ministry of Justice.

Pourgourides, C.K., Sashidharan, S. and Bracken, P. J. (1996) *A Second Exile: The Mental Health Implications of Detention of Asylum Seekers in the UK*. University of Birmingham/Cadbury Trust.

Prison Reform Trust (2004) Briefing Paper: *Forgotten Prisoners – The Plight of Foreign National Prisoners in England and Wales*. London: PRT.

Richards, M., McWilliams, B., Batten, N., Cameron, C. and Cutler, J. (1995) 'Foreign nationals in English prisons: 1. Family ties and their maintenance', *Howard Journal* 34 (2): 158–175.

Tarzi, A. & Hedge J. (1990) *A Prison Within a Prison- A Study of Foreign National Prisoners*. London: Inner London Probation Service.

Tarzi, A. & Hedge J. (1993) *A Prison Within a Prison - Two Years On: An Overview*. London: Inner London Probation Service.

Whalley, R. (2007) Disturbances at Harmondsworth and Campsfield House Immigration Removal Centres. London: The Stationary Office.

TEN

Minority Muslim Communities and Criminal Justice: Stigmatized UK Faith Identities Post 9/11 and 7/7

Basia Spalek, Robert Lambert, and Abdul Haqq Baker

Introduction

This chapter discusses Muslim communities' engagement with criminal justice agencies, principally policing and prisons, in a post 9/11 and 7/7 context. In the UK, the notion of active citizenship has become a key concept in the political agenda, with individuals encouraged to tackle a wide range of social problems through partnerships with state, private, and non-governmental organizations, in 'bottom-up' approaches to governance (Brannan, John, & Stoker, 2007). In the post 9/11 and 7/7 context, engagement with Muslim communities has taken on particular significance, and criminal justice agencies are engaging with Muslims as a way of countering the threat from terrorism, as well as engaging with individuals as offenders, victims, or witnesses of crime.

This chapter contends that, whether as victims of crime, active citizens, or young offenders, Muslims are faced with criminal justice agencies that problematize their faith identity and fail to acknowledge that, in addition to 'race'/ethnicity and culture, faith is an important identity marker for many of them. Statistical information on religious identity is limited and little credence is given to the notion of government departments and criminal justice agencies engaging with Muslims on the basis of their faith identity. Significantly, unlike racism, anti-semitism and homophobia, Islamophobia is a contested concept. The Muslim Council of Britain, an established although increasingly marginalized, mainstream representative body has warned both that Islamophobia is rife and that Muslim communities feel increasingly under siege. This chapter argues that minority Salafi and Islamist community groups are at increased risk of stigmatization and conflation with terrorists, and that a comparison between their situation and Irish Catholics, who became a 'suspect community' during a long terrorist campaign by the Provisional IRA, can provide valuable insights. The authors' research interest in a pioneering partnership project involving a small specialist police unit in London (the Muslim Contact Unit) and Salafi and Islamist community groups is proposed as an alternative community-based approach to the problems raised by 9/11 and 7/7.

Muslim: A Problematized Faith Identity

Criminal justice agencies have for some time identified and monitored racial and ethnic groupings, notably in publications arising from Section 95 of the Criminal Justice Act 1991, and used the results to guide service delivery and provision. Religious identity has not been considered until very recently, and mainly prompted by the events of 9/11 and 7/7, amid and concern about 'home-grown' terrorism and 'radicalization'. As a result, Muslims have found themselves viewed through a terrorism or extremism lens, which is disconcerting for the overwhelming majority who lead law-abiding lives. Whilst direct and institutional racism by the police, the courts, and the penal system has been extensively documented (Hood, 1992; Jefferson, Walker & Seneviratne, 1992; Kalunta-Crompton, 1999; Bowling & Phillips, 2002; Shute, Hood & Seemungal, 2005), and policies have been implemented to tackle these issues, discrimination on the grounds of religion has rarely been addressed. This is an issue that the Muslim Council of Britain (MCB) campaigned on prior to 7/7 when it had some influence with government. By way of example, in November 2003 the MCB highlighted government failure to implement the recommendations of the Runnymede Commission on British Muslims and Islamophobia published in 1997. The following extract is instructive:

> ... very little progress has been made in tackling the horror of Islamophobia in the United Kingdom after it had been brought into sharp focus by the Commission in its report published in 1997. Whilst we recognise the adverse impact of international politics on the perception of Islam generally and Muslims living in the United Kingdom, we strongly feel that the government has done little to discharge its responsibilities under international law to protect its Muslim citizens and residents from discrimination, vilification, harassment, and deprivation. The legal framework required to articulate standards of behaviour and to bring about a cohesive society remains as inadequate as it was when the report was published by the Commission in 1997 (MCB, 2003)

However, in the wake of 9/11 and more especially 7/7, influential secular commentators have sought to resist moves by all sectors of government to engage with Muslims on the basis of their faith identities (Godson, 2007; Mirza, Senthilkumaran & Ja'far, 2007). This has doubtless weakened the MCB's position, a hitherto mainstream body now cast in the role of 'extremist' and 'Islamist'. The Policy Exchange[1] report 'Living apart together: British Muslims and the paradox of multiculturalism' (Mirza, Senthilkumaran & Ja'far, 2007) illustrates this powerful secular concern that Muslims should not be encouraged by government to identify and represent themselves either as a single-faith community (which would be misleading) or as a series of religious sub-groups (Sunni, Shia, Sufi, Salafi, etc.). The report insists instead that 'Muslim' should be treated as a 'cultural' identity. However, this is not meaningful for minority sections of UK Muslim communities who reject the notion of 'secular' or 'cultural' Muslims and for whom a strong and public faith identity is crucial. This remains a hotly contested debate, and consequently criminal justice agencies do not have a clear government lead as they did in respect of diversity issues, especially post Macpherson (Macpherson, 1999).

The Equality Act 2006 established a new single Commission for Equality and Human Rights (CEHR) that brought together six strands of discrimination – 'race', age, gender, disability, religion, and sexual orientation – into one unified organization. Interestingly, when exercising its powers relating to its community functions, the CEHR is required to have 'particular regard' to race, religion, or belief (Equal Opportunities Commission, 2005), suggesting that faith identities may increasingly be monitored and used for policy development and analysis. Indeed, since 2005–06 the British Crime Survey has been recording the faith identities of respondents. The Home Office Citizenship Survey also looks at perceptions and experiences of prejudice and discrimination (though not actual experiences of criminal victimization) by faith identity. This has revealed that Hindus, Muslims, and Sikhs are substantially more likely to say that they feel very worried about being attacked because of their skin colour, ethnic origin, or religion than Christians, those of other religions, and those of no religion (Department for Communities & Local Government, 2006: 28). This fear has been shown to be heightened in the immediate aftermath of terrorist incidents such as the alleged 'airline plot' in August 2006 (Dodd, 2006). In response Ali Dizaei, a senior Metropolitan Police officer, warned government that it 'risked alienating the Muslim community over (its) reported plans to introduce airport security screening on ethnic and religious grounds' (Daily Mail, 2006). Dizaei's controversial comments resonated in Muslim communities, but were condemned by a senior police colleague as being divisive and part of a small campaign 'trying to hijack the terrorism issue and turn it into a debate on racism' (Judd, 2006). Alan Gordon, on behalf of the Police Federation went further and accused Dizaei of 'displaying blissful ignorance' and resorting to 'cheap, sensationalist

---

[1] Since this chapter was drafted, Policy Exchange has itself suffered a severe dent to its credibility following an investigation by BBC Newsnight that exposed significant flaws in the probity of its research in compiling evidence for the report The Hijacking of British Islam: How Extremist Literature is Subverting Mosques in the UK (MacEoin, 2007).

soundbites' (Judd, 2006). Gordon concluded by defending the notion of terrorist profiling claiming that it had always been used 'in one form or another' in policing (Judd, 2006). This chapter develops Dizaei's observations by contending that certain sections of Muslim communities – Salafis and Islamists – are at greater risk of a more extensive and invidious form of profiling and stigmatization.

Religious identity is an emerging field of policy and research concern within criminal justice and other contexts, but, until recently, all of the available statistics on the number of Muslims living in the UK have been estimates. Data about religious identity was first collected by the National Census 2001: 71.6 per cent of the population in the UK said that their religion was Christianity, and Islam was the next most common faith at 2.7 per cent of the population. However, these figures are likely to be underestimates as the religion question was voluntary and over 4 million people did not answer it. The English region with the highest proportion of Muslims was London (8.5 per cent), with 36 per cent of the population of Tower Hamlets and 24 per cent in Newham being Muslim. Those of Pakistani and Bangladeshi heritage comprised just under 60 per cent of the Muslim population in England and Wales. The remaining 40 per cent of Muslims were ethnically diverse, and included Afghan, Arab, Iranian, Indian, Kosovan, Kurdish, Turkish, and Somali Muslims. British Muslim communities have diverse approaches to their religion. Different religious strands within Islam extend far beyond the main Sunni–Shia divide[2] to include many competing schools of Islamic thought, including, Barelvis, Deobandis, and schools associated with Sufism and Salafism (Esposito, 2003). Such diversity of theological belief, ethnicity, and culture poses significant challenges for research and policy in this field.

More generally, a greater focus upon religious identities is required in debates on equality and diversity, alongside an acknowledgement that faith can be both a positive and negative cultural resource: for example, in some cases of domestic violence, men may use their religion to justify their violent actions (Mama, 2000), while victims of crime may draw upon their faith to help them cope with their plight (Spalek, 2002). There is much debate and controversy around the extent to which the considerations of religious groups can or should be accommodated within, and by, secular institutions (Modood, 2007), including criminal justice agencies. This is a significant issue, given that religiosity amongst Muslims may be higher than for other religious groups (Wardak, 2000). Religiosity might be understood as the degree to which an individual expresses a sincere and earnest regard for religion, which might be

---

[2]The Sunni–Shia split occurred in the decades following the death of the Prophet Mohammed in 632. Sunnis believe that Ali is the fourth of the rightly guided caliphs (successors to Mohammed as leader of Muslims) following on from Abu Bakr 632–634, Umar 634–644, and Uthman 644–656. Shias believe that Ali should have been the first caliph and that the caliphate should pass down only to direct descendants of Mohammed via Ali and Fatima.

understood as including, for example, church attendance, giving donations to religious institutions, and/or reading theological and/or sacred material (Johnson, Jang, Larson, & De Li, 2001). Indeed, as already indicated, even the hitherto 'moderate' government-friendly MCB became dangerously 'Islamist' according to another influential Policy Exchange report (Bright, 2006) in the flurry of post 7/7 polemics. The fact that the MCB was simultaneously excluded from Muslim community engagement launched by the newly formed Department for Communities and Local Government (DLCG) appeared to endorse Bright's pejorative findings (Kelly, 2006a, b, c). Lambert's (2008b) research shows real concern emerging across Muslim community divides that if the MCB can be stigmatized as 'extremist', then there might be no end to the problem.

Contrary to Bright's report, by 2006 the MCB had achieved widespread respect from diverse Muslim communities for much of its campaigning work: for example, when it raised widespread Muslim community concerns that institutional racism within the police service, as highlighted by the Macpherson report (Macpherson, 1999), had developed into institutional prejudice specifically against Muslims. Supported this argument by highlighting 2002–03 police statistics that revealed the number of stops and searches of 'Asians' conducted under the then new counter-terrorism powers had increased by 302 per cent in a year (MCB, 2004). This compared to a rise of 230 per cent for 'blacks' and 118 per cent for 'whites'. The MCB subsequently argued that:

… these figures seem to confirm that police are misusing their new powers. Police have a difficult task ensuring the safety of our country, but this is out of proportion. We think the institutional racism highlighted by the Mcpherson report [on the inquiry into the murder of black teenager Stephen Lawrence] is morphing into institutional prejudice against Muslims. We are worried a generation of young Muslim men is being criminalized in the wake of 9/11 in the same way young black men were previously targeted by police. (Quoted in Cowan, 2004: 8)

Particular attention has been given to the activities and identities of young Muslim men, the extent to which they are integrated into mainstream society, and their propensity to engage in the types of illegal or deviant activities that come to the attention of law enforcement authorities (Spalek, 2006). However, as Muslims constitute the most socially and economically deprived faith group in the UK (Choudhury, 2005), a significant number of young Muslim men, like other socially and economically deprived male youth, are likely to form subcultures, which are also likely to have strong masculinist ideals underpinning them (Archer, 2003). This chapter considers the experience of a Salafi convert community in south London, where street notions of masculinity have often led young men into gun crime. In turn, according to firsthand accounts, al-Qaida propagandists, including most notably Abdullah el Faisal[3], have exploited this vulnerability as a recruitment tool. In this way some of the skills inherent in street crime have been redeployed in a violent extremism context.

Muslim Prisoner Support and Engaging With Convert Communities

The Prison Act 1952 states that prison chaplains should ensure that all prisoners are able to practise their religions, and the Prison Service is the only criminal justice agency that systematically monitors religious affiliation. On 30 June 2005, 10 per cent of the prison population was Muslim, the third largest grouping behind Roman Catholics (17 per cent) and Anglicans (32 per cent) (Home Office, 2006: 105). The social characteristics of the prison population suggest that religious conversion is likely to be a significant feature of prison life (Spalek & El-Hassan, 2007), although the issue of conversion to Islam in prisons in England and Wales has not yet been substantially researched. According to a small-scale study of Muslim converts in English jails involving eight participants (Spalek & El-Hassan, 2007), Islam was perceived by many of the participants as a way of preventing them from carrying out illegal activities in the future, after leaving prison. Statements such as the following were typical:

> In situations like ... I think like always think about Allah is watching you and the situations how to react, how does Mohammed, if he was in this situation yeah, what would he do? And all the prayers and stuff. Cos that's what it's all about, peace init ? That's what it means to be a Muslim, being a peaceful person, that's what it's all about ... (Spalek & El-Hassan, 2007: 110)

In light of the importance of Islam to many Muslim prisoners, the involvement of Muslim communities to help re-settle those individuals who are newly released from prison should perhaps be a key element of practice. However, research has found that practitioners such as probation officers and Victim Support volunteers are often reluctant to open space for discussion of religious or spiritual issues even though these might be important aspects of their clients' lives. A limited amount of research consisting of interviews with Muslim individuals and Muslim community group representatives that provide support services for the victims of crime, including domestic violence, suggest that victims may not be accessing mainstream victim support services but rather value, and seek out, alternative forms of help that may include a focus upon religion and spirituality (Spalek, 2005). Empirical research and exploration are needed on both the appropriateness

---

[3] Abdullah el Faisal was found guilty of soliciting murder and spreading religious hatred in 2003 and was imprisoned. On release in 2007 he was deported to Jamaica, his country of origin.

and practicalities of integrating religious and/or spiritual considerations into practice. Research on religious conversion to Islam has revealed how some converts felt that they had little religious, spiritual, and practical support upon leaving prison:

> Interviewer: Do you think that it will be more difficult to practice Islam on the outside of prison?

> Much more difficult. On the outside I have no foundation for Islam, I'm living in a non-Islamic household and my friends are non-Islamic, the ones that are, they're not practising Muslims they don't go to the mosque every Friday, they talk about Islam but they don't practice the rules as such. B. (Spalek & El-Hassan, 2007:111)

UK prisons provide valuable support for Muslim prisoners in the form of prison imams. In May 2007, prison imams launched their own representative body, the Muslim Chaplain's Association (MCA), to consolidate and promote their work. At its launch the MCA chairman described prison imams' central function as helping prisoners 'to change their way of thinking through education and encourage them to develop a sense of responsibility and accountability for their actions' (Versi, 2007).

Resettlement programmes run by Muslim communities through the use of local mosques can help provide wide-ranging support to ex-offenders, such as practical help in finding accommodation and work, as well as through providing spiritual and religious assistance and guidance where this is asked for. As the substantial number of new Muslim converts are unlikely to have many family or friends who can provide them with religious and spiritual support, it is crucial for resources to be targeted at these particular individuals. In Spalek and El-Hassan's (2007) study of Muslim converts in prison, converts typically were brought up as Christians and so their families would not be able to provide them with Islamic religious/spiritual support. High-profile cases like that of the 'shoe-bomber' Richard Reid purportedly converting to Islam in or shortly after prison have also focused attention on prisons as potential sites for 'radicalization'.

A small police unit in London, the Muslim Contact Unit (MCU), has developed a close working partnership with black convert Muslim community groups, amongst others, who have firsthand experience of Reid's case, and many others of a similar nature. The essence of this work is to empower and facilitate local Muslim community groups in their efforts to educate and support convert Muslims and, where they have been released from prison, to re-integrate them into a devoutly practicing faith community. Such rehabilitation work forms part of a broader project known as 'Street', which was launched by members of the black convert Muslim community in South London in 2007. However, as we discuss below, because this is a Salafi Muslim community project, it risks opposition from powerful commentators who regularly conflate Salafism (and Islamism) with extremism and terrorism. Early research on the Street project also suggests that problems of violent extremism and gun crime can often manifest themselves in the same vulnerable youth communities and be addressed at the same time. Such connections may be self-evident at a street level but unclear if only traditional top-down approaches are applied by policy makers and researchers. Moreover, a focus on black Muslim convert street experience also helps to develop the post-Macpherson debate raised by the MCB. It may be helpful to contrast a closed approach to Muslim community groups, post 9/11, with a more open approach to black and ethnic minority community groups, post Macpherson. Muslim community engagement with police post 9/11 is reminiscent of tensions between police and black communities in the pre-Macpherson era. In addition, by highlighting the pioneering role of the MCU working in partnership with Salafi and Islamist community groups, an alternative vision for future engagement becomes apparent (Spalek & Imtoual, 2007). These groups would have otherwise been excluded from engagement processes as a result of their perceived links with terrorism, or because of their real or perceived opposition to established secular values.

Victimization

Within victim work, there is increasing acknowledgement of the need to take into consideration Muslim, alongside, other faith identities. For example, Spalek (2002) has highlighted how some Muslim women who experience victimization may turn to prayer, meditation, and their local imam as a way of helping them cope in the aftermath of crime. According to a study of South Asians living in Karachi, Pakistan, and Haslingden, England, there was a commonly shared sense of victimization amongst the South Asian Muslims around religious oppression and Islamophobia, this being linked to the concept of the 'ummah', which consists of the individual, community, and global Muslim population (Quraishi, 2005). Others have also written about the sense of identity and global solidarity that the religion of Islam provides for its adherents (Birt, 2006), so that although experiences of crime may differ vastly between individuals living in the UK and those living in other parts of the world, nonetheless, a common sense of victimization based around experiences of Islamophobia may be perceived through individuals' solidarity with the ummah.

Mainstream victim services do not at present consider the relevance of people's religious and spiritual needs, owing to the historical marginalization of religion from the public arena (Beckford, 1996). For example, support services for the victims of domestic and sexual violence generally lack an appreciation of the centrality of faith in some women's lives. This means that for women who have a religious belief, they may choose to stay in their abusive relationships rather than seek help from organizations that may, at best, ignore their religious requirements, or at worst, judge them for conforming to what is viewed as patriarchal religion (Ahmad & Sheriff, 2003). This is not to suggest that accepting domestic abuse is viewed as a religious requirement, but that where religious identity is central to an individual's sense of who they are – and as argued above, this appears particularly to be the case for Muslims – services cannot be effective without acknowledging this fact. By offering a tentative insight into the perspectives of minority Salafi and Islamist communities this chapter seeks to challenge the stereotypes that otherwise inflame the debate. By way of an introduction the authors recommend *From her Sisters Lips* (Robert, 2005) as an insider Salafi woman's view that serves as an antidote to the best-selling mainstream accounts on the subject (Ali, 2006; Spencer, 2006).

In Britain, under the Anti Terrorism Crime and Security Act 2001, a religiously aggravated element to crime was introduced, which involves imposing higher penalties upon offenders who are motivated by religious hatred. While there have been relatively few religiously aggravated prosecutions, at the time of writing the majority of identifiable victims have been Muslim. In 2005–06, out of 43 cases of religiously aggravated crime, 18 incidents involved Muslim victims, 3 involved Christians, 1 involved a Sikh, and 21 victims' religious identities were unknown or not stated (Crown Prosecution Service, 2006: 45). In Lambert's (2008b) research, one police interviewee suggested that Muslim community groups should seek to emulate the work of the Community Security Trust, which scrupulously supports individual Jewish community members who are victims of hate crime by ensuring that full details are logged and investigated by police. However, as noted earlier, there is a hotly contested debate about the very concept and existence of Islamophobia, illustrated by the following contributions for and against:

The trouble with Islamophobia is that it is an irrational concept. It confuses hatred of, and discrimination against, Muslims on the one hand with criticism of Islam on the other. The charge of 'Islamophobia' is all too often used not to highlight racism but to stifle criticism. And in reality discrimination against Muslims is not as great as is often perceived – but criticism of Islam should be greater. (Malik, 2005)

In contrast, the chairman of the MCB claimed in 2007 that Islamophobia had become so endemic and institutionalized in the UK as to make reminders about Nazi Germany worthwhile:

Every society has to be really careful so the situation doesn't lead us to a time when people's minds can be poisoned as they were in the 1930s. If your community is perceived in a very negative manner, and poll after poll says that we are alienated, then Muslims begin to feel very vulnerable. We are seen as creating problems, not as bringing anything and that is not good for any society. (Quoted in Sylvester & Thompson, 2007.)

The number of hate crimes that are prosecuted appears to be tiny in comparison to the number of hate crimes that are actually committed, particularly as most victims do not report their experiences to the police (http://www.victimsupport.org.uk/vs_england-wales/index.php). Muslim community groups, often working in partnership with local police services, play an important role in monitoring and documenting instances of hate crime. For example, the Forum Against Islamophobia and Racism (FAIR), the Islamic Human Rights Commission (IHRC), and the MCB are three organizations that monitor hate crimes committed against Muslim communities. According to the IHRC, which collected reports about attacks against Muslims from mosques and community groups, there was a rise in the number of anti-Muslim attacks during the holy month of Ramadan (http://www.ihrc.org 2006). This serves to illustrate how the incidence of faith hate crimes can be significantly influenced by cultural/religious events, as well as by national and international events, such as the London bombings, following which the Metropolitan Police Service recorded a sharp increase in faith related hate crimes, including verbal and physical assaults (European Monitoring Centre on Racism & Xenophobia, 2005).

Stigmatization – Learning from Experience

In the same way that Irish Catholic communities in the UK were often stigmatized with the terrorism of the Provisional IRA (Hillyard, 1993), so too are minority sections of Muslim communities in the UK at risk of pejorative stigmatization and conflation with al-Qaida terrorism. Similarly, just as Irish Protestant loyalists were only rarely and mistakenly conflated with Provisional IRA terrorists (and a consequent threat to UK cities like London and Manchester), so too are majority Barelvi, Sufi, or secular British Muslims increasingly less likely to be stigmatized as terrorists (and then only mistakenly) than Salafis and Islamists, minority Muslim communities in the UK that are routinely conflated with terrorism, extremism, and violent radicalism by influential commentators (Phillips, 2006; Gove 2006a; Cox & Marks, 2006; Hussein, 2007). While the events of 11 September 2001, the London bombings of 7 July 2005, and the attempted bombings of 21 July 2005 inevitably put all Muslims under the spotlight, it is increasingly apparent that Salafi and Islamist Muslim communities (like Irish Catholic nationalist and republican communities in the recent past) face the greatest risk of being cast in the role of 'suspect communities' (Hillyard, 1993).

In consequence, it becomes aposite to focus on the importance of understanding the heterogenerous nature of UK Muslim communities and especially those minority sections that are likely to be at greatest risk of stigmatization. Moreover, just as Irish Catholic communities faced this very same stigmatization it must also be noted that their young community members were often at high risk from Provisional IRA propaganda and recruitment strategies as well. So too have young members of Salafi and Islamist communities in the UK been at risk from highly developed al-Qaida propaganda and recruitment strategies since 9/11 (Lambert 2008a, b). The adverse impact of these instances of parallel stigmatization of minority communities as terrorists and susceptibility to terrorist recruitment is therefore worthy of preliminary examination. At the outset it is suggested that the best way of approaching the terms 'Salafism' and 'Islamism' is to see them as they are widely understood by the groups who apply the terms to themselves. In this respect the chapter's two non-Muslim authors are grateful to their Salafi co-author for the unique insider insight his perspective affords.

On this basis it is reasonable to recommend the *Oxford Dictionary of Islam* as a neutral entry point to the topic. Thus, stripped of pejorative usage, 'Islamist' becomes 'a term used to describe an Islamic political or social activist' and 'Salafi' is reduced to 'a name derived from salaf, "pious ancestors," given to a reform movement that emphasizes the restoration of Islamic doctrines to pure form, adherence to the Qur'an and Sunnah, rejection of the authority of later interpretations, and maintenance of the unity of ummah', that is, the Muslim community (Esposito, 2003). Salafism and Islamism, it follows, are no more significant to the profile of an al-Qaida terrorist than Catholicism was to the profile of a Provisional IRA terrorist. On the contrary, the fact that al-Qaida spokesmen often invoke and subvert Salafi and Islamist approaches to Islam in an attempt to legitimize their violence helps illustrate why it is that Salafi and Islamist community groups often have the best tools with which to undermine al-Qaida propaganda within their own youth communities. Again this follows relevant experience in Northern Ireland, where Catholic community groups (not Protestant ones) often played important roles in explaining to young Catholic community members that their religious and civic obligations did not sanction involvement in terrorist bombings.

Hillyard's (1993) seminal account of 'suspect communities' was especially concerned with the adverse impact of coercive policing and security activity licensed by the Prevention of Terrorism (Temporary Provisions) Act (first introduced in 1974 and then renewed on an annual basis) on minority Irish communities living principally in Northern Ireland, England, and Scotland. As he noted, the vast majority of over 7,000 Irish 'suspects' who had by then been arrested and detained under the emergency legislation had been subsequently released without charge. By detailing individual, often harrowing, personal accounts of the arrest, detention, and questioning of 'suspects', Hillyard was expressing a minority and poorly funded academic interest in the notion that such extraordinary and draconian police powers (first enacted by Parliament in the febrile aftermath of the Birmingham pub bombings in 1974) might unfairly alienate and stigmatize minority sections of Irish communities. The authors of this chapter share Paddy Hillyard's concerns that the 'war on terror', launched by George Bush and Tony Blair in the immediate aftermath of 9/11, has similarly licensed draconian and otherwise unlawful treatment of terrorist 'suspects' most notably at Guantanamo Bay and at various undisclosed locations under the guise of extraordinary rendition that has alienated minority sections of Muslim communities in the UK as elsewhere in the world (Hillyard, 2006; Begg, 2006).

A Partnership Policing Initiative

Now, as then, supporters of counter-terrorism measures are invariably seen to be on the side of legislation that grants increased counter-terrorism powers, for example, longer periods of pre-trial detention (Crossman and Gillord, 2005: 7) and special legislation (Clarke, 2007). At the same time, they are silent on allegations of torture and human rights abuses, such as those at Guantanamo Bay and other venues legitimized by an international 'war on terror'. However, the authors are currently researching a small strand of UK counter-terrorism involving the MCU in the Metropolitan Police (Spalek & Lambert 2007; Lambert 2008a, b) where the importance of Hillyard's earlier research has not been entirely lost. Rather, the MCU examines the implications of alienated Muslim minority communities on al-Qaida recruitment and support. Broadly speaking, this is counter-intuitive and under-researched police work that is best characterized as a 'community-based approaches to counter-terrorism' (Demos, 2006; Blick, Choudhury, & Wier, 2006).

Since January 2002 and against the grain of the war on terror, this police unit has built trusting partnerships with minority, often marginalized, Muslim community groups in London with a view to empowering their efforts to counter al-Qaida propaganda and recruitment strategies on their own terms. The MCU has assisted only those groups with a proven track record of success in this dangerous field. Employing considerable counter-terrorism practitioner experience, the MCU has approached specific Salafi and Islamist community groups in London and formed proactive partnerships with those assessed to be well qualified for the task. As a result, working in partnership with specific Salafi and Islamist groups for at least 3 years before 'home-grown terrorism', 'radicalization', 'counter-radicalization', and 'de-radicalization' became ubiquitous research agendas, the MCU was an early repository of independent, bottom-up, street-focused counter-terrorism expertise. Needless to say, this has often placed the unit at odds with more prescriptive top-down counter-terrorism advocates (Phillips, 2006; Godson, 2006a, b, 2007; Gove 2006a, b). Moreover, while the government's more recent 'prevent' agenda sets out the importance of winning Muslim community support so as to enhance the yield and quality of community intelligence (HMSO, 2006), the MCU has gone much further than this strategy allows, thereby running the risk of losing Whitehall and Association of Chief Police Officers (ACPO) support. In particular, the MCU has acknowledged the connection between the government's approach to the war on terror and an increased susceptibility of some Muslim youth to the blandishments of al-Qaida propagandists. More specifically, the unit has highlighted the potential for counter-terrorism policy and counter-terrorism operational activity that is not narrowly focused on legitimate terrorist targets, to lead to alienation in some Muslim youth communities and thereby increase the risk of al-Qaida recruitment and support (Lambert, 2008b).

Consequently, research on partnership activity between the MCU and Salafi and Islamist community groups offers a significantly different vantage point to the welter of post 7/7 government-sponsored research committed to identifying the causes of 'home-grown' terrorism and most especially the tipping point from 'radical' into violent extremism. One negative feature of this burgeoning research field is the significance it attaches to accounts of non violent radicalism of the kind articulated in *The Islamist* (Hussein, 2007). By conflating terrorism with radicalism in this way there is a danger of further problematizing Salafi and Islamist community groups, including the very ones who are at the forefront of pioneering partnership work aimed at reducing the risk of further al-Qaida recruitment and support in the UK. A useful critique of this dominant 'radicalization' research agenda is provided by an alternative group of scholars, activists, and practitioners concerned with challenging the mainstream 'radicalization' discourse at points where it 'assumes simplistic and mono-causal explanations for political violence', 'constructs everyday Muslim practices, Islamically inspired political activism and the broader Muslim community as inherently 'suspect', 'restricts the scope of legitimate criticism about foreign policy and divisive political domestic issues', and is 'counter-productive, inconsistent, and highly negative in terms of government goals of preventing further terrorist violence' (Smyth, Jackson, & Gunning, 2007). The same co-operative shares the MCU approach of seeking to understand Salafi, Islamist (and other) Muslim minority perspectives on their own terms. That also has been the underlying and prime purpose of this chapter.

Conclusion

This chapter has focussed upon Muslim communities' engagement with criminal justice agencies, principally policing and prisons, in a post 9/11 and 7/7 context. A key issue highlighted in this chapter is that criminal justice agencies have traditionally approached diversity issues through a secular, race relations framework so that currently, Muslims are faced with criminal justice agencies that problematize their faith identity. This is particularly significant in a post 9/11 and 7/7 context, whereby criminal justice agencies are increasingly engaging with Muslims as a way of countering the threat from terrorism, as well as engaging with individuals as offenders, victims, and witnesses of crime. This chapter also suggests that minority Salafi and Islamist community groups are at increased risk of stigmatization and conflation with terrorists. This chapter highlights the pioneering role of the MCU working in partnership with Salafi and Islamist community groups that have otherwise been excluded from engagement processes as a result of their perceived links with terrorism, or because of their real or perceived opposition to established secular values, thereby offering an alternative vision for future engagement. The authors of this chapter wish to stress the importance of 'bottom-up', community-based approaches to engagement in a post 9/11 and 7/7 context, whereby statutory agencies work in partnership with Muslim communities, for the purposes of counter-terrorism and counter-radicalization. Within an arguably heightened security context, partnership work between agencies of the criminal justice system and Muslim communities to tackle violent extremism is a developing, and important, area of policy and practice.

Summary

In the post 9/11 and 7/7 context, engagement with Muslim communities has taken on particular significance, and criminal justice agencies are engaging with Muslims as a way of countering the threat from terrorism, as well as engaging with individuals as offenders, victims, or witnesses of crime. This chapter highlights how criminal justice agencies have traditionally approached diversity issues through a secular, race relations framework and argues that, currently, Muslims are faced with criminal justice agencies that problematize their faith identity. Moreover, it suggests that minority Salafi and Islamist community groups are at increased risk of stigmatization and conflation with terrorists. The work of the Muslim Contact Unit is highlighted owing to its pioneering partnership work with Salafi and Islamist community groups. The chapter stresses the importance of 'bottom-up', community-based approaches to engagement in a post 9/11 and 7/7 context, whereby statutory agencies work in partnership with Muslim communities, for the purposes of counter-terrorism and counter-radicalization.

Key Texts

Choudhury, T. (ed) (2005) *Muslims in the UK: Policies for Engaged Citizens*. Budapest: Open Society Institute.
Hillyard, P. (1993) *Suspect Community: People's Experience of the Prevention of Terrorism Acts in Britain*. London: Pluto Press.
Modood, T. (2007) *Multiculturalism: Themes for the 21st Century*. Cambridge: Polity Press.

References

Ahmad, F. & Sheriff, S. (2003) 'Muslim women of Europe: welfare needs and responses', *Social Work in Europe*, Vol. 8(1) pp. 30–55.

Ali, A.H. (2006) *The Caged Virgin*. London: Free Press.

Archer, L. (2003) *Race, Masculinity & Schooling*. Berkshire: Open University Press.

Beckford, J. (1996) 'Postmodernity, High Modernity and New Modernity: three concepts in search of religion' in: K. Flanagan & P. Jupp (eds) *Postmodernity, Sociology and Religion*. 30–47, Hampshire: Palgrave.

Begg, M. (2006) *Enemy Combatant: A British Muslim's Journey to Guantanamo and Back*. London: Free Press.

Birt, Y. (2006) 'Islamic citizenship in Britain after 7/7: tackling extremism and preserving freedoms' in: A. Malik (ed.) *The State We're In: Identity, Terror and the Law of Jihad*. Bristol: Amal Press 9–20.

Blick, A., Choudhrury, T., & Wier, S. (2006) *The Rules of the Game: Terrorism, Community and Human Rights*. York: Joseph Rowntree Reform Trust.

Bowling, B. & Phillips, C. (2002) Racism, *Crime and Justice*, Harlow: Longman.

Brannan, T., John, P. & Stoker, G. (2007) 'Re-energizing Citizenship: what, why and how?' in T. Brannan, P. John, & G. Stoker (eds) Re-energizing Citizenship strategies for civil renewal 8–25.

Bright, M. (2006) *When Progressives Treat with Reactionaries*. London: Policy Exchange.

Choudhury, T. (2005) 'Overview' in: T. Choudhury (ed) *Muslims in the UK: Policies for Engaged Citizens*. Budapest: Open Society Institute, pp. 1–14.

Clarke, P. (2007). Learning from Experience. Colin Cramphorn Memorial Lecture delivered at Policy Exchange, London. http://www.policyexchange.org.uk/images/libimages/252.pdf accessed 26.8.08

Cowan, R. (2004) 'Young Muslims "Made Scapegoats" in Stop and Search', *The Guardian*, Saturday July 3rd.

Cox, C. & Marks, J. (2006) *The West, Islam and Islamism: Is Ideological Islam Compatible with Liberal Democracy?* London: Civitas.

Crossman, G. and Gillard, Z. (2005). Under Attack: Liberty and Security. Liberty newsletter. Autumn. http://www.liberty-human-rights.org.uk/publications/2-newsletter/autumn-05.pdf accessed 26.8.08

Crown Prosecution Service (2006) Racist & Religious Incident Monitoring Report 2005–2006. http://www.cps.gov.uk/publications/docs/rms05-06.pdf date accessed 27 May, 2007.

Daily Mail (2006) Airport Profiling will make Travelling While Asian an offence. Interview with Chief Superintendent Ali Dizaei *Daily Mail* 15 August http://www.dailymail.co.uk/pages/live/articles/news/news.html?in_article_id=400701&in_page_id=1770 accessed 28 December.

Department for Communities & Local Government (2006) 2005 Citizenship Survey race and faith topic report London: DCLG.

Dodd, V. (2006). Eleven Charged Over Alleged Airline Terror Plot. *The Guardian* 22 August http://www.guardian.co.uk/terrorism/story/0,,1855521,00.html accessed 28 December 2007.

Equal Opportunities Commission (2005) Parliamentary Briefing Equality Bill 21st November Commons Second Reading November.

Esposito, J. (ed) (2003) *The Oxford Dictionary of Islam*, Oxford: Oxford University Press.

European Monitoring Centre on Racism & Xenophobia (2005) *The Impact of 7 July 2005 London Bomb Attacks on Muslim Communities in the EU*. Vienna: EUMC.

Godson, D. (2006a) 'Already Hooked on Poison'. *The Times*, February 8.

Godson, D. (2006b) 'You'll Never Guess Who's to Blame for 7/7.' *The Times*, December 13.

Godson, D. (2007) 'The Old Bill Should Choose its Friends Carefully: What on Earth are West Midlands Police up to?' *The Times* August 23.

Gove, M. (2006a) *Celsius 7/7*. London: Weidenfield & Nicholson.

Gove, M. (2006b) 'We Must Engage with Moderate Muslims.' *The Guardian*, August 23.

HMSO (2006) *Countering International Terrorism: The United Kingdom's Strategy*, London: HMSO.

Hillyard, P. (1993) *Suspect Community: People's Experience of the Prevention of Terrorism Acts in Britain*. London: Pluto Press.

Hillyard, P. (2006) Speech to Critical Terrorism Studies conference, University of Manchester, October 27, 28.

Home Office (2001) 'Prison Statistics 2000 England & Wales' London: HMSO.

Hood, R. (1992) 'Discrimination in the Courts?' in: *Race and Sentencing*. Oxford: Clarendon Press. 179–192.

Hussein, E. (2007) *The Islamist*. London: Penguin.

Jefferson, T., Walker, M. & Seneviratne, M. (1992) 'Ethnic minorities, crime and criminal justice: a study in a provincial city' in: D. Downes (ed) *Unravelling Criminal Justice*. London: Macmillan 138–164.

Johnson, B., Jang, S.J., Larson, D.B. & De Li, S. (2001) Does Adolescent Religious Commitment Matter? A Reexamination of the Effects of Religiosity on Delinquency, in *Jouranl of Research in Crime and Deliquency*, 38(1): 22–44.

Judd, Teri, 2006. Police in public feud over profiling *The Independent* 21 August http://news.independent.co.uk/uk/crime/article1220622.ece accessed 28 December 2007.

Kalunta-Crompton (1999) *Race and Drug Trials*. Aldershot: Avebury.

Kelly, R. (2006a) Britain: Our Values, Our Responsibilities – Speech to Muslim Community Groups, 11 October http://www.communities.gov.uk/archived/speeches/corporate/values-responsibilities accessed 27 December 2007.

Kelly, R. (2006b) Speech at launch of Commission on Integration and Cohesion, 24 August http://www.communities.gov.uk/speeches/corporate/commission-integration-cohesion> accessed 27 December 2007.

Kelly, R. (2006c) Speech at launch of Sufi Muslim Council, 19 July http://www.communities.gov.uk/speeches/corporate/sufi-muslim-council accessed 27 December 2007.

Lambert, R. (2008a) 'Empowering Salafis and Islamists against al-Qaida: a London counter-terrorism case study' *Political Science Online* 41 (1): 31–35.

Lambert, R (2008b forthcoming) *Countering al-Qaida Propaganda and Recruitment in London: An Insider's Interpretive Case Study.* PhD dissertation. Department of Politics, University of Exeter.

MacEoin, D. (2007) *The Hijacking of British Islam: How Extremist Literature is Subverting Mosques in the UK* London: Policy Exchange.

Macpherson, Lord (1999) The Stephen Lawrence Inquiry: Report. *Cm. 4262–1.*

Malik, K. (2005) The Islamophobia Myth *Prospect*. February http://www.kenanmalik.com/essays/islamophobia_prospect.html accessed 29 December 2007.

Mama, A. (2000) 'Woman abuse in London's black communities' in: K. Owusu (ed) *Black British Culture & Society* London: Routledge pp. 89–110.

Mirza, M., Senthilkumaran, A. & Ja'far, Z. (2007) *Living apart together: British Muslims & the paradox of multiculturalism.* London: The Policy Exchange.

Modood, T. (2007) *Multiculturalism: Themes for the 21st Century.* Cambridge: Polity Press.

Muslim Council of Britain (2003) Response to Islamophobia - Identity, Inclusion, Cohesion, and equality in Modern Britain, a report by the Runnymede Commission on British Muslims and Islamophobia, 20 November http://www.mcb.org.uk/library/Islamophobia.pdf accessed 28 December 2007.

Muslim Council of Britain (2004) Counter-Terrorism Powers: Reconciling Security and Liberty in an Open Society, August http://www.mcb.org.uk/library/ATCSA.pdf accessed 28 December 2007.

National Census (2001) Ethnicity and Religion in England and Wales, http://www.statistics.gov.uk/census2001/profiles/commentaries/ethnicity accessed 30 March 30 2007.

National Statistics (2001) Religion in Britain, http://www.statistics.gov.uk/cci/nugget.asp?id=293 accessed 27 May 2007.

Phillips, M. (2006). *Londonistan: How Britain Is Creating a Terror State Within.* London: Gibson Square.

Quraishi, M. (2005) *Muslims and Crime: a Comparative Study.* London: Ashgate.

Robert, N. R. (2005) *From My Sisters' Lips.* London: Bantam Books.

Shute, S., Hood, R. & Seemungal, F. (2005) *A Fair Hearing? Ethnic Minorities in the Criminal Courts.* Devon: Willan Publishing.

Smyth, M.B., Jackson, R. & Gunning, J. (2007) The Politics of Radicalisation: Reframing the Debate and Reclaiming the Language seminar report. Centre for the Study of 'Radicalisation' & Contemporary Political Violence, Aberystwyth University/London Muslim Centre 18 October.

Souhami, A. (2007) 'Understanding institutional racism: the Stephen Lawrence Inquiry and the police service reaction' in: *Policing Beyond Macpherson: Issues in Policing, Race and Society.* Devon: Willan pp. 66–87.

Spalek, B. (2002) 'Muslim women's safety talk and their experiences of victimisation' in: B. Spalek (ed) *Islam, Crime and Criminal Justice.* Devon: Willan. 50–71.

Spalek, B. (2005) 'Muslims and the criminal justice system' in: T. Choudhury (ed) *Muslims in the UK: Policies for Engaged Citizens* Budapest: Open Society Institute. 253–340.

Spalek, B. (2006) 'Disconnection and exclusion: pathways to radicalisation?' in: T. Abbas (ed) *Islamic Political Radicalism*. Edinburgh: Edinburgh University Press.

Spalek, B. & El-Hassan, S. (2007) 'Muslim converts in prison' *The Howard Journal of Criminal Justice*, 46 (2), 99–114.

Spalek, B. & Imtoual, A. (2007) 'Hard' approaches to community engagement in the UK and Australia: Muslim communities and counter-terror responses' *Journal of Muslim Minority Affairs*, 27 (2), 185–202.

Spalek, B. & Lambert, R. (2007) 'Terrorism, Counter-Terrorism and Muslim Community Engagement post 9/11' *Social Justice and Criminal Justice conference papers*. Centre for Crime & Justice Studies, Kings College, London July pp. 202–215.

Spencer, R. (2006) *The Truth About Muhammad: Founder of the World's Most Intolerant Religion*. Washington: Regency Publishing.

Sylvester, R. & Thompson, A. (2007) 'Dr. Bari - Government Stoking Muslim Tension *Daily Telegraph* 12 November http://www.telegraph.co.uk/news/main.jhtml?xml=/news/2007/11/10/nbari110.xml accessed 28 December.

Versi, A. (2007) 'Muslim prison chaplain welcomed', in *The Muslim News Online*. 25 May http://www.muslimnews.co.uk/paper/index.php?article=2966.

Wardak, A. (2000) *Social Control and Deviance*. Aldershot: Ashgate.

ELEVEN

Policing Racist Hate Crime: Policy, Practice, and Experience

Nathan Hall

As an object of academic study, racist hate crime is a comparatively new and under-explored issue in Britain. Despite a long history of what we now label as 'hate crimes', it was the murder of Stephen Lawrence in London in 1993 and the subsequent public inquiry in 1999 that served as a catalyst for raising the profile of racist hate crime as a social, political, and policing problem deserving of serious attention in its own right. This chapter will explore a number of issues relating to the policing of racist hate crime, both historical and contemporary, and with particular focus on theoretical and practical influences that inevitably affect the police response to the hate crime 'problem'.

Defining Racist Hate Crime

Operational Policing Definitions

Between 1986 and 1999, each of the 43 police forces of England and Wales collected information on racist incidents using the Association of Chief Police Officers' definition, which referred to:

Any incident in which it appears to the reporting or investigating officer that the complaint involves an element of racial motivation; or any incident which includes an allegation of racial motivation made by any person. (ACPO, 1985)

Following the Stephen Lawrence Inquiry, the police service adopted the definition recommended by Sir William Macpherson and as such:

A racist incident is any incident which is perceived to be racist by the victim or any other person. (Macpherson, 1999 rec. 12)

This definition is held to be clearer and simpler than the original (Home Office, 2002) and purposefully removes the discretionary element from the police in determining what is and what is not a racist incident: a situation that contributed to the failure of the investigation into the murder of Stephen Lawrence. The definition, therefore, allows for anyone to be a victim of racist hate crime, and for any offence to be recorded and investigated by the police as a racist hate crime.

In England and Wales, therefore, at the reporting and recording stage of the policing process, there is no evidential test that the hate incident has to pass. The definition is simply concerned with the *prima facie* test, rather than an evidential one (i.e., 'does this appear on the surface to be a hate crime?' rather than 'is there sufficient legal evidence for this to be classified as a notifiable offence?').

Legal Definitions

Although other civil and criminal legislation is in place, the key piece of legislation relating to racist crime is the Crime and Disorder Act 1998. This legislation allows for enhanced sentencing for racially and, following amendment by the Anti-terrorism, Crime and Security Act of 2001, religiously motivated assaults, criminal damage, public order offences, and harassment. Under the Crime and Disorder Act (1998: 2, s. 28) an offence is racially aggravated if

(a) at the time of committing the offence, or immediately before or after doing so, the offender demonstrates towards the victim of the offence hostility based on the victim's membership (or presumed membership) of a racial group; or

(b) the offence is motivated (wholly or partly) by hostility towards members of a racial group based on their membership of that group.

Under the act a 'racial group' refers to persons defined by reference to their race, colour, nationality, or ethnic or national origins, and in section 28(3a) includes membership of any religious group.

The Extent and Nature of Racist Hate Crime

Official Statistics

Official figures pertaining to racially motivated offending are published annually by the Home Office under section 95 of the 1991 Criminal Justice Act. The latest figures at the time of writing show that the 43 police services in England and Wales recorded 57,902 racist *incidents* in 2004–05, of which 37,028 were recorded as racist *offences*. Of the latter, the statistics show that 61 per cent were offences of harassment, 14 per cent other wounding, 10 per cent common assault, and 15 per cent criminal damage (Home Office, 2006).

The statistics also illustrate that there is a notable *geographic* variation in the numbers of incidents recorded by the police. Broadly speaking, recorded racist hate crime is disproportionately present in metropolitan areas, most notably in London, the West Midlands, Greater Manchester, and West Yorkshire, with rural areas recording far fewer incidents. The most obvious explanation for this is the greater concentration of minority groups in large cities, but may also reflect different police practices and priorities.

Retrospectively, the section 95 statistics also illustrate a sudden increase in recorded racist incidents between 1998–99 and 1999–2000. The most notable rise occurred within the Metropolitan Police area, which saw recorded incidents rise from 11,050 to 23,346 incidents in the space of a year. In that period the Stephen Lawrence Inquiry was published, the new definition of a racist incident cited above was adopted, and police attention was sharply focussed on these types of crimes. The combined result was that officially recorded incidents of racist hate crime rose sharply.

The British Crime Survey

The most comprehensive estimate of crime available in Britain is the British Crime Survey (BCS) that records people's experience and perception of crime using a representative sample of respondents (Home Office, 2004). The BCS estimates that 206,000 racially motivated incidents occurred in 2003–04, of which 135,000 involved personal crime and 71,000 involved crimes against households (Home Office, 2004). Clearly, when compared with recorded police figures, the BCS findings illustrate that racist hate crime is vastly underreported to the authorities.

Clear-up Rates

The latest Home Office figures show that, overall, the police cleared up 36 per cent of racially or religiously aggravated offences in 2004–5 (Home Office, 2006). However, for violent crimes the clear-up rate for racially or religiously aggravated offences was lower than for their non-aggravated equivalents. For example, the clear-up rate for racially or religiously aggravated harassment was 40 per cent compared with 66 per cent for the non-aggravated equivalent. Similarly, equivalent figures for less-serious wounding and common assault were 39 per cent and 49 per cent, and 35 per cent and 43 per cent (Home Office, 2006).

Historical Context

One of the key barriers to the effective policing of racist hate crimes is the negative perception of the police held by many members of ethnic minority groups, and in particular the police action or inaction that has contributed to the formation of those perceptions.

At the numerous public forums held around the country as a part of the inquiry into the murder of Stephen Lawrence (Macpherson, 1999), one theme of particular interest persistently emerged. It was starkly apparent from the views expressed by members of the public that black people's experience of the police in England and Wales was overwhelmingly one of being 'over-policed' and 'under-protected'. It was clear that these views were not simply an angry response to the police handling of Stephen Lawrence's murder, but are in fact deeply rooted in lived experience over a significant period of time (Bowling, 1999).

Over-policing

The issue of the over-policing of black people can be traced back over a significant period of time. Indeed, one of the first studies examining this issue conducted by Hunte in 1966 stated that 'it has been confirmed from reliable sources that sergeants and constables do leave stations with the express purpose of going "nigger hunting". That is to say, they do not get their orders from superiors to act in this way, but among themselves they decided to bring in a coloured person at all costs' (1966: 12).

Hunte's study is now dated but the theme of 'over-policing' has been reflected in numerous studies conducted by various researchers and organizations throughout the 1970s, 1980s, and 1990s. From a cursory overview of existing criminological literature it would appear that the concerns expressed at the public meetings for the Stephen Lawrence Inquiry are well founded and have deep historical roots.

Reiner (1992) has suggested that these concerns are the product of 'the catastrophic deterioration of [police] relations with the black community' (1992: 102) that can be traced back to the early 1970s. Reiner explains that at that time evidence of black people being disproportionately involved in arrests for certain offences (particularly street crimes) was beginning to accumulate, and it became apparent that this situation was due in part to discrimination and racism embedded in police culture. Furthermore, a number of studies demonstrated that the police disproportionately and overwhelmingly exercised their powers against blacks, particularly in respect of 'stop and search' (Willis, 1983) and the decision to prosecute (Landau, 1981).

Under-protecting

A second crucial issue is that of the under-protection of members of minority communities. Of particular concern are the perceptions held by ethnic minority groups relating to the police response to racist hate crimes. It is widely documented that minority victims 'perceive the police response as frequently inadequately sympathetic or effective' (Reiner, 1997: 1012). In their evidence to the Royal Commission on Criminal Procedure in 1979, the Institute of Race Relations submitted a report highlighting many concerns about the police response to such incidents. The report claimed that

police officers have frequently failed to recognise the racial dimension of attacks; that there has often been a significant time delay in response to calls for assistance; an unwillingness to investigate or prosecute offenders; the provision of inadequate advice; and general hostility towards victims. (cited in Holdaway, 1996: 58)

More recent evidence demonstrates that these concerns are as relevant today as they were in 1979, if not more so, as communities have become more diverse (Holdaway, 1996; Bradley, 1998; HMIC, 1999, Macpherson, 1999). For example, in addition to surveying individuals for their experiences of victimization, Ben Bowling's empirical study of North Plaistow in London (Bowling, 1999) also examined victims' satisfaction with the police response. Whilst satisfaction varied with the ethnic and gender characteristics of the victim, overall the study showed that fewer than one in ten respondents were very satisfied with the way the police handled the matter and less than half were very or fairly satisfied. One-half were dissatisfied and one-fifth very dissatisfied. These figures concur with those of the British Crime Surveys that consistently indicate that victims of racial incidents are significantly less likely to be satisfied with the police service than victims of crime in general.

The Metropolitan Police Service (1999bd) has acknowledged this problem, stating that

many victims of race/hate crime have little knowledge of the authorities that seek to serve them other than that they do not seem to get protection from them. They have had, within their collective experience, a number of hostile and prejudiced encounters with the police that lead them to view us [the police] at best as unsympathetic and at worst actively racist. (1999bd: 90)

A salient feature of the non-reporting of racist incidents is the perception that is widely held by ethnic minority groups that the police are not interested in investigating such incidents (Fitzgerald & Hale, 1996; Bowling, 1999; Hall, 2000). This situation is reflected in the huge differences in figures that are consistently found between official police records of racist incidents and national and local victim surveys.

Explaining 'Failure'

The historical 'failure' of the police outlined above has tended to be explained in terms of individual and, more recently, institutional racism. Whilst these are of fundamental importance and will be discussed below in relation to the Stephen Lawrence Inquiry, there are two other issues that also need to be considered if we are to understand this 'failure'. These relate firstly to the nature of racist hate crime and secondly to police decision-making.

Racist Hate Crime As A 'Process'

Bowling (1999: 158) explains that racist hate crime should be viewed as an ongoing *process*, rather than as a series of isolated, distinct, and separate incidents. He suggests that

> Conceiving of violent racism (and other forms of crime) as processes implies an analysis which is dynamic; includes the social relationships between all the actors in the process; can capture the continuity between physical violence, threat and intimidation; can capture the dynamic of repeated or systematic victimization; incorporates historical context; and takes account of the social relationships which inform definitions of appropriate and inappropriate behaviour.

Put simply, crime victimization does not begin and end with the commission of an offence. Hate victimization may involve one crime or, more likely, a great many crimes to the extent that it is not always clear where one ends and the next begins. It may also involve actions that border on being criminal offences but might not be easily defined or recognized as such (a situation that can have serious implications for policing; see below). There is evidence to suggest that these events can nevertheless have a disproportionate effect on the victim and their community, and that the fear and intimidation that results will transcend far beyond just the moment when the incident or incidents occur.

Viewing hate crime in this way can help to explain the negative views of the police that many members of minority groups hold. The underlying rationale is that there is a fundamental mismatch between the nature of hate crime and the requirements of the criminal justice system. Ben Bowling (1999) argues that the problem is that whilst racist hate crime is best viewed as an ongoing *process*, the police and wider criminal justice system necessarily respond to *incidents*. For Bowling, this presents a significant problem for the agencies of the criminal justice system. These agencies recognize and respond to incidents, which Bowling defines as a one-dimensional, narrowly restricted time-slice within which only the actions of the immediate protagonists are of any relevance. In this sense, Bowling points to the fact that English criminal law understands crime only as a single event committed by an individual with criminal intent.

Bowling suggests that when the process of racist victimization is reduced to a series of isolated incidents, they become describable and measurable but appear random and inexplicable to outsiders, and are impossible to properly understand because the lived experience of the victim is drained of any context. When hate crime is reduced to an 'incident', the ongoing process of fear and intimidation becomes lost to outside view. One incident may appear minor and relatively meaningless, but the cumulative effect of the victimization is often significant. Bowling suggests that as the 'incident' is transformed from the world of the victim's experience into an object for policing it is placed in the context of the police organizational and cultural milieu, an environment that is usually antithetical to that of the victim. The net result of the 'process–incident' contradiction, according to Bowling, is that whilst the police may feel that they have responded appropriately and effectively to an *incident*, the victims are frequently left with feelings of dissatisfaction, fear, and a perception of being under-protected.

The Police 'Hierarchy of Relevance'

In addition to the 'process–incident' contradiction, Bowling (1999), citing research by Grimshaw and Jefferson (1987), argues that the existence of a 'hierarchy of police relevance' can also have an impact on the policing of racist hate crime. On attending an incident, a police officer can decide his or her course of action from a range of available options from making an arrest or conducting an investigation to simply moving on to the next call for assistance, depending on the requirements of the law and the needs of the immediate situation. When making decisions about which course of action to take, research has shown that officers utilize a hypothetical 'hierarchy of police relevance', often subconsciously, that determines their response to any given incident. At the top of the hierarchy are what Bowling terms 'good crimes'. These are clear criminal offences with innocent, reliable, and credible victims, perpetrators that are 'real' criminals, and that offer a clear opportunity of detection and arrest and a good result in terms of securing a conviction. Further down the hierarchy are 'rubbish' crimes, in which the 'quality' of the victim and perpetrator may be poor, where evidence may be lacking, where there is a much reduced chance of detection and arrest, or where there is an increased likelihood that the victim will withdraw the allegation. At the bottom end of the hierarchy are what Bowling terms 'disputes' or 'disturbances', which are frequently perceived to be legally ambiguous and of limited police relevance.

Bowling's research highlighted the extent to which, from a police perspective, racist incidents routinely fall short of the criteria required to classify them as a 'good crime' and are often regarded as 'disputes' or 'disturbances' (note the types of offences that dominate the official statistics outlined above). In other words, in all but the most serious crimes where the legal relevance to the police is clear, racist incidents tend to appear at the lower end of the hierarchy of police relevance, and as such receive less police attention than crimes where the legal duty to respond is unambiguous. Crucially, Bowling's research illustrated that this placing of racist incidents on the hierarchy, most notably by rank and file officers, remained consistent despite changes in force policy and the force prioritization of racist offences. This 'hierarchy of relevance' helps to explain the historical propensity for racist incidents not to be recorded, or treated appropriately, except where the offences are particularly serious. It is important therefore that officers are made aware of the relevance of racist incidents to the police, regardless of the 'seriousness' of the incident (see below).

The Stephen Lawrence Inquiry

Any discussion of the policing of racist hate crime would be incomplete without making reference to the Stephen Lawrence Inquiry. There is not space for a detailed discussion of the inquiry here (for this, see Macpherson, 1999; Bowling & Phillips, 2003; Hall, 2005), but it is nevertheless important to briefly note some of the key issues. The murder of Stephen Lawrence in 1993 and the subsequent public inquiry in 1999 served as a catalyst to raise the issues of race hate, crime, and policing to unprecedented levels in this country, and brought about significant changes to the way that hatred is policed in England and Wales.

The Stephen Lawrence Inquiry was divided into two parts. Part one was concerned with the matters arising from the death of Stephen Lawrence and part two with the lessons to be learned for the investigation and prosecution of racially motivated crimes. It is clear that there were fundamental errors made during the investigation of Stephen Lawrence's murder and the inquiry concluded that the investigation was 'marred by a combination of professional incompetence, institutional racism and a failure of leadership by senior officers' (Macpherson, 1999: 46.1).

In sum, the Stephen Lawrence case clearly demonstrated that the manifestation of racism within police culture at both an individual and an institutional level can have serious implications for the proper investigation of racist incidents, which in turn can have serious implications for relations with minority communities. In essence, then, two significant interrelated issues emerged from the Stephen Lawrence Inquiry. The first was the inescapable need for the police to re-establish trust and confidence in policing amongst minority ethnic communities, and the second was the equally inescapable need for a major revision of the way in which racist crime (and other hate crime) investigations are conducted and victims are treated. In all, 70 recommendations were made. An examination of all of these is clearly beyond the scope of this chapter; however, it is important to include some of the recommendations pertinent to this discussion here.

The first recommendation was that a Ministerial Priority should be established for all Police Services *To increase trust and confidence in policing amongst minority ethnic communities'* (Macpherson, 1999: rec.1). The second recommendation called for a process of implementing, monitoring, and assessing the Ministerial Priority should include Performance Indicators in relation to:

i. the existence and application of strategies for the prevention, recording, investigation and prosecution of racist incidents;
ii. measures to encourage reporting of racist incidents;
iii. the number of recorded racist incidents and related detection levels;
iv. the degree of multi-agency co-operation and information exchange;
v. achieving equal satisfaction levels across all ethnic groups in public satisfaction surveys;
vi. the adequacy of provision and training of family and witness/victim liaison officers;
vii. the nature, extent and achievement of racism awareness training;
viii. the policy directives governing stop and search procedures and their outcomes;
ix. levels of recruitment, retention and progression of minority ethnic recruits; and
x. levels of complaint of racist behaviour or attitude and their outcomes (Macpherson, 1999: rec.2).

Recommendation 13 stated that the term 'racist incident', 'outlined obove', must be understood to include crimes and non-crimes in policing terms and that both must be reported, recorded, and investigated with equal commitment. Recommendation 15 required that *Codes of Practice be established by the Home Office, in consultation with Police Services, local Government and relevant agencies, to create a comprehensive system of reporting and recording of all racist incidents and crimes*, and Recommendation 16 required that all *possible steps should be taken by Police Services at local level in consultation with local Government and other agencies and local communities to encourage the reporting of racist incidents and crimes*. This included giving the public the opportunity to report at locations other than police stations, 24 hours a day (Macpherson, 1999).

Recommendation 34 stated that

i. Police Services and the CPS should ensure that particular care is taken at all stages of prosecution to recognise and to include reference to any evidence of racist motivation.

Crucially, Recommendation 48 stated that there should be an *immediate review and revision of racism awareness training within Police Services to ensure that there exists a consistent strategy to deliver appropriate training within all Police Services, based upon the value of our cultural diversity, and that training courses are designed and delivered in order to develop the full understanding that good community relations are essential to good policing and that a racist officer is an incompetent officer*. Finally for our purposes, Recommendation 49 highlighted the need *for all police officers, including CID and civilian staff, to be trained in racism awareness and valuing cultural diversity* (Macpherson, 1999).

Policing After the Stephen Lawrence Inquiry

John Grieve, who was responsible for leading the Metropolitan Police's response to the Stephen Lawrence Inquiry, wrote this of his experiences:

> Hate crimes are complex events to investigate. The impacts they have on communities are far reaching. The way the investigation is handled and, in particular, how the family of the victim of a hate crime is supported, can be crucial to ways in which policing is viewed by the community. We now know more about the skills that the investigation of hate crimes requires. These include: fairness; proactivity; the effective use of knowledge; a focus on outcomes; regular contact with community leaders; sound communication; cunning; integrity; resilience; cooperation with communities (and not just keeping in touch with them); an understanding of families and their community context; and a detailed knowledge of law, especially about evidence and exhibits. These are all essential investigative policing skills that need to be intelligence-led. There is also an increasing need to be an 'intelligent customer' of intelligence services. (Cited in Hall, 2005: xv)

Following the Stephen Lawrence Inquiry, the Metropolitan Police (Met) identified six strategic approaches for improving the policing of hate crime, which were encompassed in their Diversity Strategy first published in 1999. These approaches were broadly categorized under the headings of (1) leadership, (2) resolving problems and investigating and preventing crime through an inclusive approach, (3) challenging processes and procedures, (4) increasing the diversity and knowledge of the workforce, (5) training, and (6) a coordinated communications strategy. Related activities included the investigation and prevention of hate crime, developing an appreciation of diversity, creating an organization people want to work for, and interacting with the public (Metropolitan Police Service, 1999a; Grieve, 2004). These six strategic approaches represent what Grieve (2004) labels as 'key success factors' for the investigation and prevention of hate crimes.

In accordance with the philosophy of the Diversity Strategy, the Met developed and implemented a number of structural and tactical changes designed to improve their response to racist and other hate crimes. These included the introduction of specialist investigative units with officers dedicated to hate crime investigations, the development and use of proactive and intelligence tools, partnership approaches, family liaison, community outreach, independent involvement, minimum standards for investigation, and victim-, perpetrator-, and offence-based prevention strategies (there is not the space here to discuss all of the post-Lawrence policing initiatives but see ACPO [2005], Hall, [2005] for a detailed discussion of these).

Outside of London, different forces have responded in different ways to the hate crime 'problem'. Some forces have employed some or all of the initiatives alluded to above, others have not. Many have responded with initiatives tailored to the particular demographics of the area they police. An examination of the initiatives employed in other forces is therefore beyond the scope of this chapter, but the ACPO Hate Crime Manual (2005) contains examples of good practice from around the country.

The Relevance of Racist Hate Crime to the Police

Fostering an understanding of why hate crime is relevant to the police is clearly important in underpinning strategies for combating racist hate crime. Indeed, an effective and appropriate police response is crucial for a number of reasons.

The Impact of Hate Crime

First, there is a growing body of evidence to suggest that hate crimes have disproportionate physical and psychological impacts upon both the victim and the wider community as compared to equivalent 'non-hate' crimes (Chahal & Julienne, 2000; Craig-Henderson & Sloan, 2003); that hate crimes are socially divisive and can heighten tensions between communities (Levin, 1999); that they are more likely than other crimes to involve repeated victimization (ACPO, 2005); and that they can increase the risk of civil disorder through retaliatory attacks along intergroup lines (Levin, 1999).

Critical Incidents

Second, because of the factors mentioned above, there is a very real possibility that hate crimes will be, or will become, 'critical incidents' (critical incidents are defined as *any incidents where the effectiveness of the police response is likely to have a significant impact on the confidence of the victim, their family and/or the community*). This is a crucial consideration given the Ministerial Priority for all police services to increase trust and confidence in policing among minority communities, as advocated by the Stephen Lawrence Inquiry.

Policing by Consent

Third, as ACPO (2005: 7) suggest, how well the police service protects vulnerable members of society and provides an effective and appropriate service to an increasingly diverse community 'is a mark of sophistication in the thinking and action of a contemporary police service'. Furthermore, in a modern democratic and diverse society, protecting all the composite groups of that society in accordance with their needs is crucial if the service is to continue to police by consent.

Limitations to Change

It should not be assumed that the implementation of strategies such as those introduced after the Stephen Lawrence Inquiry will inevitably prove to be a panacea to the problems of policing racist hate crime. Research has consistently demonstrated that the transformation of police policy into effective practice is a complex and vulnerable process. (Grimshaw & Jefferson, 1987), and that this is particularly true of policies relating to racist hate crime (Bowling, 1999; Hall, 2002, 2005). This is largely attributable to issues previously discussed in this chapter pertaining to the nature of racist hate crime, the hierarchy of relevance, individual and institutional racism, elements of police culture, the amount of discretion afforded to police officers in responding to incidents, and the historical legacy of negative experience.

Supply, Demand, and the Problem of Resources

A further limitation to change worthy of consideration, albeit briefly, is the issue of resourcing. Following the Stephen Lawrence Inquiry, forces increased resourcing to help meet Macpherson's recommendations and to help challenge the problems facing the police. At face value it would seem logical to expect that increases in funding and resources in this area should result in improvements in police performance in relation to racist hate crimes. It is, however, a feature of public services that this is not likely to be the case, certainly in the long term. As Lipsky (1980: 33 *[emphasis added]*) explains:

> A distinct characteristic of the work setting of street-level bureaucrats [such as the police] is that the demand for services tends to increase to meet the supply. If additional services are made available, demand will increase to consume them. If more resources are made available, pressures for additional services utilising those resources will be forthcoming.

In other words, in public services such as the police, it is not unusual for more people to need the services on offer than the police can provide services for. Demand will usually outstrip supply, and perceived availability of a service will fuel demand for that service, rather than the other way around as is often the case in private industry. The situation becomes particularly acute when the increases in resourcing are relatively moderate in quantity and relatively short in duration, as is often the case when different issues compete for political and police priority. This is of course not to suggest that resources should not be allocated – indeed they should and it is important that responses to hate crime are adequately resourced – but rather that simply employing additional resources should not be viewed as a panacea to the problem of hate crime.

Limitations in Practice

Whilst many of the post-Lawrence policing strategies are aimed at minimizing the negative influence of the factors discussed above, it is clear that policing racist hate crime remains somewhat problematic. Whilst this chapter has considered a number of *theoretical* limitations to improving the policing of racist hate crimes, there is evidence of their *practical* impact in the 'real world'. For example, research by Victim Support (2006) examining service provision by a range of agencies to victims of hate crime found that the police were rated poorly by 80 per cent of those surveyed. Areas of dissatisfaction included perceptions that the police did not provide enough support, did not keep victims informed of case progress, criminalized the victim, did not treat cases seriously, and were not culturally aligned to victims. It is of concern then that these views mirror those aired at the public meetings held as part of the Stephen Lawrence Inquiry a decade ago. However, the Victim Support study also found that many victims held positive views of specialist police investigative units, leading Victim Support to recommend that the police should examine ways of mainstreaming the features of specialist units into mainstream policing.

This latter point mirrors my own research findings relating to positive victim perceptions of Community Safety Units in London (Hall, 2000, 2002, 2005, 2008 forthcoming), although perhaps unsurprisingly in light of the theoretical limitations discussed in this chapter, some of the findings suggest that although overall police performance and satisfaction levels are often good, the public frequently still have a poor perception of hate crime management and investigation in general. This suggests that despite the increased efforts of forces in recent years, and the development of some significant good practice, there is further work to be done to improve service delivery and shift public perceptions.

In addition above, we briefly considered *why* an understanding of hate crime is relevant to the police, but this is not always fully recognized by police officers. Some officers still hold the view that crime is crime, do not always understand why hate crimes should be treated differently, and also perceive hate crimes as 'problematic' or 'griefy' to deal with (Hall, 2005, 2008 forthcoming; Crane & Hall, 2008; note also the significance of this in relation to the hierarchy of relevance discussed, above).

Encouragingly, however, there is also ample evidence that front-line officers are committed to providing a good-quality service to all members of the community that need police assistance (HMIC, 2008). However, research has also revealed that officers often express deep frustration that the sheer volume of work does not allow them to commit the time they would like to spend with hate crime victims (Crane & Hall, 2008; Hall, 2008 forthcoming). This finding should perhaps not be particularly surprising given the significant increase in the number of recorded hate crimes since the Stephen Lawrence Inquiry, and the volume of other incidents that similarly require police attention at any given time.

This situation can, however, have very real effects on communities and their perceptions of the police. For example, Crane and Hall (2008), reflecting previous research in this area (Reiner, 1997; Bowling, 1999; Metropolitan

Police Service, 1999d), found that victims often perceive that the police are not aware of the extra significance they feel hate crimes have in their lives, and that they are just recorded as minor incidents of anti-social to behaviour. This is supported by findings from a report commissioned by the Crown Prosecution Service (CPS; John, 2003) which mirrors submissions to the Royal Commission on Criminal Procedure in 1979 (discussed above). The CPS report found that:

> ...of the 46 cases reviewed in 19 of the cases the police failed to recognise that racial aggravation was involved, despite there being evidence to the contrary primarily from the victim but also from the perpetrator. Evidence of this is provided in 10 separate cases where the victims clearly state that they regarded the incidents as racially motivated and provided evidence of racial aggravation, yet the police took no notice and charged on a less serious basis, without taking into account the racially aggravated aspect. (John, 2003: 18)

Such situations can further compound the view, rightly or wrongly, that the police do not take such matters seriously. This mirrors the historical context discussed above, and raises some important questions concerning the training and educational needs of police officers in this area.

Despite the issues raised above, recent research by HMIC (2008) has yielded some encouraging results in this area. In 2006 and 2007 HMIC conducted an inspection, *Duty Calls*, which covered the impact on service delivery and organizational capability of compliance with race equality legislation, notably the Race Relations (Amendment) Act (2000) and related provisions. Fieldwork was conducted in six police forces with a focus on hate crime, stop and search, Black and Minority Ethnic (BME) staff progression and retention, and procurement as well as comment on community engagement and consultation. HMIC (2008: 1) was encouraged to find, on the whole, 'a palpable commitment to do what is right, many people working hard to good effect, and significant progress since 2001'.

With particular reference to hate crime, HMIC (2008: 1) concluded that:

> In responding to reports of alleged hate crime, the forces had much of the necessary infrastructure in place, were demonstrating effective leadership in many areas, and were using third party reporting processes effectively. Overall performance and satisfaction levels were up to standard. Attention was required to internal hate crime, training and supervision and full compliance with the ACPO manual... *The way ahead involves building on what has been achieved to date.*

Conclusion

This chapter has examined a number of issues pertinent to the policing of racist hate crime. Whilst there have been improvements since the Stephen Lawrence Inquiry, concerns still exist about the way that racist hate crimes are policed.

Indeed, despite the encouraging HMIC (2008) findings it is clear that there is no room for complacency and much still remains to be done. Given the theoretical 'limitations to change' discussed in this chapter, this should not come as too much of a surprise. Hate crimes are complex events, and there are many issues both internal and external to the police, and over which they have varying degrees of control, that inevitably impact upon the ability of the police to provide a service appropriate to the needs of victims and wider communities.

Summary

In April 1993, Stephen Lawrence and his friend Duwayne Brooks were subjected to an unprovoked racist attack by five white youths. Stephen Lawrence was stabbed twice and died shortly afterwards. The police investigation failed to bring the killers to justice and was later to be condemned by a public inquiry as having been "marred by a combination of professional incompetence, institutional racism and a failure of leadership by senior officers" (Macpherson, 1999: 46.1). The Stephen Lawrence Inquiry was by no means the first report to critically examine the issues of race, policing and criminal justice. However, it has been described as "the most radical official statement on race, policing and criminal justice ever produced in this country" (McLaughlin 1999: 13). In essence, two significant interrelated issues emerged from the Lawrence Inquiry. The first was the inescapable need for the police to re-establish trust and confidence amongst black and minority ethnic (BME) communities and the second was the equally inescapable need for a major revision of the way in which racist crime (and, by analogy, other hate crime) investigations are conducted and victims are treated.

This chapter examines the policing of racist hate crime in England and Wales. In addition to providing historical context, the chapter outlines some of the problems and challenges, both in theory and in practice, that the police face when responding to racist hate crime. It concludes that whilst there have been improvements since the Stephen Lawrence Inquiry, there is still cause for concern about the way that racist hate crimes are policed. Hate crimes are complex events, involving many issues both internal and external to the police, and over which they have varying degrees of control. This inevitably impacts upon the police's ability to provide a service appropriate to the needs of victims and wider communities.

Key Texts

Bowling, B. (1999) *Violent Racism: Victimisation, policing and social context.* New York: Oxford University Press.

Macpherson, W. (1999) *The Stephen Lawrence Inquiry*. Cm 4262. London: The Stationary Office.

Rowe, M. (Ed.) (2007) *Policing Beyond Macpherson*. Cullompton, Willan Publishing.

References

Association of Chief Police Officers (1985). *Guiding Principles Concerning Racial Attacks*. London: ACPO.

Association of Chief Police Officers (2005). *Hate Crime: Delivering a Quality Service; Good Practice and Tactical Guidance*. London: ACPO.

Bowling, B. (1999). *Violent Racism: Victimisation, policing and social context*. New York: Oxford University Press.

Bowling, B. and Phillips, C. (2003). *Racism, Crime and Criminal Justice*. Harlow: Longman.

Bradley, R. (1998). Public Expectations and Perceptions of Policing. Police Research Series, Paper 96. London: Home Office.

Chahal, K. and Julienne, L. (2000). *'We Can't All Be White!': Racist Victimisation In The UK*. York: York Publishing Services Ltd.

Craig-Henderson, K. and Sloan, L. R. (2003). After the Hate: Helping Psychologists Help Victims of Racist Hate Crime. *Clinical Psychology: Science and Practice*, 10(4), 481–490.

Crane, B. and Hall, N. (2008). Talking a Different Language? Racist Incidents and Differing Perceptions of Police Service Provision. Paper presented to the Winter Conference, Institute of Criminal Justice Studies, University of Portsmouth, February 2008.

Fitzgerald, M. and Hale, C. (1996). Ethnic Minorities, Victimisation and Racial Harassment. Home Office Research Study No. 154. London: HMSO.

Grieve, J. (2004). The investigation of hate crimes: art, science or philosophy? In N. R. J. Hall, N. Abdullah-Kahn, D. Blackbourn, R. Fletcher and J. Grieve (eds) *Hate Crime*. Portsmouth: Institute of Criminal Justice Studies.

Grimshaw, R. and Jefferson, T. (1987). *Interpreting Policework*. London: Allen and Unwin.

John, G. (2003). *Race for Justice: A Review of CPS Decision Making for Possible Racial Bias at Each Stage of the Prosecution Process*. London: CPS.

Hall, N. (2000). Meeting the Needs of Ethnic Minority Victims in London? An Assessment of a Metropolitan Police Service Community Safety Unit. Unpublished MSc Thesis, University of Portsmouth.

Hall, N. (2002). Policing Racist Hate Crime in London: Policy, Practice and Experience After the Stephen Lawrence Inquiry. Unpublished research report presented to the Metropolitan Police Service.

Hall, N. (2005). *Hate Crime*. Collumpton: Willan Publishing.

Hall, N. (2008 forthcoming) Policing Hate Crime in London and New York City: Policy, Practice and Experience. Unpublished PhD thesis. Institute of Criminal Justice Studies, University of Portsmouth.

Her Majesty's Inspectorate of Constabulary (1999). *Winning The Race: Revisited*. London: Home Office.

Her Majesty's Inspectorate of Constabulary (2008). *Duty Calls*. London: Home Office.http://inspectorates.homeoffice.gov.uk/hmic/

Holdaway, S. (1996) *The Racialisation of British Policing*. Basingstoke: Macmillan Press Ltd.

Home Office (2002) *Statistics on Race and the Criminal Justice System: A Home Office Publication under Section 95 of the Criminal Justice Act 1991*. London: Home Office.

Home Office (2004) *Statistics on Race and the Criminal Justice System: A Home Office Publication under Section 95 of the Criminal Justice Act 1991*. London: Home Office.

Home Office (2006) *Statistics on Race and the Criminal Justice System: A Home Office Publication under Section 95 of the Criminal Justice Act 1991*. London: Home Office.

Landau, S. (1981) Juveniles and the police. *British Journal Of Criminology*, 21(1), 27–46.

Levin, B. (1999) Hate crimes: worse by definition. *Journal of Contemporary Criminal Justice*, 15(1), 6–21.

Lipsky, M. (1980) *Street-level bureaucracy: dilemmas of the individual in public services*. New York: Russell Sage Foundation.

Macpherson, W. (1999) *The Stephen Lawrence Inquiry*. Cm 4262. London: The Stationary Office.

Metropolitan Police Service (1999a) *Protect and Respect: The Met's Diversity Strategy*. London: Metropolitan Police Service.

Metropolitan Police Service (1999bd) *Action Guide To Race/Hate Crime: Consultation Draft*. London: Metropolitan Police Service.

Metropolitan Police Service (2000a) *Third Party Reporting*. London: MPS.

Metropolitan Police Service (2000b) *The Investigation of Racist, Domestic Violence and Homophobic Incidents. A Guide to Minimum Standards*. London: MPS.

Metropolitan Police Service (2000c) *Tackling Hate Together: Community Safety Units – Protecting our Communities*. London, MPS.

Metropolitan Police Service (2001a) *Protect and Respect: Everyone Benefits*. London: MPS.

Metropolitan Police Service (2001b) *Athena Spectrum. A Menu of Tactical Options for Combating Hate Crime*. London: Metropolitan Police Service.

Metropolitan Police Service (2002) *Guide to the Management and Prevention of Critical Incidents*. London: MPS.

Reiner, R. (1992) *The Politics of The Police*. (2nd edn.). Hemel Hempstead: Harvester Wheatsheaf.

Reiner, R. (1997) Policing and the police in M. Maguire, R. Morgan, and R. Reiner (eds) *The Oxford Handbook of Criminology* (2nd edn.). New York, Oxford University Press.

Victim Support (2006) *Crime and Prejudice*. London: Victim Support.

Willis, C. F. (1983) *The Use, Effectiveness and Impact of Police Stop and Search Powers*. Home Office Research And Planning Unit Paper No. 15. London: Home Office.

TWELVE

Racism, Ethnicity and Drug Misuse: A Brief Introduction

Karen Mills

Introduction

In recent years there has been a growing body of research into the drug treatment needs of black and minority ethnic groups in the UK, although the same is not true across Europe (EMCDDA, 2000; Fountain *et al.*, 2004). This research shows that the social and treatment needs of black and minority ethnic drug users are as varied as those of any other set of individuals. Drugs of choice and mode of administration vary between communities – drugs of greatest prevalence are different in the black Caribbean and Asian communities for example, and are affected by both geography and life experience (Sangster *et al.*, 2002; Mills *et al.*, 2007). A balance must be struck between developing broad provision and meeting individual need. With a new drug strategy in place (Home Office, 2008), the time is now ripe to review drug service provision as it relates to black and minority ethnic communities and consider how well-judged changes might serve to translate research evidence into best practice.

This chapter explores the prevalence and nature of drug use in black and minority ethnic communities, as well as the treatment needs of black and minority ethnic drug users and the extent to which they are being addressed. This discussion is complemented by research evidence into good practice in the area. The chapter concludes with an examination of the ways in which drug treatment services might need to develop to respond to Britain's constantly changing demography.

Black and Minority Ethnic Communities and the Prevalence of Drug Misuse

The history of drug use in Britain abounds with stereotypes and assumptions (Manning, 2007). In the broad context of endemic and institutional racism

(Macpherson, 1999) it is unsurprising that many of these centre on the prevalence and perceived dangerousness of black drug users. Thompson (2001) has created a seminal model for the understanding of racism in the British context. His description of racism as operating at the *personal*, *cultural*, and *structural* levels can be seen in operation in wider British society and in relation to the assumptions concerning race and drug misuse. For example, at a cultural level racism attaches the negative stereotypes of drug misuse to particular cultures. Though they mutate over time, these cultural stereotypes are remarkably persistent, whether it be in the form of the evil drug-wielding 'oriental' menace of Dr. Fu Manchu (Rohmer, 1913), the association between African-American jazz music and a supposed drugs 'epidemic' (Yates, 2002), or the violent threat posed by Jamaican 'Yardy' drug dealers (Thompson, 2003). The reality of the situation is rather more complex, and as a result, very difficult to map accurately. Baker (1997) describes the paucity of knowledge about drug use, particularly in minority communities, as inviting 'wishful thinking, anecdotal assertions, propaganda, rumour, exaggeration, and potentially wildly inaccurate guesswork' (Baker, 1997, quoted in Wanigaratne *et al.*, 2003: 40).

One study developed a model for extrapolating drug use overall from the numbers of drug-related deaths (De Angelis, 2004), but this was restricted to opiate use and offered only limited evidence of the much wider range of drugs used by minority ethnic communities. Furthermore, since problem drug users form only a small proportion of the population[1], and since minority ethnic groups form only a small sub-section of that group, even very large minority population samples can yield imprecise results as to the prevalence of drug use and problem drug use (Ramsey *et al.*, 2001). In an attempt to overcome this problem, the 2000 British Crime Survey incorporated 'booster samples' of larger minority groups (Ramsey *et al.*, 2001), a notable finding being the relatively higher use of illicit drugs amongst people of dual heritage (Aust and Smith, 2003).

Sangster *et al.* (2002) were able to provide a clearer view of the nature and extent of drug use in minority populations. Focusing on the issue directly and combining literature search with targeted interviews to examine specific needs, they highlighted the pattern of crack cocaine and cannabis use among black Caribbean people and the preference for smoking (rather than injecting) heroin in South Asian communities. They also point out the subtle geographical differences and difficulties in categorizing cultural difference. Among new communities (Mills *et al.*, 2006, 2007), drug use can be seen to be influenced both by the trends they experience in the UK (e.g., Polish migrants being influenced by *khat* use among the London Somali community) and by the patterns of use brought from a country of origin (e.g., opium as a drug of choice among Peterborough's Iranian community). However, as Fountain *et al.* (2003)

---

[1] Hough (2002: 987) estimates that while some two million individuals use illegal drugs each month, the 'number of problem drug users is unlikely to exceed 200,000'.

point out, some trends are judged by the numbers presenting to services and are therefore possibly skewed by the services available, rather than being a reliable measure of actual need (see also Shaw *et al.*, 2007).

Drug Misuse, Social Inequality, and Race

A large body of research, dating back to the 1980s, highlights the fact that drug misuse is concentrated in areas of greatest deprivation (Fountain *et al.*, 2003). Seddon (2006) elaborates upon the social context of the drugs–crime nexus, and Buchanan (2006) stresses the extent to which disadvantage acts to limit and fracture the lives of drug users. McIntosh *et al.* (2000) offer a powerful description of the ways in which drug users must repair these 'spoiled identities' (p. 181) if they are to protect themselves from relapse into drug misuse in the long term. Housing, employment, and social structures – the hallmarks of full inclusion within society – are key to this process of restoration (see also Reid *et al.*, 2001).

The 2001–02 British Crime Survey draws out a connection between poverty and heroin use, just as there is an association between affluence and the use of powder cocaine (Aust & Condon, 2003). However, the link between ethnicity, social exclusion, and drug use is by no means clear. The Social Exclusion Unit (1998) commented that the majority of England's black and minority ethnic communities are concentrated in some of the most deprived inner city areas. Furthermore, many of these communities are young and growing, with large numbers of under-25s. As drug use is more likely amongst younger age groups, higher usage would therefore be expected amongst black and minority ethnic communities. However, the evidence indicates that, nationally, the prevalence of illegal use is actually less among minority ethnic communities than white communities (GLADA 2003, 2007). This is particularly the case among South Asians, who report much lower drug use than white people. (Fountain *et al.*, 2003). Theories about the reasons for this lower reported prevalence among minority groups include protective factors afforded by strong family supports and cultural taboos against admitting to drug use (Sangster *et al.*, 2002)[2]. Sangster *et al.* (2002) point to the fact that drug seekers of all races and ethnicities visit areas of 'known' drug prevalence in order to purchase drugs to consume elsewhere. Since the drugs market operates strictly within the laws of market forces, open and closed drugs markets – street sales and crack houses – develop to provide for this 'need'. In the process these neighbourhoods become places of high crime, noise, and nuisance and crack houses develop in the homes of the most vulnerable (GLADA, 2003). This developing of markets in response to a myth of availability reconciles the apparent opposites that levels

---

[2]As noted earlier, the only substantial difference from this trend is higher use among individuals of dual heritage than would seem to be the case among other minority groups (Aust & Smith, 2003). However, this needs to be replicated in other studies before it can be seen as a conclusive difference.

of drug use are actually higher among white users than black and minority ethnic users but that, nevertheless, drug misuse tears minority communities apart (Sangster *et al.*, 2002).

Community Stigmas and Strengths

Social exclusion is not the only factor which influences the lives of black and minority ethnic drug users. Low levels of drug awareness are discernible in all minority communities (Bashford *et al.*, 2003; Mills *et al.*, 2007). These levels of ignorance can cause problems in themselves – for example, in some Asian communities young people with addictions might be sent back to Pakistan in the belief that this will offer some respite, while in fact heroin is nearer its source and cheaper for the user (Bashford *et al.*, 2003). Furthermore, a lack of parental knowledge can intensify pressures upon Asian young people who are conversant with and under pressure to use drugs but have an important avenue for advice and discussion closed to them (Mills *et al.*, 2007).

In newer communities, and among established communities where older members remain non-English-speaking, there may quite literally be no shared language to discuss drugs problems. Some languages (e.g., Farsi) simply have no pejorative words that equate to 'illegal drugs' and must rely on more generic terms (medicines). Some minority groups display a strong element of denial, wanting to see drug problems as affecting the host community and not their own lives (Mills *et al.*, 2006). Such attitudes risk feeding stereotypes that some minority communities – particularly those from South Asia – are a low-risk group with no need for services (Bashford *et al.*, 2003). This sense of the betrayal of fundamental cultural mores, sometimes described as the 'stigma' attached to drugs, is often associated with Asian or Muslim communities. It is linked to issues of cultural and religious doctrine and is a significant feature affecting the openness with which drugs issues can be discussed in some black and minority ethnic groups (Pearson & Patel, 1998). Stigma applies both to the use of drugs and to talking about drug-related issues – with a sense that such discussion serves to normalize and offer encouragement towards drug use. In breaching these rules, individuals risk exclusion from family, and families risk exclusion from the wider community. Evidence of stigma can be seen both in established minority communities and among newly arrived populations. Mills *et al.* (2007) comment that this reticence can extend to community members denying the impact of drugs upon their lives even though, in their experience of migration and displacement, they have witnessed or faced the use of drugs as a weapon of war. In these newer community groups, stigma is made more acute by the fact that networks are limited and communities are sometimes vanishingly small – ostracism in these circumstances is total and potentially lifelong (Mills *et al.*, 2007).

Patel *et al.* (2004) explore the vulnerability to drug misuse of unaccompanied minors arriving in the UK. These young people, without the points of reference provided by family, are subject to influences from new friends and street culture. Patel *et al.* (2004) point out that young refugees are not a homogenous and easily defined group. Mills *et al.'s* (2007) research found that some of these young people had been sent abroad by their parents to escape the repercussions of a regime change, and that a previously privileged background had left them unfit for their new life. In seeking acceptance amongst new peers they turned to the credibility they felt was offered by drugs.

However, these vulnerabilities are only part of the picture and great strength lies at the heart of minority communities. Most asylum seekers travel only as far as the borders of the next country (Refugee Action, 2005). Only the richest, most powerful, and most capable are likely to journey as far as Europe and to the UK (Mills *et al.*, 2007). Studies in Lambeth, London (see Mills *et al.*, 2007), show that 48 per cent of the borough's Somali community are educated to degree level or above. Harnessing this untapped potential (and a similar percentage of that community are unemployed) might be the key to overcoming social exclusion in these communities and consequently to helping address and prevent drug misuse.

Delivering Services to Black and Minority Ethnic Groups

Widespread drug misuse in the UK is a relatively recent phenomenon. Prior to the 1980s addiction was limited to a small number of white, middle-class users dependent upon heroin (Strang & Gossop, 2005; Pearson & Patel, 2007). During the 1980s, however, the availability of heroin in UK cities mushroomed (Yates, 2002). At this time the issue was refracted through the lens of public health and the main problem was seen as the transmission of HIV/AIDS (Robertson, 2005). The response from the UK press was fierce and triggered the public health responses of mass HIV-awareness advertising and a rapid growth in treatment services (ACMD, 1982; Edwards, 1989). At this stage, however, heroin use was seen as a white, male issue. Treatment services concentrated their efforts on this section of the population, and treatment grew up around these needs (Pearson & Patel, 2007). The focus of treatment since has been upon substitute prescribing, and since no comparable treatment option exists in relation to crack cocaine, these services were slow to grow (Bottomley, 1999), with negative consequences for black crack users. Similarly, the fact that services for opiate users grew up in response to HIV/AIDS meant that stress was laid on the dangers of injection as a mode of administration, and the substitution of heroin smoking as a less dangerous form of use. For South Asian users, however, where the chosen mode of administration is smoking (Cottew and Oyefeso, 2005), such advice can lead to needs being marginalized and underestimated (Sangster *et al.*, 2002).

This history casts a long shadow. While services might have changed dramatically, black and minority ethnic service users remain estranged from services that are perceived as unwelcoming and inappropriate (Home Office, 2002; South, 2002). Interestingly, in some areas, evidence is emerging that where young black men are engaged by services, their retention is as good as it is for white service users[3]. If this is confirmed to be the case, then there are learning points to make good practice more widespread and issues for services in advertising their presence.

More recently the focus – and the funding – of drug treatment has been upon those drugs that cause greatest harm in terms of crime. While this has led to a growth in the development of crack services – many offering cognitive behavioural therapies – this does cause a further set of tensions. Firstly, minority communities have tended to have negative experiences of the criminal justice system (Bowling and Philips 2002; Skellington, 1996; see also Smith's Chapter 2 in this volume). Unless actively overturned, the misgivings stemming from a history of negative experiences can have a similarly negative impact upon an individual's engagement with the treatment process. If such treatment is quasi-compulsory via a drug rehabilitation requirement (McSweeney et al., 2006), this has implications for equal access to justice. If retention is compromised by previous negative experiences, then the consequent breaching of an order will serve to accelerate an individual's journey through the criminal justice system.

Furthermore, there is a neglect of those drugs and, consequently, of the communities more associated with particular drugs and are not strongly connected to crime and disorder. *Khat* is a particular case in point here. Used extensively by the Somali and Yemeni communities and strongly associated with deprivation, unemployment, and exclusion (which would not appear to be the case in Somalia and Yemen itself), this drug has until recently received only low priority in strategy documents as it is not a Class 'A' drug (Havell, 2004), and its use not a cause of crime (Null *et al.*, 2007). Indeed it can be argued that within the current framework – focusing as it does upon crime and disorder – to include *khat* use would be inappropriate (Mills *et al.*, 2007) and serve to criminalize a whole new section of the public. While *khat* use does create problems for the families and individuals who use it the solution lies not in judicial measures, but in inclusive, community solutions to what is in fact a symptom of social exclusion (Havell, 2004; Buchanan, 2004). Buchanan (2006) goes so far as to argue that if the problems of drug misuse stem from social exclusion, then drug treatment cannot act to resolve them (McKeganey, 2008). It is heartening to observe that the latest drug strategy makes specific mention of wider problems (Home Office, 2008), possibly heralding a broadening of strategy to include the much more intractable problem of social inclusion.

---

[3]This is a finding of an unpublished study commissioned by the National Treatment Agency. Source: personal communication with senior NTA official.

Service Responses

Responding to the drug treatment needs of black and minority ethnic groups requires effort at all levels. Fundamental requirements are enshrined in law (Drug Strategy Directorate, 2003), and the Race Relations (Amendment) Act 2000 speaks of the need to eradicate discrimination and develop action plans for race equality. In practical terms the starting point for developing services is a local needs assessment, and increasingly needs assessments accentuate the needs of black and minority ethnic service users within local crime reduction partnerships. From this starting point, however, clear guidance is required to support commissioners and providers in promoting good practice. Sangster *et al.* (2002) emphasize the importance of 'cultural competence'. This concept, underlining the need for provision to be sensitive, specific, and appropriate (Sangster *et al.*, 2002), is active and incremental, with services striving to build upon existing good practice. The Race and Drugs Project (2005) offers explicit action points to services at every stage of development in order to support them in making race equality explicit.

Good practice, then, begins with policy development. Here it is crucial that policies are developed and reviewed in conjunction with local minority communities, and with key partners to ensure that all participants in service delivery are committed to processes of equality (Race and Drugs Project, 2005). In implementation, there is a need to embed race equality at all levels and to ring-fence funding for its delivery. This includes the representation at all levels of black and minority ethnic staff (Havell, 2004). Sangster *et al.* (2002) stress the dangers of interpreting this last point as crude 'ethnic matching'. It cannot be assumed that clients will wish to see a worker from their own ethnic background. Indeed, concerns about confidentiality may mean that staff from outside the community are preferred (Mills *et al.*, 2006, 2007), though a balance must be struck in each case between the requirement to demonstrate privacy actively and the possibility of offering services in an individual's own language (Fountain *et al.*, 2003). Clearly at its best, a process of training and cross-fertilization can occur within staff groups to a point where all frontline staff are meshed into community needs and are able to offer an appropriate and responsive service (Bashford *et al.*, 2003).

When delivering services there is a need to target publicity appropriately, including giving specific thought to the needs of women from minority ethnic groups (Race and Drugs Project, 2005), and to ensuring that service users can recognize that services are not threatening. This might include the presentation of a waiting room with provision of culturally specific pictures and newspapers to show to new service users that the diverse needs of local minority groups are considered from the first (Sangster *et al.*, 2002). Alone, however, these symbols are tokenistic and alienating. They must be backed up with a familiarity with the needs of communities (Home Office, 2006), proper staff training, and adequate resources.

For some communities, services need to be reconfigured entirely. Differences of opinion are evident about the extent to which it is the goal of services to be delivered via mainstream mechanisms (Mills *et al.*, 2007). These have the advantage of greater stability via core funding (Sangster *et al.*, 2002; Havell, 2004), but not all service users are at a point where access to these is possible. While Sangster *et al.* (2002) envisage a process whereby over time specialist services might be integrated into mainstream provision, it must be remembered that the demography of the UK is fluid and that new groups might always require some degree of separate provision. In developing new models for services, a balance must on occasion be struck between the need to maintain the privacy of individual service users and the capacity to draw upon the strength that family networks can provide (Mills *et al.*, 2006). In Mills *et al.*'s (2006) research, service users from Asian communities expressed a strong desire to enter into discussion with parents and family but needed mediation and education to facilitate this. Overall there is a need for the democratization of services, that is a sharing of power and the cross fertilization of ideas and knowledge so that the voices of minority communities can be heard more clearly and responded to more actively (Race and Drugs Project, 2005; Fountain *et al.*, 2003).

Conclusion: Translating Knowledge into Action

While it is not possible to draw general conclusions that apply to all places at all times, existing research shows that, in general terms, drug use is lower in black communities than in white. The relatively higher level of crack cocaine and cannabis use amongst black Caribbean people should be seen in this context. Heroin use is highest among white service users and there is relatively low usage of any drug amongst South Asians. In terms of any drug treatment needs, historically, members of black and minority ethnic communities have been described as 'hard to reach'. However, it might be more accurate to say that the nature of the treatment need among these groups is different and that it is service provision that has neglected to conform itself effectively to their needs. The impact of poverty and exclusion, together with individuals' own experience of migration trauma and of racism, combine to catalyse vulnerability. While research into good practice has advanced, there is considerable delay in the implementation of findings. New research indicates the persistence of issues of shame and stigma, continued fears of a lack of confidentiality, and a lack of cultural and religious competence (LDAN, 2007). In part, problems persist because the challenges are diffuse and the landscape apparently shifting. But the guidance offered centrally also lacks specificity. For example, in advising best practice in relation to asylum seekers, the Home Office diversity manual states 'Service providers need to be able to address the differing needs of all these groups' (Home Office, 2006: 35). While at the same time, demands in relation to waiting times, overall numbers in treatment, and attrition are extremely specific, couched as targets and increasingly cash-linked (NTA, 2007). Behn's aphorism about performance management: 'what gets measured is what gets done' (Behn, 2003: 599), is clearly relevant here.

In the meantime, the demography of the UK changes with new minority groups arriving – for example, from an expanding European Union and asylum seekers from the world's most troubled nations. The new Drug Strategy, set to direct policy until 2018 (Home Office, 2008), does emphasize the need for attention to the needs of black and minority ethnic communities. Drugs like *khat*, which have not previously been given attention, are now noted and responses to local needs assessment in relation to minority communities are stressed. It remains to be seen whether and when strategy becomes action.

Summary

This chapter examines the racist stereotypes that underpin many of the assumptions about drug use by members of minority groups, before exploring the rather more complex reality of drug use within minority ethnic communities. While the evidence does not lend itself to many firm conclusions, it does show that overall drug use is actually less prevalent among minority ethnic groups. The specific risk factors that apply to minority ethnic communities are investigated, with a particular focus on the part played by social exclusion. The chapter assesses how these risks are counterbalanced by protective forces in play for some communities – these include community, family, and faith – although these forces can also alienate and exclude individual drug users.

A brief history of the development of drug treatment services shows how minority groups have often been excluded from provision. The treatment needs of service users from minority groups are outlined, together with an assessment of the efforts which providers have made to meet these needs. While research is providing a fuller picture of what is required, progress by treatment providers remains slow. The chapter concludes with some thoughts about recent policy developments – it remains to be seen if the expressed aspirations can improve the quality of service delivery.

Key Texts

Fountain, J., Bashford, J. and Winters, M. (2003) Black and Minority Ethnic Communities in England: A review of the Literature on Drug Use and Related Service Provision. National Treatment Agency for Substance Misuse and the Centre for Ethnicity and Health, London: NTA.

Mills, K., Brooks, S., Sender, H. and Green, R. (2006) *Accessing Drug Services in Peterborough: A Study of Black and Minority Ethnic Communities*. London Home Office and Centre for Community Research University of Hertfordshire Hatfield. http://drugs.homeoffice.gov.uk/publication-search/dip/Peterborough_BME_report?view=Binary.

Sangster, D., Shiner, M., Patel, K. and Sheikh N. (2002) *Delivering Drug Services to Black & Minority Ethnic Communities*. DPAS paper 16. Home Office.

References

Advisory Council on the Misuse of Drugs (ACMD). (1982) Treatment and Rehabilitation. Report of the Advisory Council on the Misuse of Drugs. London: HMSO.

Aust, R. & Condon, J. (2003) Geographical Variations in Drug Use. Key Findings From the 2001/02 British Crime Survey. 4 December 2003. London: Home Office.

Aust, R. & Smith, N. (2003) *Ethnicity and Drug Use: Key Findings From the 2001/2002 British Crime Survey*. Home Office Findings Number 209. London: HMSO.

Baker, O. (1997) *Drug Misuse in Britain*. London: Institute for the study of Drug Dependence.

Bashford, J., Buffin, J., & Patel, K. (2003) *The Department of Health's Black and Minority Ethnic Drug Misuse Needs Assessment Project. Report 2: The Findings*. Preston: Centre for Ethnicity and Health.

Behn, R.D. (2003) 'Why measure performance? Different purposes require different measures', *Public Administration Review*, 63(5), 586–606.

Bottomley, T. (1999) 'Life in the slow lane: are we serious about services for stimulant users?' *Druglink*, May/June, 12–14.

Bowling, B. & Phillips, C. (2002) *Racism, Crime and Justice*. Harlow: Longman.

Buchanan, J. (2004) 'Missing links? Problem drug use and social exclusion', *Probation Journal*, 51(4), 387–97.

Buchanan, J. (2006) 'Understanding problematic drug use: a medical matter or a social issue?' *British Journal of Community Justice*, 4(2).

Cottew, G. & Oyefeso, A. (2005) 'Illicit drug use among Bangladeshi women living in the United Kingdom: An exploratory qualitative study of a hidden population in East London', *Drugs: Education, Prevention and Policy*, 12 Issue 3.

De Angelis, D., Hickman, M. & Yang, S. (2004) 'Estimating long-term trends in the incidence and prevalence of opiate use/injecting drug use and the number of former users: back-calculation methods and opiate overdose deaths', *American Journal of Epidemiology*, 160(10), 994–1004.

Drug Strategy Directorate (2003) *Diversity fact sheet February 2003 Race relations amendment act 2000: what does it mean in practice?* http://drugs.homeoffice.gov.uk/publication-search/diversity/RRAA-diversity-factsheet.pdf?view=Binary accessed 01.03.2008.

Edwards, G. (1989) What drives British drug policies? *Addiction*, 84 (2), 219–26.

European Monitoring Centre for Drugs and Drug Addiction (2000) EMCDDA Scientific Report, Mapping Available Information on Social Exclusion and Drugs, Focusing on 'Minorities' Across 15 EU Member States. Lisboa: EMCDDA.

Fountain, J., Bashford, J. & Winters, M. (2003) Black and Minority Ethnic Communities in England: A Review of the Literature on Drug Use and Related Service Provision. National Treatment Agency for Substance Misuse and the Centre for Ethnicity and Health, London: NTA.

Fountain, J., Bashford, J., Underwood, S., Khurana, J., Winters, M., Carpentier, C. & Patel, K. (2004). Drug use amongst Black and minority ethnic communities in the European Union and Norway. *Probation Journal*, 51(4), 362–78.

Greater London Alcohol and Drug Alliance (GLADA) (2003) *London: The Highs and Lows*. London: Greater London Authority.

Greater London Alcohol and Drug Alliance (GLADA) (2007) *London: The Highs and Lows 2*. London: Greater London Authority.

Havell, C. (2004) *Khat use in Somali, Ethiopian and Yemeni communities in England: Issues and Solutions*. London: Turning Point & Home Office.

Home Office (2002) *Updated Drug Strategy*. London: Home Office.

Home Office (2006) *Home Office Diversity Manual*. London: HMSO. http:// drugs.homeoffice.gov.uk/publication-search/diversity/DiversityManual?view= Binary accessed 28.01.2008.

Home Office (2008) *Drugs: Protecting Families and Communities. The 2008 Drug Strategy*. London: Home Office.

Hough, M. (2002) 'Controlling/policing substance use(rs): drug user treatment within a criminal justice context', *Substance Use & Misuse*, 37(8–10), 985–96.

London Drug & Alcohol Network (LDAN) (2007) *LDAN News*. December 2007. London: LDAN.

Macpherson, W. (1999) *The Report of the Stephen Lawrence Inquiry*. London: The Stationery Office.

Manning, P. (2007) *Drugs and popular Culture*. Devon: Willan.

McIntosh, J. & McKeganey, N. (2000) 'The recovery from dependent drug use: addicts' strategies for reducing the risk of relapse', *Drugs: Education, Prevention and Policy*, 7(2), 2000.

McKeganey, N. (2008) Recovery is key. *Druglink*, March/April 2008, 18–19.

McSweeney, T., Stevens, A. & Hunt, N. (2006) The Quasi-compulsory Treatment of Drug-Dependent Offenders in Europe: Final National Report – England. EISS, Kent; QCT Europe: Institute for Criminal Policy Research.

Mills, K., Brooks, S., Sender, H. & Green, R. (2006) *Accessing Drug Services in Peterborough: A Study of Black and Minority Ethnic Communities*. London: Home Office and Centre for Community Research University of Hertfordshire Hatfield. http://drugs.homeoffice.gov.uk/publication-search/dip/Peterborough_BME_report?view=Binary. Accessed 01.03.2008.

Mills, K., Knight, T. & Green, R. (2007) *Beyond Boundaries: Offering Substance Misuse Services to New Migrants in London.* University of Hertfordshire.

National Treatment Agency (NTA) (2007) *Waiting Times and Access to Treatment* http://www.nta.nhs.uk/areas/waiting_times/default.aspx accessed 28.01.2008.

Nutt, D., King, L.A., Saulsbury, W. & Blakemore, C. (2007) Development of a rational scale to assess the harm of drugs of potential misuse. *The Lancet.* 369(9566), 1047–53.

Patel, K., Buffin, J., Underwood, S., Khurana, J., McQuade, C., Brako, M., Keeling, P. & Crawley, H. (2004) *Young Refugees and Asylum Seekers in Greater London: Vulnerability to Problematic Drug Use.* London: GLADA and the Centre for Ethnicity and Health.

Pearson, G. & Patel, K. (1998) Drugs, deprivation and ethnicity: outreach among Asian drug users in a Northern English City. *Journal of Drug Issues* 28(1), 199–224.

Pearson, G. and Patel, K. (2007) *Drugs, Deprivation and Ethnicity: Outreach Among Asian Drug Users in a Northern English City.* Faculty of Health, Centre for Ethnicity & Health & Institute for Philosophy, Diversity and Mental Health. University of central Lancashire http://www.uclan.ac.uk/facs/health/ethnicity/reports/drugsdeprivationandprivacy.htm accessed 01.02.2008.

Race and Drugs Project (2005). *An Organisational Aide Memoir for Drug and Allied services. Action Points for Change: Enhancing Good Practice by Making Explicit the Dimension of Race Equality. Revised EU version.* Enfield: University of Middlesex.

Ramsey, M., Baker, P., Goulden, C., Sharp, C. and Sondhi, A. (2001) *Drug Misuse Declared in 2000: Results from the British Crime Survey.* Home Office Research Study 224. London: Home Office Research, Development and Statistics Directorate.

September 2001 http://www.homeoffice.gov.uk/rds/pdfs/hors224.pdf accessed 01.02.2008.

Refugee Action (2005) *Briefing: Journey of the Asylum Seeker.* http://www.refugee-action.org.uk/information/learningaboutasylum.aspx.

Reid, G., Campbell, A., Beyer, L. & Crofts, N. (2001) 'Ethnic communities' vulnerability to involvement with illicit drugs'. *Drugs: Education, Prevention and Policy*, 8(4), 350–74.

Robertson, R. (2005) 'The arrival of HIV' in J. Strang, & M. Gossop, (eds), (2002) *Heroin Addiction and the British System: Volume 1 Origins and Evolution.* Oxford: Routledge.

Rohmer, S. (1913) *The Mystery of Dr. Fu Manchu.* London: Cassell & Co.

Sangster, D., Shiner, M., Patel, K. & Sheikh, N. (2002) *Delivering Drug Services to Black & Minority Ethnic Communities.* DPAS paper 16. London: Home Office.

Seddon, T. (2006) Drugs, crime and social exclusion: social context and social theory in British drugs–crime research. *British Journal of Criminology.* 46, 680–703.

Shaw, A., Egan, J. & Gillespie, M. (2007). Drugs and Poverty: A Literature Review. A report produced by the Scottish Drugs Forum (SDF) on behalf of the Scottish Association of Alcohol and Drug Action Teams. Glasgow: Glasgow Caledonian University.

Skellington, R. (1996) *'Race' in Britain Today*. London: Sage.

Social Exclusion Unit (SEU) (1998). *Bringing People Together: A National Strategy For Neighbourhood Renewal*. London: Stationery Office.

South, N. (2002) 'Drugs, alcohol and crime' in M. Maguire, R. Morgan & R. Reiner (eds), *The Oxford Handbook of Criminolog*, Oxford: Oxford University Press.

Strang, J. & Gossop, M. (2005) *Heroin Addiction and the British System. Volume 1 Origins and Evolution*. Oxford: Routledge.

Thompson, N. (2001) *Anti-Discriminatory Practice* (3rd edn.) Basingstoke: Palgrave.

Thompson, T. (2003). 'Without a gun, you're dead', *The Observer*. London: September 21, 2003.

Wanigaratne, S., Dar, K., Abdulrahim, D. & Strang, J. (2003) Ethnicity and drug use: exploring the nature of particular relationships among diverse populations in the United Kingdom. *Drugs: Education, Prevention & Policy*. 10(1), 2003.

Yates, R. (2002) A brief history of British drugs policy, 1950–2001. *Drugs: Education, Prevention & Policy*. 9(2), 2002.

Index